Scandals of the Civil War

"There were heroes and there were villains in the mid-1800s, just as there have always been. When the American Civil War erupted and ran its bloody four-year course, people were still human beings, still imperfect, and some still inclined to follow paths which they no doubt wanted hidden from the public record. *Scandals of the Civil War* is a fascinating glimpse at the people of that era which examines in detail the human failings: the heavy drinking; the illicit romances; the illegal gambling; the parties and the prostitution; the political corruption; the get-rich schemes by such leading industrialists as Vanderbilt, Morgan and Gould; the arrogance and downfalls of generals Benjamin Butler and Dan Sickles; the tragedy of Mary Lincoln. All come together in this exceptional addition to the treasury of Civil War-era historical records. The intent, says author Douglas Lee Gibboney, is not to demean the men and women of that period but rather to show that they were real people, flesh and blood, not lifeless monuments from a long-ago time."

—**William G. Williams**, author of *Days of Darkness: The Gettysburg Civilians* and other works.

Scandals of the Civil War

by
Douglas Lee Gibboney

BURD STREET PRESS
SHIPPENSBURG, PENNSYLVANIA

This Burd Street Press publication
was printed by
Beidel Printing House, Inc.
63 West Burd Street
Shippensburg, PA 17257-0708 USA

The acid-free paper used in this book meets the guidelines for permanence and durability of the Committee on Production Guidelines for Book Longevity of the Council on Library Resources.

For a complete list of available publications
please write
Burd Street Press
Division of White Mane Publishing Company, Inc.
P.O. Box 708
Shippensburg, PA 17257-0708 USA

Library of Congress Cataloging-in-Publication Data

Gibboney, Douglas Lee, 1953-
    Scandals of the Civil War / By Douglas Lee Gibboney.
        p. cm.
    Includes bibliographical references and index.
    ISBN 1-57249-364-X
    1. United States--History--Civil War, 1861-1865--Anecdotes. 2. Scandals--United States--History--19th century--Anecdotes. 3. United States--History--Civil War, 1861-1865--Biography--Anecdotes. I. Title.

E655.G53 2005
973.7--dc22

                                                    2004065967

Dedicated to the memory of both Alexander Gibboney, who served in Colonel Hand's Pennsylvania Regiment of the Continental Army, and Lieutenant James P. Gibboney, 45th Pennsylvania Volunteers, killed near Petersburg, Virginia, in July 1864. Alexander fought to create this country. James died to preserve it.

Contents

A Yankee cavalryman posed for this photo in Nashville, Tennessee, a town which offered a great many other amusements for lonely soldiers.

INTRODUCTION

This book is the result of too much time spent standing in line at the grocery store. Having filled my cart with the many sundry items deemed necessary by my wife for the health and welfare of our happy household, I frequently find myself stuck behind hordes of other happy shoppers waiting to go through the checkout. One's options for entertainment are limited in this lonely public limbo. I generally peruse the pages of the weekly scandal sheets placed for the convenience of the impulse-buying public at the front of each register.

The tabloids offer an advanced education in human nature. The odd and the unusual, the liquored and the licentious, the naked yin and yang of mankind appear for all to see between the sheets of these entertaining and enterprising newspapers.

Reading this view of the modern world made me ponder how much things have changed since the days of our ancestors. What kind of stories would tabloid readers of the 1860s have seen? What were the juicy scandals of the Civil War? Standing there by the bubble gum and candy bars, I decided to write this book.

Participants in the great battles of the Civil War frequently wrote conflicting accounts of what had happened—even when their impressions were recorded immediately after the event. Though the historian attempts to reconcile these primary sources and reach some truth as to what actually occurred, the mists of time can make that an increasingly difficult task. Fact becomes history, history becomes legend, and legend becomes myth.

This problem is compounded when it comes to bad behavior. No one wants their naughty bits known by their peers, let alone preserved for the amusement of future generations. Yet man is a social animal and, for many, nothing is more delightful than comparing nasty notes on what someone else supposedly has done.

In a letter preserved by the Vermont Historical Society, Corporal Edwin Horton of the 4th Vermont Infantry advised his wife not to show anyone what he wrote to her. As for her correspondence to him, he said, "I burn them because I don't think it is a good plan to keep a lot of old letters for others to read and chuckle about as soon as a man's back is turned." One can only imagine how many scandals of the Civil War disappeared into a roaring fireplace as the war's veterans and their families had second thoughts about what they had written.

In this book, you will find a potpourri of titillating tales taken from before, during and after the War Between the States. I have for the most part avoided subjects such as slavery, massacres and prison camps to concentrate on the less sweeping and more individual episodes from the era.

Nothing written here is in any way meant to demean or degrade the men and women of the Blue and the Grey. If anything, the intention is to humanize them so that we can understand that they were not lifeless bronze-and-granite heroes but flesh-and-blood people just like us. Indeed, that makes their sacrifices and struggles all the more impressive.

In many ways, this book reminds me of some of the popular tomes I read decades ago upon first becoming interested in the Civil War. My hope is that this effort will have a similar effect upon its readers and encourage them to learn more about this period of our history.

William G. Williams, author of *Days of Darkness: The Gettysburg Civilians*, was kind enough to take valuable time away from his own writing and offer comments on a draft of this text. The staff of Burd Street Press has my sincere appreciation for their help in bringing this book to fruition; Nicole

Riley, in particular, has been very helpful and patient with my e-mails, phone calls and questions. Marianne Zinn served as copyeditor while Angela Guyer designed the cover and interior layout.

Loving thanks also go to my wife, Carolyn, for her suggestions on this text. For a quarter century, she has somehow managed to put up with me and, for that alone, she deserves some kind of hazardous duty medal.

Please note that bibliographical information has been combined with the endnotes following the chapters section.

D.L.G.
December 2004

Georgia's Robert Toombs hoped to be the president of the Confederacy but his ambitions were undone by his conspicuous consumption of alcohol.

Chapter One
Drunk from the Same Canteen

In 1820, historians estimate that the average American man consumed a half pint of whiskey daily. Instead of coffee, farm workers routinely passed around a jug of spirits during breaks from their labors. In part, the alcohol helped them endure the hard life of early America and was a continuation of the frontier tradition. It was also the result of an overabundance of corn, much of which was then distilled into potable and profitable whiskey. As a result, whiskey prices dropped and made spirits even more affordable. Alcoholic beverages could also be safer to drink than water that was frequently contaminated.[1]

There were many legendary boozers of the antebellum era. One of them was Junius Booth, an English actor who had fled to America to escape his wife and live happily with his new love, a Covent Garden flower girl named Mary. Booth became one of the leading thespians on the American stage. He was also one of its most prodigious drinkers. His nose had been flattened during a rehearsal when he was howling drunk and became so threatening in his character role that a fellow actor smashed him with a fireplace poker.

Another time Booth sold himself to a New York pawn shop for the price of a drink. He stood in the showroom window with a sales tag around his neck until he was redeemed by friends. In Philadelphia, a stage manager locked the wayward star in his dressing room to ensure that he would be sober for the evening's

performance. Booth hired a bellboy to stand outside the door with
a saucer of brandy and the actor sucked the contents through the
keyhole using a pipestem.

Eventually Booth's abandoned wife tracked him down in
America and, in 1851, they were divorced. This left him free to
finally marry Mary, his live-in girlfriend, and give legitimacy to
their children, including a boy named John Wilkes.[2]

Sam Houston, one of the fathers of Texas independence and
the state's Unionist governor at the start of the Civil War, also
made a name for himself as a legendary booze hound and possible opium user. The Indians who adopted Houston into their
tribe named him "Big Drunk." When Houston's second wife tried
to convince him to stop boozing, he agreed and restricted himself
to eighty-proof bitters and orange peel.[3]

By the 1850s, Sam actually did quit drinking and was a popular speaker on the temperance circuit. This greatly amused his
old friends who had first-hand recollections of the Texas governor's
wild ways. Not entirely coincidentally, Houston had a touch of
presidential fever and hoped that the temperance vote could be
of help there.

President James Buchanan was renowned for his ability to
consume large quantities of alcohol without effect. He maintained
a fine wine cellar at his Pennsylvania home and reportedly would
consume two or three bottles at a sitting, though starting first
with a stiff glass of cognac and ending with a nightcap or two of
old rye whiskey. His favorite distiller, located just ten miles from
Buchanan's estate, was named Jacob Baer. Baer branded his ten-
gallon casks with the name "Old J.B. Whiskey." Buchanan encouraged his guests to believe that he was the J.B. in question.
The two laborers who cut Buchanan's lawn received ten dollars
and a gallon-and-a-half of whiskey as payment.[4]

* * *

Despite growing up on the frontier, where alcohol could be
a balm to harsh reality, Abraham Lincoln was not a drinker.
Unlike some abstainers, he was tolerant of people who did par-
take, which was a practical necessity given the liquid nature of

frontier politicking. Like Sam Houston, Lincoln also spoke before temperance groups in a bid to gain their votes. Supporting the reelection of Illinois Congressman Richard Yates, who had a reputation as a drinker, Lincoln said he "would much prefer a temperate man to an intemperate one; still I do not make my vote depend upon whether a candidate does or does not taste liquor." In 1861, a few years after Lincoln's endorsement, Yates appeared drunk when he was inaugurated as governor of Illinois.[5]

Early in his career, Lincoln and a partner, William Berry, struggled to make a living as storekeepers in the tiny village of New Salem, Illinois. Hoping to save the failing business, a license to sell liquor by the drink was obtained; Berry may have done this without Lincoln's knowledge. Years later this led to a charge from political opponent Stephen Douglas that Lincoln had been a tavern keeper. Lincoln scored his own points in this regard when he paid a social call on Douglas and "the little giant" offered him a libation. Lincoln refused and Douglas asked if Lincoln was a member of a temperance society. Lincoln responded that he was not a temperance member but he was temperate in that he did not drink liquor. The conversation was soon repeated to prohibitionist groups by Lincoln's political allies.[6]

Years later a committee of temperance advocates came to the White House and told Lincoln that Northern defeats were due to God's displeasure that the army drank so much whiskey. Lincoln responded that seemed unfair since the other side drank more and worse whiskey than the Union troops.[7]

When the lanky log-splitter won the Republican nomination for president in 1860, a delegation of party big wigs came to call at his Springfield home. For the occasion, Mary Lincoln arranged a fashionable buffet that included cakes, sandwiches, champagne and brandy. This was potentially offensive to several temperance attendees and the spirits were removed from view, despite Mary's objections.

As one of the Todds of Kentucky, Abe's wife had grown up in a society where all gracious hostesses offered bourbon and branch water and kindred refreshments. Later, when gifts of liquor were sent to the White House, Mrs. Lincoln forwarded them to the soldiers' hospitals. Family friend and White House staffer Noah Brooks recalled that wine was served at dinner only when special guests were present. To be sociable, the president would touch his wine glass to his lips and occasionally even take a few swallows.[8]

Lincoln's law partner, William Herndon, greatly enjoyed his liquor, which was one of the several reasons that Mary Todd Lincoln never cared for the man. When the new president-elect prepared to depart from Springfield for Washington in 1861, he bade farewell to Herndon with instructions to keep the Lincoln name on their door because he would return someday and resume practice.

Out of the blue Lincoln suddenly switched topics. He said, "Billy, there is one thing I have, for sometime, wanted you to tell me, but I reckon I ought to apologize for my nerve and curiosity in asking it even now."

"What is it?" Herndon asked.

"I want you to tell me how many times you have been drunk."

Surprised, Herndon stammered some kind of an answer and Lincoln dropped the subject.[9]

On a steamboat trip to Grant's headquarters at City Point, Virginia, in 1864, Lincoln suffered a bout of seasickness. An eager staff officer offered the president a remedy in the form of a glass of champagne. Lincoln declined, saying that he had "seen too many fellows seasick ashore from drinking that stuff."[10]

* * *

In the decades prior to the Civil War, the temperance movement attracted increasing support in America. Not only was the country divided between North and South but also between boozers and teetotalers.

Abolitionist Wendell Phillips, in a temperance address at the Boston Music Hall in 1857, boasted, "Twenty years ago, you only had to enter a hotel to see the character of an American gentleman. Now you have to go downstairs. Much has been gained in twenty years; a drinking life has come to be looked upon with disgust; public opinion was the controlling power in this country. Get the ideas right and the customs will follow."[11]

The war, however, reversed the progress that the temperance movement may have been making. Given a soldier's perspective of "live for today, for tomorrow we may die," what did a little sip of whiskey matter?

Speaking before the American Temperance Union in May 1864, John Marsh alluded to this shift in the national mood and tried to put the best face on it. He said, "If the war has given increase to drunkenness, it has also shown intoxicating liquors to be the nation's greatest foe, by endangering and bringing certain ruin upon the nation's army of defense. It has justified the most rigorous measures for the suppression of the liquor traffic and rendered contemptible all complaints of prohibitionary law as unconstitutional and an interference with the liquor dealer's rights."[12]

A surprising number of the Civil War's hell-for-leather generals stuck to the straight-and-narrow of the temperance road. Confederate cavalryman Nathan Bedford Forrest, despite his reputation as a rough-hewn slave trader, never touched the stuff. Reportedly he had once gotten inebriated as a young man and swore off the hooch after recovering from his hangover. When offered a friendly glass during the war, he would reply wryly, "My staff does all my drinking."[13]

The celebrated Confederate general Patrick Cleburne gave up liquor after emigrating from Ireland to America. During his off-hours from the Helena, Arkansas, drug store where he worked, Cleburne had tried social drinking with his buddies. He found that he was somewhat of a mean drunk. After one particular session, a friend tried to rouse the sleeping Cleburne, who angrily awoke and threatened to kill the man. Abashed, the future general became a teetotaler.[14]

Dashing James Ewell Brown Stuart was very fond of parties but not of liquor. As a child, his mother had made the future cavalier promise that he would not drink. Stuart stuck to his word throughout the war, even warning aides not to give him alcohol if he should be wounded. When he actually was shot at Yellow Tavern in May 1864, a surgeon suggested whiskey might ease the dying man's pain. Stuart at first refused but then relented, taking his first and last drink of liquor.

George Armstrong Custer, on leave home from the army in the autumn of 1861, was found stumbling drunk on the streets of Monroe, Michigan. What's more, he had the misfortune to be observed by Judge Bacon, the man who would eventually become his father-in-law. Custer's sister sobered up the young officer and insisted that he take a vow of abstinence. "Yellow Hair" did not touch liquor again.[15]

Robert E. Lee is often believed to be a non-drinker but the record shows he sometimes sipped brandy for "medicinal purposes" and would enjoy an occasional glass of wine with dinner. By no stretch of the imagination, however, was he a regular imbiber.[16]

"Stonewall" Jackson rarely drank but admitted to his aide, Henry Kyd Douglas, that he liked the taste of all alcoholic spirits. He confided, "I am the fondest man of liquor in this army and, if I had indulged my appetite, I would have been a drunkard."[17]

In January 1862, Jackson led his soldiers out of Winchester, Virginia, on an expedition toward Romney. En route the weather turned bitterly cold, leading Doctor Hunter McGuire to produce a bottle of brandy which he had been given. At the physician's suggestion that it would be healthful for him, Jackson filled a glass and drank it down without pause. As the troops continued their march through the bitter winter weather, the normally taciturn commander began chatting away freely. He wiped his perspiring forehead, unbuttoned his overcoat and spoke of how the day had become surprisingly warmer. Suffering in the winter cold, the general's staff knew that no climate change had occurred; "Old Jack" was simply feeling his liquor.[18]

* * *

As the fathers of secession gathered in Montgomery, Alabama, to formally organize the Confederates States of America, there was much speculation over who would win the presidency of the new country. Robert Toombs, who had represented

Georgia in both houses of the United States Congress, was considered the frontrunner by many observers.

Toombs, however, greatly enjoyed his liquor and, along with many another conventioneer past and present, he indulged himself after each day's work session had ended. In fact, during Georgia's state secession convention, Toombs did not wait for the end of the day; he began drinking champagne during a committee meeting and falsely announced that Fort Sumter had been fired upon. While in Montgomery, fellow Georgian Alexander Stephens admitted that Toombs "was in the habit of getting tight everyday at dinner."[19]

Unfortunately for Toombs' presidential aspirations, his fellow delegates took note of this behavior which was capped by a particularly memorable evening just as the selection process came to a conclusion. Toombs got drunk at dinner and then went on to a party where he got even more drunk. The gathering was hosted by South Carolina's James Chesnut, husband of diarist Mary Chesnut, and many members of the convention were present to view Toombs' performance first-hand. His chance of winning the top job ended that night.

Toombs went on to serve briefly as the Confederate secretary of state and then became a general in the Army of Northern Virginia until resigning his commission in March of 1863. Following the war, he fled to England and, upon his return, refused to accept a pardon from the United States government. His end was a sad one. His wife died and Toombs' eyesight began to fail. He found comfort in large quantities of drink. On his death bed, he was told that temperance advocates were meeting in his hometown of Washington, Georgia. The dying lawyer responded, "Prohibitionists are men of small pints." Robert Toombs was a man who liked his pints large.[20]

* * *

Jefferson Davis, the person selected to be the Confederacy's chief executive, was not present when the presidential vote was taken in Montgomery; instead he remained at home and out of trouble in Mississippi. However alcohol had nearly derailed the

Confederate leader's own career several times, starting when Davis attended the U.S. Military Academy.

Benny Havens was a legendary grog house located along the Hudson River two miles from West Point. The place was strictly off limits to cadets, which made them all the more eager to find their way there. Future Confederate general Henry Heth recalled that, while at the academy, he spent more time thinking up ways to get to Benny Havens than he did studying calculus.

On July 31, 1825, Captain Ethan Allan Hitchcock, a grandson of the famous Revolutionary War hero, entered the Havens barroom and interrupted the partying of Jefferson Davis and four other cadets. The offenders were quickly whisked away to the guard house. A court-martial convened where all five were found guilty and sentenced to be dismissed from the academy. The court, however, recommended a pardon for Davis and one other offender. In Davis' case, it was possibly because Captain Hitchcock had not actually seen Davis with a drink and possibly because Hitchcock was acquainted with Davis' older brother, Joseph. The Mississippian narrowly escaped expulsion and continued on at West Point.[21]

One might imagine that would have ended Cadet Davis' sub rosa revelries at Benny Havens—but one would be wrong. The following year, Davis and another student were back at the barroom when word came that a West Point professor was on his way in. The two students raced out a back trail toward the academy but Davis tripped and tumbled down a sixty-foot embankment. He suffered serious injuries and spent most of the next four months recovering at the post hospital. Somehow though, he managed to again avoid prosecution for being at Benny's.[22]

Davis recovered just in time for the Christmas holidays but it might have been better if he had remained in the infirmary. Some of his barracks mates planned to hold a traditional Christmas party and Davis secured the necessary eggnog booze at Benny Havens. Suitably supplied with cheer, the illegal celebration began in the wee hours of December 25. The merrymakers grew merrier and merrier as dawn approached. Their noise attracted the attention of Captain Hitchcock who came to investigate and discovered thirteen cadets in one room. Jefferson Davis was not among them but, a moment or two later, he burst in and shouted a belated warning to "put away the grog" for Hitchcock was coming.

Hitchcock ordered Davis to return to his quarters and fortunately the Mississippian did so. Shortly thereafter an "eggnog riot" erupted which resulted in the arrest of twenty-three cadets, nineteen of whom were expelled from West Point. Davis probably escaped only because he had followed Hitchcock's order, returning to his room to sleep off the alcohol.[23]

In the winter of 1838, yet another booze-tinged adventure nearly killed Davis. He then was in Washington, making contacts to possibly restart his military career after becoming bored with life on his Mississippi plantation. One evening he attended a reception given by the secretary of war which was followed by a post-midnight champagne supper. Afterward Ohio Senator William Allen led Davis back to his boarding house, walking through the dark streets of the capital. Allen however had drunk too freely of the champagne and stumbled off a bridge into Tiber Creek. Jefferson Davis followed right behind him, a plunge that almost proved fatal when Davis' head struck a rock. Allen, drunkenly reciting a campaign speech, pulled Davis to safety and managed to get him back to his quarters. The next morning, Davis was unconscious, and it took several hours for the doctors to revive him.[24]

* * *

Virginia's war-time governor, John Letcher, was, in the view of some critics, a habitual inebriate who gave high commands in the Virginia forces to his drinking buddies. A prominent feature of the governor's official reception area was its liquor cabinet, the contents of which were made freely available to visitors.

Early in 1861, a political ally cautioned Letcher about the overly abundant use of whiskey in his office. The friend suggested that the open bar should be moved to a more discreet location and made accessible only to special guests. The governor was also warned about serving drinks to delegates attending the state's secession convention out of concern that, if they appeared drunk during the convention's business sessions, the governor would be blamed.

Later that year, the Richmond *Examiner* castigated Letcher for doing nothing but drinking whiskey and eating hogfish while on an official trip to Norfolk. Throughout his term, rumors of intemperance dogged the governor. He dismissed the gossip as the work of his political enemies. Nevertheless, in 1863, he lost a bid to serve in the Confederate Congress, in part due to public concern about his boozing. The *Examiner* noted that Letcher bid adieu to the gubernatorial mansion "with a bowl of 'apple-brandy toddy' and a festive speech."[25]

Similarly, Confederate general and politician Louis T. Wigfall developed a reputation as a drinker. Serving in northern Virginia during the autumn and winter of 1861, Wigfall took a particular fancy to hard cider and appeared intoxicated before his Texas troops on several occasions. The liquor probably also inspired several late-night false alarms where his sleeping soldiers were roused to fight off non-existent Yankees. This disgusted two of the general's subordinates, Colonels John B. Hood and James Archer, to the point that they quit answering the long roll of the drummers unless they received specific orders to do so.[26]

In February 1862, Wigfall resigned from the army to enter the Confederate Senate. There he distinguished himself by making drunken anti-administration speeches in the saloons of Richmond hotels. As a legislator, however, Wigfall did strike a blow for sobriety. He insisted that guards be posted at the city's hospitals to prevent wounded soldiers from "straggling off and poisoning themselves at whiskey shops." The senator obviously understood that particular danger all too well.[27]

The Confederacy's wartime demand for grain resulted in unsuccessful legislative attempts to ban whiskey stills. No such laws ever made it through the Confederate Congress but several states passed their own prohibitions. In March 1862, Virginia outlawed making whiskey from corn, wheat, rye or other grain but later amended the measure to permit production for medical and manufacturing purposes. Alabama authorized the seizure of stills but allowed some small manufacturers to continue production under a price-control scheme. Georgia Governor Joe Brown banned his state's railroads from hauling whiskey and allowed its manufacture only by licensed agents twenty miles or more from the railroad, with all of the product going to government use.[28]

The Confederacy's need for liquor was great; in 1864, the army alone required two million gallons. To meet demand, the national government set up distilleries in North Carolina and South Carolina, which ensured a better quality product but also brought complaints that all the local grain supplies were being used up. Newspapers reported rumors that Jefferson Davis' in-laws were profiting from "a fat contract" in the distilling business. The president's secretary, Burton Harrison, did his best to disavow these stories.[29]

As the Union forces advanced through the South, many farmers believed that it was better to turn grain into transportable liquor than to allow it to be captured by the bluecoats. Despite the war, the sons and daughters of Dixie who fancied a drink probably never went thirsty for very long.

* * *

Ulysses S. Grant is undoubtedly the most famous drinker of the Civil War era. Grant's taste for the hard stuff entered in everyday folklore with Lincoln's famous remark that he'd like to know what brand whiskey the man drank so that some could be sent to the less successful commanders.

Grant acquired his reputation for insobriety when the army sent him to California in the early 1850s. Separated from his family, he was bored and drank more than he should have. Defenders state that Grant simply had a low tolerance for alcohol, the same argument occasionally put forth for the poet Edgar Allan Poe. In any event, in 1854, Grant resigned his commission. The circumstances of the resignation are unclear; he may have been forced out after his commander, Captain Robert Buchanan, saw him drunk—though that was hardly an unusual event among soldiers of the frontier army. Grant said in his memoirs that he resigned because he had a wife and two children and "saw no chance of supporting them on the Pacific coast out of my pay as an army officer." Another story had Grant spending all his money on alcohol while he waited in San Francisco for a ship to take him back east. Reaching New York City, he had to call on his friend, future Confederate General Simon Buckner, for financial assistance.[30]

Regardless of the specifics, Grant returned to civilian life with a damaged reputation due to his drinking habits. When Grant's father sought to have his son reinstated in the army, Secretary of War Jefferson Davis refused.[31]

The next years were difficult ones for the future president as he shuffled from failure to failure while trying to support his family. At one point, he was reduced to peddling firewood on the streets of Saint Louis and even pawned his gold pocket watch for twenty-two dollars. When the war started, his military career quickly came back to life. He received a colonel's commission in the 21st Illinois Volunteers, and political influence brought a brigadier generalship to him a few weeks later.[32]

Joining Grant's staff was his friend, John Rawlins, an attorney whose father had been a heavy drinker. Rawlins strongly disliked alcohol and, throughout the war, carefully monitored Grant's consumption while working to quell rumors—true and false—that the general had gone on a spree. Rawlins' close relationship with his superior allowed him to deliver stern temperance lectures whenever required. Most of the time, Grant was a model of sobriety. Another staff member, Horace Porter, wrote that coffee, tea and water were the only available beverages at the headquarters table. While Grant might have had an occasional toddy after a hard day's ride, he never followed the common custom of army officers in offering liquor to visitors.[33]

The gossip spread by the general's enemies did far more damage to Grant's reputation than any of the occasional benders that he might have gone on. Had Grant been less successful in battle, these rumors could have badly hurt or even ended his career. In war, as in life, it is difficult to argue with success.

Still Grant's actions did provide fodder for his ever-observant critics. In June 1863, he was not feeling well and may have taken some wine for medicinal reasons before boarding a Yazoo River steamboat. Eyewitness accounts published after Grant's death claim that he subsequently became inebriated on board and had to be locked in his stateroom. The next day he supposedly repeated the performance on land, even galloping off on a drunken madcap horseback ride.[34]

A year later, Major General William "Baldy" Smith believed that his rival, Ben Butler, had gotten Grant drunk as a form of blackmail to retain command of the Army of the James. Butler and Grant had toured the lines outside Petersburg on June 29, 1864, and supposedly Grant had freely indulged in the refreshments offered at each of the headquarters that they visited. Smith quickly dashed off a note to Rawlins informing him of the general's bad behavior. For his part, Butler later denied that he had ever seen Grant drink a glass of spirituous liquor. Several eyewitnesses though observed that Grant was indeed under the influence on that day. A review of Butler's department had been in the works; when it finally appeared, the controversial Butler remained in place. It was quarrelsome tattletale "Baldy" Smith who soon afterward got the axe.[35]

In December 1864, the Congressional Joint Committee on the Conduct of the War visited Grant's headquarters at City Point, Virginia, and the commanding general joined them for dinner. It came as "a painful surprise" to the distinguished guests that Grant drank freely to the point of intoxication. They wondered quietly what impact his condition might have upon the great movements of the army.[36]

The drinking stories followed Grant to the White House and beyond. During a postwar political visit to Pennsylvania, legend has it that he overindulged while sitting on the porch of a Cameron family mansion near the state capitol in Harrisburg. In Lancaster County, on the same trip, a door supposedly had to be taken off its hinges to carry the unconscious drunken hero to meet his train.[37]

During Grant's world tour that lasted from 1877 to 1879, the British viceroy in India hosted a dinner party where he reported that Grant got "drunk as a fiddle." After causing an uproar by groping and kissing the ladies who were present, the distinguished American was carried back to his room by six English sailors. There he supposedly began an amorous encounter with his wife, Julia, but the mood was broken when he became sick and vomited. The less-than-chivalrous viceroy reported that "if you have seen Mrs. Grant," you would understand why he became ill.[38]

* * *

With the mass mobilization of so many young men for the army, drunken free-for-alls could occur whenever given the slightest opportunity. Consider this account from the Harrisburg, Pennsylvania, *Morning Telegraph* of July 26, 1861:

> *The city was filled with drunken men yesterday afternoon and last night, and fights occurred at various grog shops. A number of men were badly beaten, and some stabbed with knives. A row occurred at Warfield's tavern in Market Street, in which twenty or thirty persons participated, and all were more or less injured. A Lieutenant of a Pittsburg company, whose name we did not learn, having repeatedly threatened to kill the proprietor of the tavern, a warrant was issued by Alderman Kline for his arrest. Equally disgraceful scenes were enacted at other drinking establishments. Fights also occurred on Capitol hill, at Camp Curtin, at the Baptist church, and on the streets, and broken heads and bloody faces were the order of the day and night. Two or three men were so badly injured that fears are entertained of their wounds proving fatal.*
>
> *The proprietors of some of the rum mills became alarmed and closed their establishments at an early hour of the evening. Had all of them pursued a similar course, much of the disorder and rioting which disgraced our*

city, flowing directly from the whisky traffic, would have been avoided. While the great mass of volunteers behaved themselves like men and true soldiers, a few conducted themselves like ruffians, and rioted with impunity. On occasions like the present the public peace and safety demand the closing of all the grog shops, and the Mayor should issue a proclamation to that effect. He certainly has the authority to do so, and it is his duty to exercise it.

Also in that same day's Harrisburg newspaper was another similar story:

Served Right—Last night a drunken soldier insulted a respectable woman on Third street. A citizen who witnessed the affair knocked the ruffian down and castigated him severely. Just now it is not safe for ladies to go on the streets unprotected after dark.

Such episodes were common in towns North and South throughout the war. For example, on February 25, 1864, members of the 1st Michigan Cavalry found themselves waiting for a train connection south at the Elmira, New York, rail depot. The soldiers drifted off to nearby saloons where they became drunk and then rampaged through the town, destroying property and threatening shopkeepers. When a small military guard attempted to interfere, they were overwhelmed by the cavalrymen. Several companies of infantry were called from camp, and the rioters were brought to bay only after one of them had been killed and four others wounded. One member of the provost guard lost an arm as a result of the melee.[39]

Elmira, which served as both a training and prison camp, experienced problems through the end of the war. On March 25, 1865, the camp commander ordered that guards be posted in front of all saloons near the barracks to stop any enlisted man from entering. But with Lee's surrender and the influx of thousands of veterans returning to town for discharge, it was impossible to stop the celebratory flow of liquor.

Drunken soldiers gathered on the town's Lake Street Bridge where they enjoyed the sport of harassing the locals. The situation grew out of control. One evening, while trying to clear the bridge, the provost guard fired shots and wounded five soldiers. It would take a bit of imagination to explain such a post-surrender injury to the folks back home.[40]

* * *

Some soldiers steadied their nerves before going into battle by imbibing a little "Dutch courage" or "fear tonic." During the Seven Days' fighting of June 1862, Texas Brigade Private William Fletcher observed Yankees passing back and forth to a barrel that he believed contained whiskey. He feared that the enemy's drunken condition might make them reckless and lead to uncalled-for killing.[41]

In that same campaign, Sergeant John Cook of the 3rd Vermont wrote a letter home about visiting the battlefield of Savage Station. He saw Rebels lying in rows—some places three and four deep—with groaning wounded trapped under the dead. He noticed a strong smell of rum and found that some of the Confederate canteens were filled with "rott gutt." Cook believed that the Rebels were nearly all drunk and that accounted for their willingness to attack so recklessly. Cook theorized that, while alcohol might deaden a man's awareness of danger, it detracted from the ability to fight hand-to-hand.[42]

Of course, it was not only the fighting men who were tempted by alcohol in the heat of battle. Union quartermaster Montgomery Meigs offered the following defense to criticism about the slow removal of the wounded from the battlefield of Second Bull Run:

> *You describe the drunken excesses of an ambulance driver. Would that man have been less likely to drink had he been hired by a surgeon? Is the quartermaster the only officer who, in the enormous demand for labor and for men, sometimes hires a man who drinks? Ask the Surgeon-General how many surgeons have been dismissed for drinking to excess. How many surgeons, nurses, and*

stewards have been guilty of stealing and drinking the liquors provided for the sick? He will tell you a story which will fill you with horror. Yet how unjust it would be to give the public impression that it is because they are hired by the Medical Department that these things occur. As it is, the burden of complaint has been that ambulance drivers get drunk. They are hired by the quartermasters; therefore the Quartermaster's Department is in fault.[43]

Even the aftermath of battle was enough to drive a man to drink. Following the fighting at Antietam in September 1862, civilian Alexander Root recalled that the stench of decaying corpses and dead horses was so bad that he would take a swallow of whiskey as soon as he rolled out of bed in the morning. Otherwise, Root claimed, the overpowering smell would make him throw up.[44]

* * *

Corporal Charles Moulton of the 34th Massachusetts Volunteer Infantry wrote his mother in December 1862 to reassure her that the accounts of soldier drunkenness she had read in the newspaper were "mere bosh." The dutiful son noted that enlisted men had no opportunity to get liquor and, if they did, they risked a heavy penalty of fines and imprisonment. All the overindulgence that Moulton noticed came primarily from the commissioned officers. Four months later Moulton again wrote home and confessed that "intemperance and debauchery" were "entirely common." He complained that an officer might get "as drunk as a beast" but, if a lowly private followed that example, he was tossed in the guard house and had ten or twenty dollars taken from his pay. As soldiers before and after Moulton have agreed, there was just no justice in it![45]

* * *

At the end of June 1863, the 35th Virginia Cavalry, nicknamed the "Comanches," found themselves on the outskirts of Gettysburg, Pennsylvania, where they scattered a Northern militia unit before entering the town. The grey horsemen rode wildly through the streets, shouting and firing their pistols randomly into the air. Though the locals were hardly pro-Southern, they treated the Rebel invaders to all the liquor they could drink, probably in the hope of giving the routed home guards more time to escape. According to regimental biographer Captain Frank Myers, the "Comanches" were soon in a "half-horse, half wild-cat condition, and each man imagined himself to be the greatest hero of the war." They told the terrified town-folk exaggerated tales of the bloody work that they had done with their sabers. The party ended two hours later, when Major General Jubal Early arrived, and ordered the "Comanches" to go off in search of the Yankees.[46]

Further back in the army's line of march, Hood's Texas Brigade captured a supply of enemy whiskey just after fording the Potomac River. The troops had halted and built fires to dry their clothes, so a good-humored General Hood ordered a liquor ration of one gill per man—about a quarter of a pint—to be distributed. Private William Fletcher recalled that the Rebs had empty stomachs and the mash made a mighty impact. Some soldiers stood around joking and laughing while others began fighting and still others tried to break up the fighting. One private slightly wounded an officer with a bayonet but the transgression went unpunished. When the march resumed, Fletcher and others paid for their partying as they staggered northward, wanting nothing more than to lie down by the road and sleep it off. Corps commander James Longstreet took note of the straggling and ordered that all future captured whiskey be destroyed.[47]

Likewise, alcohol was a strong temptation to the Army of the Potomac on its journey through Maryland en route to Gettysburg. The provost marshal warned the tavern owners and storekeepers of each town not to sell liquor to the soldiers. The warnings, however, proved ineffective, as Colonel Charles Wainwright discovered when he found several of his artillerymen drunk. To ensure that the inebriates kept up with their commands, he had them tied by the hand to their cannon. Wainwright then rode ahead as they entered each village to dump out all the whiskey that he could find.[48]

Wainwright personally was no teetotaler. A month after Gettysburg, back in camp in Virginia, he complained that, though he had a little ice, the claret supply was exhausted. His mess had six or eight cases of wine waiting in Washington but they had been unable to get them down to the army.[49]

The colonel was, however, appalled by the conduct of some of the soldiers when the Pennsylvania Reserves presented a sword to their old commander, Major General George Meade, on August 28. Champagne and whiskey were served in great quantity and quite a lively party followed. Privates assigned as guards at the event were hugging the officers. A drunken old man who was there with Pennsylvania Governor Andrew Curtin stood on a table and began singing ribald songs. The officers stole plates and cutlery for use in camp, and one man walked off with a half-dozen bottles of champagne. Wainwright felt the best way to avoid such scenes in the future was to ban sword presentations until after the war ended.[50]

In December 1864, Wainwright participated in a raid out of the Petersburg trenches through southeastern Virginia. Applejack was both plentiful and potent along their route, and the officers had difficulty keeping it away from the men. One unfortunate fellow drank so much that he literally could not put one foot in front of the other. His exasperated comrades finally marched off without him. While the blue column was still within sight, a group of Rebels grabbed the downed Yank. When they discovered that their prisoner was too drunk to walk, they shot him in the head, stole his boots and left the bloody body in the roadway.

Wainwright proudly noted that the drinking was mainly among the infantry and cavalry. He saw only one of his artillerymen under the influence, and that soldier was forced to march roped behind a cannon. Every so often a sergeant tossed a bucket of cold water on the carouser to help sober him up—rough treatment indeed given the winter weather![51]

Another officer during the Petersburg siege, Captain Samuel Elder of the 1st U.S. Artillery, went on a drinking spree and blundered his way into Confederate lines. The next day he was both hung-over and a prisoner.[52]

* * *

The monotony of camp life could be dangerous to officer and enlisted man alike. Dr. Thomas Lowry's book, *Tarnished Eagles*, documents a colorful case of alcoholic excess, involving Colonel Charles Summalt, commander of the 138th Pennsylvania Volunteers. The regiment was mustered into service during August 1862 and found itself assigned to the unexciting chore of guarding the Relay House rail junction near Baltimore and Washington. One soldier wrote home, "We have good times here, plenty to eat and drink and not much to do."[53]

Colonel Summalt certainly had plenty to drink and he began at once to demonstrate his lack of fitness for command. On the night of September 20, he shot his revolver, sending a wave of excitement through his green troops who no doubt were still jittery over the Rebel army's just-ended excursion into Maryland.

On November 4, the colonel was so drunk that the lieutenant colonel took over the command.

On December 2, he was again intoxicated and vomited in the officers' mess tent.

On December 4, he assembled his regiment for not one but two separate dress parades. During the second, Summalt delivered a lengthy, alcohol-influenced speech.

On December 6 and 13, he was drunk again.

On December 20, he was unfit for duty due to alcohol.

On December 25, the colonel was "dead drunk" from Christmas cheer.

On January 2, a post-New Year's spree caused him to be "unseemly and disgusting."

On January 13, he called the guards from their posts and ordered them to drink with him.

At his subsequent court-martial, witnesses testified of Summalt's visits to the home of a well-known secessionist, where he declared his affection for the South and revealed his support for John Breckinridge during the 1860 presidential contest. Breckinridge was then serving as a general in the Confederate army.

During another well-lubricated visit to the same home, Summalt quoted Shakespeare before offering his classical interpretation of "Ajax defying the lightning"—a performance that was no doubt quite memorable. This exertion so tired the colonel that he passed out on the settee and missed dinner. Upon awakening, he asked for coffee, which he laced with whiskey. He then requested that the daughter of the house sing the Rebel anthem, "Maryland, My Maryland."

On yet another occasion, Lieutenant Edward Moon tried to beg off the colonel's invitation to visit the Relay House Tavern by claiming he was too tied up with regimental business. Summalt, already inebriated, ordered Moon to forget work and come along. After playing a sloppy game of billiards, the colonel turned to leave the bar but only got as far as the porch before falling off into a water-filled ditch. Despite Lieutenant Moon's objections, Summalt fired his gun in the air four times. The sergeant of the guard arrived, and, although the commander had forgotten that evening's password, the sentries permitted him to continue back to his quarters.

The 138th Pennsylvania would eventually leave its routine railroad duty and see horrific fighting during the Virginia campaigns of 1864 and 1865. Men from the 138th, in fact, would kill the Confederate general, A. P. Hill, during the capture of Petersburg. Fortunately, by the time the regiment saw heavy action, Colonel Summalt was no longer in command. On March 30, 1863, a military court dismissed him from the army.[54]

Brigadier General James Ledlie was busy drinking rum while his troops met disaster during the July 1864 Petersburg mine assault.

CHAPTER TWO
MORE DRINKING

For the thirsty private in camp, alcoholic beverages were generally prohibited although army sutlers were not above selling an illicit dram if they could do so without getting caught. For a time, some merchants circumvented the rules by selling potent canned brandy peaches to the enlisted men. When Ben Butler discovered illegal liquor sales to his troops at Fortress Monroe, he drove the offending sutlers from camp and banned booze for officers and men alike—even though that meant Butler himself had to forego his wine at dinner!

In February 1862, the 44th Virginia camped near Crab Bottom in the Shenandoah highlands. One of the officers, J. S. Hubbard, complained that the locals would rather "trade in horses and whiskey" than serve in the army. To keep them from peddling their moonshine to his soldiers, Hubbard destroyed every barrel within five miles of camp, noting that the populace was "getting quite uneasy" since he declared war on the liquor business.[1]

The 1st Maryland Potomac Home Brigade found a bonanza when camped near the Baltimore-and-Ohio Railroad in the spring of 1862. A train had been switched off onto a siding, and it included an entire car loaded with whiskey! It took a day or two for the unit's officers to discover the source of their men's liquid delight. During the search, Captain Albert Hunter spied a wooden bucket in the bushes. Suspecting that it contained liquor, he raised his carbine to put a bullet through it after first calling out that he was about to shoot. No one answered the warning and Hunter fired. The whiskey bucket flew into the air as one of the enlisted bluecoats bolted out of the bushes.

The railroad car was rolled closer to camp for safekeeping. Captain Hunter slept inside to guard the contents. That night he awoke to the sound of an auger boring through the car's wooden slats. Peering out the door, the captain spied a corporal hoping to drill straight through to one of the kegs and tap its contents.

The following night, someone slid open the freight car door and Hunter took a potshot at the intruder with his revolver. When one of the men pleaded for whiskey to ease a heart condition, the unsympathetic officer suggested that the soldier drink some coffee instead.

Railroad officials finally collected the troublesome whiskey wagon but not before two more barrels of hooch disappeared. One of these Hunter managed to track down. The other was not found until it was completely empty.[2]

* * *

Occasionally whiskey might be issued as a reward for special service or medicinal reasons. Upon taking command of the Army of Tennessee in December 1863, Confederate General Joe Johnston won favor with the men when he introduced a twice-weekly whiskey ration. For those who wanted a tad more, an enterprising fellow with several canteens around his neck stationed himself between the camp and town to sell "pine top" at two dollars a pop. Payment in Confederate money, of course![3]

Men of the 8th Illinois Cavalry clamored for a whiskey ration during harsh weather in the first winter of the war. Their request was sent to regimental surgeon Abner Hard who disappointed them by instead offering hot coffee and crackers after sentry duty.[4]

The frequency of a whiskey ration varied greatly from unit to unit. John Billings of the 10th Massachusetts Light Artillery recalled it only being issued to his company on three or four occasions and then after especially hard service. According to Billings, the men believed the officers would siphon off the supply for their own satisfaction. Captain N. D. Preston of the 10th New York remembers but one time that he was ordered to give the men whiskey, that being after Sheridan's 1864 Richmond raid. Others received more frequent distributions though the small quantity often caused complaint. Sometimes it was not much more than a tablespoon—hardly enough for a man to get "oskerfoodled." The 45th Pennsylvania Volunteer Infantry received a whiskey ration in June 1864 during the Virginia overland campaign. It consisted of four spoonfuls per man.[5]

The men also suspected that whiskey rations served to mask a dose of quinine which army doctors used as an all-purpose aid for good health. Teetotalers found eager bidders for their unwanted allotment of army-issued liquor.

During an "emergency," an officer could write an order for an enlisted man to be given a full canteen of whiskey. As a result, some of the soldiers in Company G of the 45th Pennsylvania learned to write their lieutenant's signature even better than he could do it himself. No one in the company was ever punished for such a forgery.[6]

Packages from family and friends received careful inspection to ensure that they did not include a contraband bottle of booze. One trick was for the folks at home to hide liquor inside a stuffed turkey or in a hollowed-out spot beneath a cake. In early 1863, guards on the Potomac bridges near Washington were confiscating five-hundred dollars worth of contraband army-bound liquor every day.[7]

In September 1863, the 2nd Vermont Infantry traveled from Virginia to New York City to keep order after the summer's violent draft riots. Camped in Washington Square, the temptations of town life were irresistible and the soldiers snuck past the guards as often as possible. Private Wilbur Frisk reported that the penalty for becoming drunk and starting a small row was twenty-four hours of "log drill." The penalty was twice that for getting drunk and starting a major altercation.[8]

Private Charles Tillison of the 2nd Vermont Infantry wrote his son, Dudley, from Brandy Station, Virginia, in February 1864, with instructions for a money-making scheme to smuggle spirits via the mail: *"if yo send the Box bee cafule And pack it so it wont wratle for they are gitin very strick fill the canes full And cork them tight And pack them well with saw dust And if I can git it heare it will bring me a good too hundred dolars the minet I git it if you cant git the wines git what yo can eny thing that is licker."*[9]

John Worsham of the 21st Virginia Infantry remembered chasing David Hunter's Yankees west from Lynchburg in June 1864. The Confederate column marched by a handsome residence where two attractive young women and their maids stood with two huge washtubs. The tubs contained ice water and brandy julep and the passing Rebels were invited to help themselves. Worsham stated that no second invitation was needed. The tubs were repeatedly refilled as the soldiers continued past.[10]

U.S. sailors had traditionally received a grog ration, consisting of whiskey or rum diluted with water. Meddlesome temperance advocates, however, successfully lobbied the U.S. Congress to pass legislation ending the practice as of September 1, 1862. In lieu of booze, the sailors got an extra five cents per day—hardly a fair trade. The old salts were understandably upset, especially since their officers were still permitted to tipple. The secretary of the treasury licensed merchant schooners to serve as sutler ships to the blockading fleets, and these vessels conducted a lively trade in alcohol. One officer dubbed them "floating grogshops." Confederate sailors received a regular ration of one gill of spirits or a half-pint of wine per day. Seamen on both sides eagerly sought out the liquor cargos of captured vessels.[11]

Even those poor souls being held as prisoners of war searched for ways to wet their whistle. At the infamous Andersonville camp in Georgia, Union prisoners made and sold an alcoholic concoction of "corn beer." The recipe called for cornmeal to be added to a barrel of water which then fermented in the hot Southern sun. A bit of black strap molasses and possibly some sassafras root tea was added for taste before the brew was sold at ten to fifteen cents a half pint. Several dozen outlets in the prison retailed the mixture.[12]

Private Robert Sneden of the 40th New York survived the Andersonville stockade to be transferred to another Georgia prison in September 1864. There Sneden volunteered to become a hospital clerk for his Confederate captors. When that prison was evacuated due to Sherman's march, Sneden unexpectedly found himself lodged at a Savannah hotel in charge of the medical stores, including a good supply of whiskey. Rebel officers congregated all day long in his storeroom, playing cards and sipping the hard stuff. One time the celebrants stayed in the storeroom all night and woke there the next morning in a drunken stupor. Sneden was ordered by the hospital surgeon to either turn the officers out at 9 p.m. or else lock them in until daybreak. Had he locked them in, the prisoner would have become the jailer of his own captors![13]

John Winder, the controversial commissary general for all Southern prisons east of the Mississippi, had his headquarters in that very same hotel. Sneden learned that the general had a ten-gallon cask of imported brandy hidden beneath his bed. The resourceful Yankee made a syphon from a flexible smoking tube and somehow tapped the cask without discovery. The brandy was fine-tasting stuff, smuggled to the port of Wilmington by a blockade runner. From then until the cask emptied, Sneden ignored the rough hospital whiskey and secretly helped himself to the Rebel general's top-shelf stock.[14]

* * *

In March 1865, Private Henry Robinson Berkeley was captured when Phil Sheridan's Yankees routed what was left of Jubal Early's Rebels at Waynesboro, Virginia. Berkeley and the other prisoners were force-marched without rations the one hundred miles to Winchester. From there, they were taken by train to confinement at Fort McHenry in Baltimore. Their new quarters were primitive; the exhausted men were forced to sleep outdoors in the mud, pelted by a cold, sleety rain. Berkeley thought he would certainly die that night as some others, in fact, did. He believed that his life was saved by a fellow prisoner, Major Don

Halsey, who gave him a full glass of whiskey and a cup of hot coffee. After drinking both, Berkeley felt amazingly better.[15]

Phoebe Yates Pember, the forty-something matron of Chimborazo military hospital in Richmond, kept her medicinal whiskey locked in the pantry. The key she carefully stowed in her pocket. She noticed, however, that the ward officer requested a new quart of whiskey every morning—even when none had been issued to patients. Inquiring the reason, she was told that rats apparently knocked over the bottles during the night. This curious answer failed to satisfy Pember, who investigated further. She discovered the lost whiskey had been decanted into several champagne bottles and hidden behind a bed. Pember accused the ward officer of the theft and threatened to have him reassigned to the front lines. A short time later the ward surgeon came to her and protested the charge, stating that the ward officer did not drink. Pember responded angrily to the surgeon, "I know he does not, and I also know who does." Caught in his deception, the doctor eventually resigned from his hospital post.

Chimborazo's matron faced her most serious challenge after Richmond was evacuated by the Confederates. An unruly gang of patients broke into her room and announced that they had "come for the whiskey." Pember defiantly refused, determined to keep the hospital's thirty gallons of liquor out of trouble-making hands. The ringleader cursed and called her "a name that a decent woman seldom hears" as he moved to push her aside. He abruptly halted when Pember produced a revolver. She warned that if she missed once, there were still five more shots and "the room is too small for even a woman to miss six times." Muttering threats, the ringleader backed away and the whiskey was saved.[16]

* * *

The remarkably candid writings of Captain Francis Donaldson, published as *Inside the Army of the Potomac*, contain repeated references to the use of liquor and its impact upon the army's fighting force. Donaldson began his military career in the 1st California Regiment and was captured in October 1861 at Balls Bluff, Virginia. One of his grey-clad guards demanded that

Donaldson surrender his canteen, which he reluctantly did. He was surprised when, a short time later, the guard returned the canteen half-filled with whiskey, instructing the prisoner to use it sparingly. Such acts of kindness grew less and less common as the war continued and its brutality increased.[17]

Upon Donaldson's exchange and return to service, he spotted an enlisted man with a canteen of whiskey as his regiment marched up Pennsylvania Avenue in Washington. When a halt was called, the soldier had the poor judgment to offer his captain a drink. The dutiful officer seized the canteen and poured its contents into the street, much to the regret of all concerned—including the man who dumped it.[18]

Subsequently, Donaldson became a captain in the 118th Pennsylvania, nicknamed the "Corn Exchange" Regiment because it had been funded by that Philadelphia concern. In his letters home, he wrote candidly of frequent hard drinking in the army. Donaldson had a stormy relationship with his superior, Lieutenant Colonel James Gwyn, partially due to that officer's freewheeling ways with whiskey. During one of their early meetings, Gwyn visited Donaldson's tent when a gallon jug of liquor accidentally broke. Gwyn grabbed a tin wash basin and saved much of the booze but he immediately helped himself to a long draught of it. A disgusted Donaldson decided at that moment that the Irishman was "a very low person."[19]

Preparing for action in front of Marye's Heights at Fredericksburg in December 1862, Donaldson noted that Gwyn steadied himself by getting "pretty full of liquor." While the unit remained under fire, another officer had his canteen struck by a bullet and a stream of whiskey gushed forth. A quick-thinking lieutenant grabbed the canteen and drank its contents before the owner even knew what had happened.[20]

The following month, the 118th Pennsylvania took part in General Ambrose Burnside's ill-fated "Mud March." When road conditions stalled the movement, the regiment went into a temporary bivouac. To pass the time, Lieutenant Colonel Gwyn tippled "quite freely" with Colonel Charles Johnson of the 25th

New York. The pair decided to wager over which regiment's pioneers were best with an axe, and a representative from each command was chosen to chop down a tree. When Gwyn's man won the contest, a general riot broke out between the two regiments, fueled in part by a whiskey ration that had just been issued. It took the threat of a battery of artillery loaded with canister to break up the violent fracas. Gwyn subsequently challenged Johnson to a duel. The New York officer quickly agreed to fight, but Gwyn decided that the issue was better settled with a bottle than a bullet. Another "big drunk" ensued, which included officers, enlisted men and teamsters, both black and white.[21]

In a May 1863 letter home, Captain Donaldson claimed to have personally witnessed General Joseph Hooker "guzzling wine" during the battle of Chancellorsville. Historians generally agree that the hard-drinking general had sworn off the sauce while he led the Army of the Potomac. Donaldson, however, visited the headquarters tent after Hooker had been injured by cannon fire striking the columns of the Chancellor house. Donaldson saw the commanding general reclining and busily drinking champagne. Informed of Hooker's injury, another officer opined that the bubbly was a more likely reason for the general's prostration.[22]

Donaldson complained that the high-ranking officers "drink, drink, drink, always and all the time" to celebrate victory, to celebrate defeat, because of rain and because of sunshine. Shortly after Chancellorsville, one of Donaldson's fellow officers invented a cocktail of whiskey, water, sugar and nutmeg; this was dubbed a "Hooker's Retreat" or more simply a "Joe Hooker."[23]

Later that month, a gala sword presentation took place for brigade commander James S. Barnes. These affairs always served as an excuse for celebration. Refreshments included two barrels of gin cocktail, two barrels of "Fish House" punch, two barrels of claret punch and two casks of ale. That night the spacious reception tents were filled with men getting a "lordly load on" and dawn found many of them passed out under the tables.[24]

As the armies rested following the battle of Gettysburg, one of the 118th's lieutenants stayed drunk for weeks, before disappearing into his tent for two days. Concerned, Donaldson looked in to see the man in a filthy condition with maggots crawling over him. Two days later, the drunken officer's rum was ordered to be destroyed, and the inebriate stripped of his clothes and given a bath.[25]

A short time later, another officer held a party to celebrate construction of his new log hut, with those in attendance drinking to the point of sickness. The next morning it took over an hour for their black servants to clean up the mess.[26]

Ongoing conflicts with his commanding officer, Colonel James Gwyn, eventually drove Captain Donaldson out of the army. In 1906, the two men met again on a streetcar in Philadelphia. They put their old antagonisms aside and talked of the wartime days. Gwyn confessed that he had been a "pretty free drinker" back then and had kept it up until just a year earlier when his health made him quit. He planned, however, to get "pretty full" come the 4th of July. Donaldson urged him not to do so and reminded him of the many problems that liquor had caused while they were in the service.[27]

Incidentally, many Civil War melodramas have used the plot device of a family divided by the conflict. Donaldson was an actual member of one. His brother, John, served as a captain in the 22nd Virginia Infantry, and the pair always feared that their units would meet on the field of battle. Fortunately, they never did.

* * *

Allegations that an officer was intoxicated in battle were not uncommon. After First Bull Run, a court of inquiry found that Colonel Dixon S. Miles had been drunk on doctor's brandy during the fighting. A veteran of nearly four decades in the U.S. Army, Miles narrowly escaped being cashiered—although his loopy battlefield behavior actually may have been due to the medication he was taking for dysentery. The following year his command was trapped by "Stonewall" Jackson at Harpers Ferry, and Miles was mortally wounded while waiting to surrender. Some said that Miles' men were so distraught by his decision to give up that they would have been willing to shoot the old man themselves. Unsubstantiated rumors went through the ranks that the ill-starred officer had been drinking again.[28]

A West Point classmate of Joe Hooker, General Henry Benham, commanded the engineers who were to bridge the Rappahannock River for Sedgwick's three corps during the Chancellorsville campaign of 1863. Unfortunately, Benham had been up all night drinking whiskey and was "as tight as a brick"— even to the point of falling off his horse and badly scratching his face. As a result, the laying of the pontoons was delayed about four hours.

Another Northern general at Chancellorsville, Amiel Whipple, was thought by some soldiers to be too plastered to dismount from his horse when he came under enemy fire. A Rebel sniper's bullet struck and mortally wounded him. One of Whipple's officers defended the general, saying that, in fact, he was not drunk but merely slow and unsteady in the saddle.[29]

During the crucial first day's fighting at Gettysburg, Union Brigadier General Thomas Rowley had just assumed division command when his erratic behavior brought charges that he was under the influence. A native of Pennsylvania, Rowley rode his horse up and down the battle line, waving a sword and shouting, "Here's for the old Keystone State!" After Major General John Reynolds was killed, Rowley mistakenly assumed that he had become acting corps commander and started issuing orders to troops that he did not really command. As the Union soldiers retreated pell-mell through the streets of Gettysburg, Rowley tumbled from his saddle and landed in a ditch.

Somehow Rowley reached the relative safety of Cemetery Hill. There he made himself so obnoxious that a lowly lieutenant serving with the provost marshal placed the general under arrest and had guards escort him to the rear. A subsequent court-martial found Rowley guilty although one fellow officer remarked that his performance would not have been any better even if he had been sober.

Rowley never saw combat again. He was shipped off to oversee implementation of the draft in Maine. Despite his colorful but less-than-stellar performance of July 1, Rowley's name is prominently memorialized in large stone letters on the temple-like Pennsylvania monument near Gettysburg's "high water mark."[30]

* * *

One of the most notorious cases of an officer drunk in battle was that of James Ledlie. An ambitious New York civil engineer, Ledlie rose through the ranks to become a brigadier general in the Army of the Potomac. On May 24, 1864, Ledlie's men encountered Confederates under "Little Billy" Mahone on the south side of Virginia's North Anna River. The Rebels were strongly entrenched but Ledlie refused to see that as an insurmountable problem. Witnesses report that the general's judgment was befogged by alcohol.

While Ledlie prepared his brigade to charge the fortifications, a messenger brought orders from his superior, Major General Thomas Crittenden, warning against making any assault. Nevertheless, Ledlie sent his soldiers forward as Mahone's men gleefully prepared to slaughter them. That is exactly what happened. The Yanks lost 450 men while the Rebs sustained about 75 casualties. As the beaten Federals made their way back to their own lines, Ledlie turned over command of his brigade and went to sleep off the effects of the liquor.

Despite this sorry performance, Ledlie received a promotion to division command on June 8. It was a move the army's leaders would soon regret.[31]

By July 1864, Grant's army had pinned Lee's men down in defenses around the strategic city of Petersburg, Virginia. Capture Petersburg and the Confederate capital of Richmond would fall. But a line of increasingly strong earthworks surrounded the "Cockade City," making a direct assault impossible. A group of former coal miners in the 48th Pennsylvania were given the go-ahead to dig a shaft under the grey lines and blow open a gateway.

On July 30, the explosives were detonated. James Ledlie's division received the task of leading the advance. The orders were to pass through the depression created by the blast and secure a position on the crest beyond. When Ledlie's men reached the enemy's line of works, they found a crater that was fifty to sixty yards long, twenty yards wide, and twenty to twenty-five feet deep. There the Yankees stopped while successive waves of support troops tumbled into the hole behind them. "Little Billy" Mahone, the same commander Ledlie faced on the North Anna, rallied the shocked Southerners and launched a counterattack. The result was a humiliating and bloody fiasco for the Union side. The Federals were gunned down in the crater until the survivors could make a run for it back from where they came.

While this tragedy transpired, the commander of the lead division, General Ledlie, sat in the safety of a bombproof, bumming rum from Surgeon H. E. Smith of the 27th Michigan Volunteers. Smith told an investigating committee that Ledlie complained of "malaria" and being hit by a spent ball. Brigadier General Edward Ferrero, commanding a division of black troops who were also trapped in the crater, partook of a toddy as well; perhaps he feared contracting Ledlie's "malaria."[32]

The scandalous defeat and his shameful behavior ruined Ledlie's military career. The general resigned from the service in January 1865. He returned to his occupation as a civil engineer, working with the Union Pacific Railroad. This work took Ledlie to the town of Battle Mountain, Nevada, which claims him as a favorite son. In 1879, U. S. Grant visited the town while Ledlie was there but it is unlikely that the two met; in Grant's opinion, Ledlie was "the greatest coward" of the conflict. Battle Mountain, incidentally, had the distinction of being named "the armpit of America" by *Washington Post Magazine* in 2001. It has since begun an "armpit festival" to showcase local pride.[33]

* * *

Accusations of drunkenness, justified or not, surrounded many Civil War failures. For example, when Brigadier General Edward McCook's bluecoat cavalry botched a July 1864 raid on the Atlanta railroads, newspaper accounts placed the blame on captured whiskey. The rebuttal came back that only six barrels of liquor had been seized and those had been destroyed. What's more, even if the soldiers did drink the liquor, there was only a half pint per man and that would hardly be enough to keep them intoxicated for two full days![34]

That autumn, shortly after the battle of Allatoona, Georgia, a Confederate regiment under the command of Colonel R. H. Shotwell demonstrated that booze could also be an incentive for victory. The Rebs had just stacked arms following a long day's march of twenty-nine miles. A courier rode up with orders for Shotwell's men to advance another three miles before making camp. There was much grumbling but the weary veterans shouldered their muskets, formed ranks and headed off as they were told. After two miles, they encountered a Yankee garrison guarding the Chattanooga and Atlanta Railroad. New orders came for the regiment to capture the position.

Shotwell's men had suffered badly in a similar attack at Allatoona and the prospect of a nighttime fight after a fatiguing march held little appeal. What's more, the soldiers were hungry, having received only two ears of corn per man as rations in the past two days.

To boost morale, Shotwell engaged in a little hyperbole, telling the men that capturing the post would yield a fine feast of Federal food and drink. The attack was made and the Yankee garrison, learning that they were in the path of the entire Confederate army, surrendered.

Lo and behold, Shotwell's prediction came true. The hungry Rebs found quantities of sugar, coffee, crackers, bread, bacon and two barrels of whiskey. Shotwell's men engaged in an orgy of eating and drinking which lasted until daylight. Their commander reported that they were "the most promiscuously and universally drunk set of men...that ever occupied the same amount of territory."[35]

* * *

Confederate partisan John S. Mosby's favorite wartime beverage was coffee—not the ersatz Confederate stuff but the real thing that could be captured from a Yankee haversack. Mosby avoided alcohol during the war though, in later years, he enjoyed an occasional beer or whiskey. The Rebel raider fully appreciated the stupefying effect that alcohol could have upon his Yankee opponents.

One of Mosby's early antagonists, Major Joseph Gilmer of the 18th Pennsylvania Cavalry, was cashiered from the army for drunkenness after a sorry performance against the partisans at Aldie, Virginia, in March 1863. A few days later, when Mosby captured General Edwin Stoughton at Fairfax Court House, he noted empty champagne bottles in Stoughton's room, leftover reminders from a party earlier in the evening.[36]

The biggest favor alcohol ever did for Mosby came in December 1864 while he was eating a late-night dinner at the hospitable farmhouse of Ludwell Lake. Federal cavalry surrounded the residence, and a stray shot fired through a window struck the guerilla chieftain. Reacting quickly, Mosby concealed the uniform coat which bore his insignia of rank as the Yankees entered the house to examine their capture.

Mosby later recalled there was "a good deal of whiskey among them." The Northerners failed to recognize the injured man. After their doctor pronounced the wound fatal, the Yankees took Mosby's pants, boots and hat but left behind the supposedly dying soldier. In their befuddled state, they forgot to take Mosby's horse and pistols. An Irish trooper, thinking more clearly than the rest, took a last look at the Rebel raider and declared prophetically, "He is worth several dead men yet."

Had the night not been so cold, perhaps there would have been less need for whiskey to warm the spirits of the lonely Union cavalry patrol. In that case, the career of the "Grey Ghost" might have come to a much different conclusion. As it was, Mosby survived to bedevil the Yankees until the war's end.[37]

Mosby's own soldiers, however, were not immune to the call of demon rum. Their commander actively sought out and destroyed local stills to prevent his men from imbibing. He also sent raiding parties to empty the liquor stocks of grog shops.

When a group of Mosby men arrived to destroy one old woman's store of liquor, she pleaded poverty, saying that she had no other means of making a living in the tough wartime economy. The soldiers took her words to heart. Recalling that Mosby's orders were only to "pour out the liquor," they secured a large washtub and dumped it all in there for her to recover. The rangers did help themselves to a couple of complimentary canteen-fulls, of course.[38]

On April 28, 1864, some two dozen of Mosby's men went on a springtime spree at the Pickett House Hotel in Leesburg. Preoccupied in the barroom and on the veranda, their revelry was such that Union cavalry rode within two hundred yards of the establishment before the rangers took notice. One of the Rebels, John DeButts, influenced by far too many drinks, stumbled onto the street and commenced a regular "Wild West" gunfight with one of the Federals. DeButts' unsteady shot went astray but, in reply, he received a bullet in the shoulder. According to Federal records, one Confederate was killed and twenty-two others were captured that day, including all of those in the barroom. One might imagine that the "Grey Ghost" was not amused.[39]

* * *

The outlaw-soldiers who rode with William Quantrill and "Bloody Bill" Anderson literally drank whiskey like water. Many of their most dastardly deeds occurred when they were intoxicated. Anderson's men found a barrel of whiskey during their capture of the train station at Centralia, Missouri, on September 27, 1864. The liquor was enjoyed by the raiders while they sacked the town. Later they proceeded to massacre all but one of the Union prisoners that they had taken.

Anderson himself approached the horrified townspeople, waved a bottle of booze and asked if anybody wanted a taste. Amazingly, one fellow actually accepted. As the raiders rode away, newly captured boots filled with whiskey were slung across their saddles.

The sole surviving Union prisoner was Sergeant Thomas Goodman of the 1st Missouri Engineers. "Bloody Bill" hoped to exchange Goodman for one of his own men who had been taken captive. Sometime later at the guerilla camp, Goodman watched in amazement as the bushwhackers guzzled liquor until many of them were falling down drunk. Goodman thought that this might be an opportunity to escape until he realized that his guards were the only two teetotalers in the entire outfit. Goodman bided his time but later did find his way to freedom.[40]

* * *

Alcohol, a woman and/or drugs may have played a role in one of the Confederacy's last chances to win a significant battle. In November 1864, Union Major General John Schofield was in a race with his old West Point classmate, John B. Hood, to prevent Schofield's forces from uniting with those of George Thomas at Nashville. Elements of Hood's army arrived at Spring Hill, Tennessee, in time to block the crucial Franklin and Columbia Turnpike but, as darkness fell, they failed to do so. Instead the Rebels went into camp within sight of the escaping Yankees. Ever since, controversy has raged over what went wrong.

There are many theories. One, naturally, is that some of the generals were drunk. Many Tennesseans were overjoyed to see the return of the Rebel army to their state and had freely offered fine sipping whiskey to the important officers. Major General John C. Brown, whose division could have spearheaded the necessary assault, is one possible suspect rumored to be under the influence. There are also solid reports of lively drinking by the high command at the mansion which served as Hood's headquarters that evening.[41]

As for the woman, it was the notorious Jessie Peters. Her physician husband had shot and killed Confederate General Earl Van Dorn a year earlier for having an affair with his comely wife. Since Dr. Peters had fled the area following Van Dorn's murder, Jessie was no doubt lonely that chilly autumn evening. Corps commander Benjamin Cheatham is rumored to have stopped by to pay his regards. If the story is true, Cheatham, a bachelor and frequent imbiber, was another key officer who let pleasure get in the way of the business at hand.

And what of the drugs? Rebel army commander John Hood had suffered mightily in the war, being seriously wounded in the arm at Gettysburg and losing a leg at Chickamauga. His injuries had been bothering him during the cold and exhausting march north, and rumors persist that he may have been using laudanum or other opiates to ease his pain. He went to bed, seemingly unconcerned by reports that the Yankees were fleeing up the highway. Apparently he thought the enemy would still be there in the morning. When he awoke and discovered they were gone, he unleashed his anger on his subordinates. In that black mood, he led his army to a disastrous defeat at Franklin later in the day.[42]

The full details of what truly happened that evening at Spring Hill will probably never be fully known. Clearly the Confederate command structure had suffered a major breakdown with plenty of blame to go around for all. The result was the ruination of the proud old Army of Tennessee.

* * *

As the war neared its conclusion in April 1865, Tom Rosser invited two other Confederate generals, Fitz Lee and George Pickett, to join him for a midday shad bake. The officers disappeared from their lines for several hours, enjoying their repast and possibly a sip or two. Unfortunately, that was the same moment that Union forces under Philip Sheridan struck the vital position at Five Forks, which Pickett and company had pledged to protect at all costs. Sheridan's men sent the Confederates reeling and Richmond was soon doomed to capture. Afterward, in an effort to place blame for the ruinous defeat, rumors spread that the three key Confederate generals were drunk. Even had the trio been sober and at their assigned posts, however, it is unlikely that they could have restrained Sheridan's overwhelming onslaught.[43]

There is no doubt that, at various stages of their lives, George Pickett, Fitz Lee and Tom Rosser certainly enjoyed their liquor.

Confederate soldier John Wise described Pickett as "a high and free liver" who frequently declared that "to fight like a gentleman, a man must eat and drink like a gentleman." As a student at West Point, Pickett had passed out in a snowbank returning from a drinking bout at the off-limits Benny Havens Tavern. A classmate on sentry duty rescued the Virginian before he was discovered and dismissed.[44]

Fitzhugh Lee also had a fondness for Benny Havens during his academy days. He was caught there not once but twice. His uncle, Robert E. Lee, was then the superintendent of West Point, and he dutifully recommended that his delinquent nephew be expelled. Fitz though managed to remain in military school and went on to command cavalry in his Uncle Bobby's Confederate army.[45]

Thirty-one years after Pickett's famous charge at Gettysburg, Kirkwood Otey, formerly a major in the 11th Virginia, came forth with an interesting but unlikely story. He reported seeing two of Pickett's staff officers standing with tin cups by the whiskey wagon on the afternoon of July 3, 1863. This was while the broken grey ranks struggled back from their assault on Cemetery Ridge. Otey had been wounded in the action and was then in search of his own medicinal libation. His inference was that Pickett had been drinking as the fighting took place. Otey's recollection is questionable both for the time it took him to come forward and his own subsequent army court-martial for drunkenness on duty.[46]

Otey is also contradicted by the recollection of Brigadier General Cadmus Wilcox who offered his flask to Pickett just before the charge, saying that "in an hour, you'll be in hell or glory." Pickett declined because he had given his word to a young lady in Virginia that he would not drink alcohol. The young lady, Sallie Corbell, was young indeed—more than two decades Pickett's junior. He would marry her two months later.[47]

After the war, Tom Rosser bought a farm of two hundred acres, and a friend asked what he was going to do with the land.

"Grow grapes, make brandy and raise hell" came the carefree response.

Rosser's drinking days, though, ended on a poignant note. His daughter, Elise, contracted tuberculosis and died in 1886 at the age of twelve. Her father's fondness for alcohol worried the young girl. She had once written him, "I is so afraid you is drunken." She asked Rosser never to drink again and that promise to his dying daughter he kept for the remainder of his life.[48]

* * *

Union Major General Oliver Otis Howard was a pious Medal of Honor winner who had lost a limb at the battle of Fair Oaks in 1862. Nevertheless, he returned to the army to command the unfortunate XI Corps in its sorry experiences at Chancellorsville and Gettysburg. Shuffled off to the western theater, he served under William Tecumseh Sherman during the Georgia campaigns of 1864. Though Howard was only in his early thirties, his troops nicknamed him "Old Prayer Book."[49]

Howard was a staunch temperance man whereas his new commander could often be seen sipping from a flask while on the march or in battle. One day Sherman met with Howard in the latter's tent. They were joined by an army surgeon who decided to offer "Uncle Billy" a stiff toddy. Knowing of Howard's objections, the doctor slyly suggested that the army commander looked tired and should come with him to take a Seidlitz powder. This was an effervescing salt containing sodium bicarbonate, rochelle salt and tartaric acid.

Catching the medicine man's drift, Sherman agreed to the treatment. At this, Howard quickly interjected that Sherman need not leave as Howard had some of the prescribed powder right there. Trapped by his own words, Sherman reluctantly drank the distasteful potion.[50]

Following Lee's surrender at Appomattox Court House in April 1865, Sherman conferred with Confederate General Joe Johnston about the capitulation of the Army of Tennessee. Meeting at the Bennett Farmhouse near Durham Station, North

Carolina, Johnston was accompanied by Confederate Secretary of War John Breckinridge.

Sherman, at one point, pulled a container of whiskey from his saddlebag and offered a drink to his friends, the enemy. Both Southerners gratefully accepted. As the negotiations continued, Sherman helped himself to another taste but forgot to share with the other two. After the conference ended, according to Johnston's recollection, Breckinridge was highly miffed by the slight. He told Johnston that Sherman was "a hog" for drinking by himself. The former vice president of the United States angrily declared, "No Kentucky gentleman would have ever taken away that bottle. He knew we needed it and needed it bad."

Asked about the story years later, Sherman said that he did not recall the particulars but "if Joe Johnston told it, it's true. Those fellows hustled me that day. I was sorry for the drink I did give them."[51]

Breckinridge biographer William C. Davis doubts the substance of this tale and credits it for falsely creating the Kentuckian's reputation as a heavy drinker. The anecdote's source is the John Wise memoir, *End of an Era*, in which he recounts a postwar visit with Joe Johnston. Elsewhere in his book, Wise describes Breckinridge at a Confederate White House reception as having "brought the perfume of Kentucky Bourbon with him."[52]

* * *

Andrew Johnson, the stocky Tennessee tailor who made it to the White House, had his own unfortunate encounters with alcohol. Johnson had spent five terms in Congress, been Tennessee's governor and served in the U.S. Senate when the war broke out. An opponent of secession, he was later installed as the military governor of his home state after Union forces captured Nashville. Assistant Secretary of War Charles Dana visited Johnson's office there in September 1863. Though it was still morning, Johnson produced a jug of whiskey and offered his guest a drink. Johnson mixed his own whiskey with water in a tumbler, instead of sipping a small amount neat. From this, Dana concluded that Johnson was not a "philosophical" drinker but a man who took more liquor than most and took it pretty often.[53]

Hoping for reelection in 1864, Abraham Lincoln discarded his first-term vice president, Hannibal Hamlin of Maine; he instead chose Southern Democrat Johnson as his running mate on a Union-Republican ticket. On March 4, 1865, Johnson was sworn in as vice president of the United States.

Unfortunately, the night before, Andy had been celebrating at a party hosted by Colonel John Forney, clerk of the Senate. In fact, he celebrated too much and got drunk. The next day, the embattled nation's new number two had a terrible hangover. Hoping to make himself feel better, he coaxed a "hair-of-the-dog" drink from his predecessor, Hamlin, just before entering the Senate chamber for the official ceremonies.

Johnson made a fool of himself, giving a rambling, boozy speech that amazed the gallery. At one point, Johnson interrupted his address to ask the name of the secretary of the navy. Hamlin tugged at the tails of Johnson's coat while Senate clerk Forney hissed for him to sit back down. Ignoring this advice, Johnson rattled on. Lincoln quietly gave instructions that Andy should not to be allowed to speak when the gathering moved outside for the president's own swearing-in.[54]

The *New York World* called Johnson "a drunken clown." The performance shocked official Washington, which was now certain that the new vice president was unfit for his high office. Massachusetts Senator Charles Sumner gathered the Republican caucus to urge that they demand Johnson's resignation. Lincoln defended his running mate by assuring friends that, while Andy had made a bad slip, Lincoln had known him for many years and he was no drunkard. Still, the damage was done; it was a debacle from which the Tennessean's reputation never recovered.

A little over a month later, Andrew Johnson was in his room at the Kirkwood House, while a German with a droopy mustache sat downstairs in the hotel barroom. That man was George Atzerodt—his assignment that evening was to kill the vice president. Throughout the day, Atzerodt had been drinking, trying to find the courage to do the deed. Finally the booze got the better of the would-be assassin and Andy Johnson went unharmed.

A few blocks away was the Star Bar. According to one scenario, John Parker, a Washington policeman with a less-than-stellar record, was there taking a little liquid refreshment. In any event, Parker was not where he was supposed to be, guarding the president of the United States.

Another Star Bar patron called out to a handsome fellow who was concentrating on his whiskey and water, "You'll never be the actor your father was!"

"When I leave the stage, I will be the most famous man in America," came the reply. Then John Wilkes Booth finished his drink and walked next door to shoot Abraham Lincoln at Ford's Theater.[55]

Alcohol played a role in the capture and death of Booth. On April 24, 1865, the assassin and his accomplice, David Herold, were hiding out at the Garrett farmhouse not far from Port Royal, Virginia. Booth badly needed rest; he was suffering from a leg broken during his escape after shooting Lincoln. Leaving the actor at the farmhouse, Herold went off with a couple of Confederate soldiers to a countryside barroom, known as "The Trap." Run by a Mrs. Carter and her four daughters, the log roadhouse had a reputation as a place where a man might find some fun. Herold and the others enjoyed a few drinks and amused themselves with the other entertainments that the joint had to offer. It was the last good time of David Herold's life.

The next day Union cavalry looking for the fugitives came to call at "The Trap." As good Southerners, the Carter women refused to cooperate with the Yankees' questions until they were told that the men being sought had molested a young girl. This lie changed the ladies' view of the situation and they told the

Federals where they could find one of the men, Willie Jett. The Yankees rode off to nab Jett who, in turn, took them to the Garrett farmhouse. Booth was mortally wounded while resisting capture. David Herold was taken alive, tried by a military court and hung three months later. His final drinking spree at "The Trap" had indeed led to a trap.[56]

General Hugh Judson Kilpatrick was a reckless adventurer on the battlefield and in the bedroom.

CHAPTER THREE
ROMANCE IN WAR AND PEACE

The family of Robert E. Lee might seem an unlikely place to look for a scandal of any kind, let alone a sex scandal. Alas, there is one. To understand it, a little history on the Lee clan is in order.

Robert E. Lee's father was Henry Lee III, popularly known as "Light Horse Harry" for the gallant service that he had rendered as a young cavalry commander in the Revolutionary War. "Light Horse Harry" married his cousin, Matilda Lee, who was the heiress of the magnificent Stratford Hall estate in Virginia's Northern Neck. To them four children were born, one of whom was named Henry Lee IV. Henry the Fourth would later earn the dubious nickname "Black Horse Harry."

"Light Horse Harry" dabbled in politics and served three terms as Virginia's governor. Unfortunately, he was a reckless businessman who lost great sums of money in questionable ventures and was often hounded by his creditors. Probably for this reason, Matilda created a trust for her holdings; upon her death, they would bypass her husband and go directly to the children.

Matilda died in 1790. "Light Horse Harry" became custodian of the Stratford estate that his son, Henry the Fourth, would inherit when he came of age. At loose ends, the father cast about looking for something to do. He briefly considered sailing to France and lending his military skills to the revolutionaries there but fate intervened. He fell in love with Ann Carter. She was the

47

daughter of one of the richest men in Virginia and seventeen years the junior of "Light Horse Harry." The pair married and their son, Robert Edward Lee, was born at Stratford Hall in January 1807. There is a recurring legend that, prior to Robert's birth, Ann Carter was thought to have died during an illness and was buried alive. A servant supposedly heard moaning coming from the crypt and rescued her. A good story, it is, nevertheless, not true.[1]

This second marriage did not improve "Light Horse Harry's" head for business. Heavy chains were strapped across the doors of the great Stratford house to keep the creditors at bay and family possessions were sold off to pay bills. The Revolutionary War hero was twice jailed for debt.

In 1808, "Black Horse Harry" came of age, leaving his father and his new family in the awkward positions of guests at Stratford. They departed for more modest but quite comfortable quarters in Alexandria. There they lived off a trust from the estate of Ann's father which "Light Horse Harry" was prohibited from squandering.[2]

"Light Horse Harry" had a sad end. In 1812, a Baltimore mob beat him nearly to death in a wild riot over the war with Britain. "Light Horse" had gone to the aid of Alexander Hanson, the son of a close friend, whose newspaper offices were under siege because of its anti-war editorials. On the evening of July 27, four hundred angry protestors surrounded the building where Hanson, Lee and a handful of supporters waited with loaded muskets. The mob tried to storm the place but was driven back. The attackers brought a cannon to blast the building to pieces when the militia arrived and maintained an unsteady peace until morning. Having no alternatives, Hanson, Lee and company agreed to surrender their weapons and were taken to jail where perhaps they might be better protected. En route the prisoners were stoned and cursed.

The next evening the still-agitated mob broke into the jail and grabbed the trapped men who were beaten and stabbed. Some had hot candle grease poured in their eyes and others were covered with tar. One thug tried to cut the nose off "Light Horse Harry."[3]

The fifty-six-year-old soldier barely survived the brutality and he would never truly recover. Hoping to regain his health, he sailed for Barbados, leaving behind his wife and family. Little Bobby Lee never saw his father again.

Meanwhile "Black Horse Harry" soon proved that, in addition to Stratford, he had also inherited his father's losing ways with money. By 1828, his debts were such that they forced the sale of the great estate. The fine property was purchased by one of the creditors, Henry D. Storcke, for $11,000.

"Black Horse" fell back upon his political connections, hoping that with Andrew Jackson's influence, he could become chief clerk of the United States Senate. When that fell through, "Old Hickory" offered him a consul post in Morocco. "Black Horse" accepted and set off for Africa.

Here is where Henry the Fourth earned his nickname. With "Black Horse" already sailing to his new job, Senate confirmation hearings were held, and what they uncovered was not pleasant.

"Black Horse" was married to Anne McCarty, who along with her sister, Betsey, was heir to one of the largest fortunes in that part of Virginia. "Black Horse" and Anne conceived a child, but the infant died tragically by tumbling down the steep steps of the Stratford mansion. To ease the pain of her loss, Anne abused morphine while her husband sought comfort elsewhere.

"Black Horse" served as the guardian of his sister-in-law, Betsey, but it was an instance of the "fox-in-the-henhouse." He became sexually attracted to her and the two had an affair which produced a stillborn child. Subsequent investigators discovered missing monies from Betsey's trust account while it was in the questionable care of "Black Horse."[4]

As a result of these shocking revelations, not one senator voted to confirm the appointment of "Black Horse Harry" Lee as consul to Morocco. In disgrace, Henry the Fourth fled to Europe where he was joined by his wife, Anne, who had somehow managed to forgive him. Robert E. Lee's older brother died in Paris seven years later.

And what of Anne's sister, Betsey? She married Henry D. Storcke and took her place as the mistress of Stratford Hall![5]

Historians have made much of these family scandals in shaping the character of Robert E. Lee, and there is no doubt that they impacted the young man's outlook on life. He always dreamed of purchasing Stratford Hall, thereby restoring what once had been. Robert E. Lee's wife, Mary, had inherited the magnificent Custis Mansion of Arlington, and that was Lee's home in the antebellum years. When the Federal government first occupied and later confiscated the estate during the Civil War, the loss must have seemed like a case of *déjà vu.*

On Christmas Day 1861, with the war underway, Robert Lee wrote wistfully to his wife: *"In the absence of a home I wish I could purchase Stratford. That is the only place I could go to, now accessible to us, that would inspire me with feelings of pleasure and local love. You and the girls could remain there in quiet. It is a poor place, but we could make enough cornbread and bacon for our support and the girls could weave us clothes. I wonder if it is for sale and how much."*[6]

* * *

The years before, during and after the American Civil War fall neatly into the Victorian era, when a premium was placed upon respectability and appearance. Affairs of a carnal nature were not to be openly discussed in polite circles—particularly in mixed company. Even so, human desire does not change, regardless of social mores.

This was a time of a strong double standard. The sexual urges of men were understood to be part of the animal male nature. A good wife might accept her husband's visit to a bawdyhouse as long as he was discreet and came home in time for dinner. Lusty female behavior, on the other hand, was not tolerated in good society.

Confederate raider John Hunt Morgan, though a married man with a sickly wife, had a reputation in the prewar years as someone who "lived freely." In the words of his brother-in-law,

Confederate General Basil Duke, Morgan enjoyed amusements that would "have shocked a New Englander almost as much as the money he spent in obtaining them." His associates in the wool and slave-trading businesses urged Morgan to come visit New Orleans and Memphis; in the former city, they promised "50 Acres of whores" including "some very pretty ones" while the latter place featured nice women of "any size or color."[7]

In Morgan's hometown of Lexington, Kentucky, slave dealer Lewis Robards specialized in acquiring attractive mulatto "fancy girls" who could be sold into the New Orleans flesh trade. Most of these young women were the result of sexual relations between master and slave. Often Southern wives disliked having pretty mixed-race females around their plantations, either because they were reminders of their husbands' indiscretions or out of concern that their sons might be tempted. One woman explained that the "fondness of our young men for some of the negro girls" was because "as babies they were suckled by negro women."[8]

Most major cities had their disreputable sections where paid female companionship was easily available. In 1860, Britain's Prince of Wales made a well-publicized visit to the United States. While in New York, he allegedly ducked his handlers to spend an evening visiting many well-known brothels. His mother, Queen Victoria, would have been shocked—although even the very proper Royal Highness enjoyed her own close relationship with Scottish servant John Brown.[9]

Venereal disease was the great scourge of the nineteenth-century Don Juan; there was no remedy for it at that time, and, according to some estimates, 50 percent or more of the era's menfolk suffered from it. Women feared their husbands might bring the incurable disease home to the marital bed.[10]

West Point records indicate that Confederate General Ambrose Powell Hill and Union General George Armstrong Custer both contracted gonorrhea during their student days, probably from prostitutes in New York City. In Hill's case, recuperating from the effects of the disease took so long that he was forced to repeat his third year at the military academy. While he may have thought his recovery was complete, it is probable that the lingering disease was the source of the many illnesses which would plague his entire military career.[11]

When Hill fell in love with Ellen Marcy, the girl's mother learned of Hill's affliction and used the knowledge to end the engagement. Instead Miss Ellen married another rising young officer, George B. McClellan, who later would command the Union's Army of the Potomac.[12]

Custer always liked the ladies; in fact, the influential father of one of his early girlfriends may have helped secure his appointment to West Point in order to get George out of town and away from his daughter. On August 29, 1859, shortly after returning from a furlough, the young cadet reported to the academy infirmary with the symptoms of gonorrhea. The disease possibly left him sterile; his later marriage to Libbie Bacon was childless.[13]

Rumors of sexual shenanigans seemed to follow the yellow-haired soldier. During the war, he employed an ex-slave named Eliza Brown as his cook, and Custer's detractors maintained that she shared his bed. While Eliza was an important enough fixture at headquarters to earn the nickname "Queen of Sheba," reliable evidence of any intimate coupling is lacking. What's more, Eliza remained with the Custer household even after the war ended and she enjoyed a close relationship with the general's wife.[14]

Annie Jones from Massachusetts, however, is another case entirely. Annie was a teenage camp follower who had tagged along with the Army of the Potomac since 1861. She reportedly became a favorite of several generals, including Franz Sigel, Julius Stahl and Edwin Stoughton. She latched on to Custer at Warrenton, Virginia, in the fall of 1863 and remained with him, as he later reported, while seeking employment as a nurse. By then, Annie would have been seeking such "employment" for at least two years. She described Custer as her "friend and companion."

Annie later hooked up with Custer's superior officer, Hugh Judson Kilpatrick, who, despite having a wife and infant child at home, found her an appealing bunkmate. Kilpatrick dressed his paramour in a major's uniform and gave her a horse to ride, but apparently he was not as much fun as her previous patron. Annie returned to Custer's camp. Naturally this angered Kilpatrick who had her arrested and hauled away to Washington as a suspected spy. The wayward girl was briefly booked into the Old Capitol Prison before agreeing to stay out of Virginia and the District of Columbia if she was released. She later claimed that several of her jailers became her lovers.

No doubt Custer and Kilpatrick figured that they had heard the last of the troublesome trollop, but they were wrong. On March 13, 1864, authorities in Washington arrested Annie Jones once more. This time Annie boasted of her close ties to Custer and Kilpatrick and both generals were asked to explain the relationship. Custer, by then newly married, submitted a reply putting things in the best light possible and denied intimate relations. Kilpatrick simply did not respond.[15]

After the war, Custer may have had an intimate relationship with an Indian woman named Me-o-tzi or Mo-nah-se-tah while serving on the frontier in 1869. Me-o-tzi rode with the 7th Cavalry for several months as an interpreter, and Custer wrote of her great beauty in his book, *My Life on the Plains*. Custer's detractors and Cheyenne tradition say that the relationship became sexual and a child was born. The parenthood claim seems unlikely from both a timing standpoint and the question of whether Custer could actually father children. Supposedly Me-o-tzi refused all offers of marriage after Custer left, believing that her white "husband" would someday return. But Me-o-tzi knew of and had, in fact, met Custer's wife, Libbie, so the actual truth of the relationship remains in question.[16]

Of course, taking a "campaign wife" was not unknown. While serving in the Washington Territory in 1856, Captain George Pickett married an Indian maiden named "Morning Mist" in both tribal and white ceremonies. On December 31, 1857, they had a son, James Tilton Pickett, but childbirth was difficult and the mother died early in the new year. Tragically, Pickett's first wife had also died as the result of childbirth.

When the war came, the Virginian returned east to fight for the South. He left young James in the care of friends, given the uncertainties of military life and the unhappy reaction a mixed-race child might produce back home. Though he provided money for James' upbringing and left the child mementoes of his army career, Pickett never saw his son again. James grew up to be a talented artist before dying of tuberculosis in 1889. Pickett's third wife, Sallie, explained away the child in one of her books by saying that he had been a gift from an Indian chief—which probably sounded better than claiming he had been found in a pumpkin patch.[17]

Union General Hugh Judson Kilpatrick continued his rakish ways for the remainder of his life. Shuffled out of the Virginia theater, he received orders to join the western army for its 1864 Georgia campaign. Sherman said that he knew Kilpatrick was a damned fool but that was just the kind of fellow he wanted to command his cavalry. Near the close of the "March to the Sea," Kilpatrick acquired a new mistress in the form of a Chinese laundry girl named Molly. When Molly became pregnant, the ungallant general ordered her from his camp but Molly would not leave. She demanded that he take responsibility for the unborn child.

As the Federal invaders headed north to the Carolinas, Molly trailed along. Kilpatrick turned his attentions elsewhere and even proposed marriage to one cute Southern belle. The woman declined. Though Kilpatrick had made the marriage offer in jest, he was, in fact, a bachelor again. His wife and young child had recently died.

The Yankee rogue found another lover in Columbia. Marie Boozer was an attractive nineteen-year-old who had just left her fourth husband. Marie's mother was the Northern-born wife of a Columbia shopkeeper and, during the war, she and her daughter had helped hide escaped Federal prisoners. As the bluecoats departed the smoking ruins of South Carolina's capital, Marie went along, often riding in a carriage with Kilpatrick's head on her lap.

On the morning of March 10, 1865, the lovers occupied a white frame cabin near Monroe's Cross Roads, North Carolina. Wade Hampton's Rebel cavalry had been dogging the Union horsemen and here they found their chance to launch a surprise attack. Preoccupied with his lady, Kilpatrick had failed to post an adequate number of sentries. Marie and her general awoke to the sound of gunfire as grey horsemen galloped into the Yankee camp.

Clad only in boots and a nightshirt, Kilpatrick ran onto the porch to see mounted Rebels riding right at him. "Where is General Kilpatrick?" one of them demanded.

An expert at self-preservation, Kilpatrick pointed at a distant officer desperately trying to mount a black horse and shouted, "There he goes!" As the Confederates gave chase to the decoy, Kilpatrick scrambled onto the back of another steed and made his getaway.

Marie was left to rescue herself. She dressed quickly and rushed out to her carriage to which no horses were hitched. She was dangerously stranded in the middle of a hot little skirmish until, as chivalry required, one Southern trooper helped her find safety in a roadside gully. Hidden beneath Marie's skirt was Kilpatrick's battle flag.

In time, Union infantry arrived, Kilpatrick's troops rallied and the Rebs took their plunder and retreated. The early morning "shirttail skedaddle" drew laughter from the ranks of both armies.[18]

Shortly thereafter, the Yankees reached Fayetteville and Marie bid her soldier adieu to take the Union tugboat *Davidson* down the Cape Fear River to Wilmington. She secured passage to New York City by marrying a Union officer from Philadelphia. Later she traveled to Europe and married yet again—this time to a French count. If one wants to believe the legend, she eventually ended up in Asia as the concubine of a Chinese warlord. Marie's oriental lover supposedly cut her tendons to prevent her from running away and fed her until she weighed over three hundred pounds. The warlord apparently liked a woman with some meat on her bones!

Kilpatrick wasn't lonely long. A Southern woman, whom he had first met in Georgia, showed up in his camp to renew their relationship. She was married but on the run from her husband. After the "shirttail skedaddle," Kilpatrick was trying to keep his love life low profile, so he dressed the woman in an army uniform and called her "Charlie." His adjutant also had a mistress who dressed in men's clothes and went by the name of "Frank." Needless to say, the fancy dress costumes fooled no one, least of all the many soldiers who saw that the general and comely "Charlie" were sharing the same quarters.[19]

When the war came to an end, Kilpatrick shipped a favorite horse, "Spot," back to his New Jersey farm. He left Molly, the pregnant Chinese laundress, behind in North Carolina.[20]

The general turned his sights to a career of public service, hoping to become the governor of New Jersey and perhaps someday even president. In the meantime, he settled for an appointment as United States envoy to Chile; that set the stage for one of the strangest romantic escapades of his life.

On a U.S. Navy ship en route to his new post, Kilpatrick encountered a "Mrs. Williams" who was bound for Panama to join her naval officer husband. Arriving in Panama, Kilpatrick met the husband who confessed that he had a problem. He and his wife were headed to San Francisco but his military ship would not arrive there for some time due to the frequent official stops that it planned to make. It would be impossible for his wife to accompany him. Could she follow the general on his journey to Chile and sail from there to meet her husband?

One might think Kilpatrick would have found something fishy with this proposal but perhaps he was too enticed with the prospect of being alone with "Mrs. Williams." In any event, he agreed to help a brother officer by looking after the man's wife.

Naturally Kilpatrick and his new charge soon became lovers. When they arrived in Chile, he actually introduced her into society as his spouse. Unfortunately, when it came time for "Mrs. Williams" to leave, she did not go. In fact, she began plying her trade as a prostitute on the streets. Those who knew her as the new envoy's wife were horrified. Kilpatrick sent awkward letters of apology to those who had wined and dined him and his illicit companion. Word of "Mrs. Williams" reached Washington in the form of sensational press reports and Kilpatrick tried to concoct a satisfactory explanation for the State Department.[21]

Though his wife had died, Kilpatrick had invited his mother-in-law to accompany him to South America as his official hostess. The mother-in-law was an eyewitness to all that had happened. After Kilpatrick's death, she petitioned the court to remove her daughter's body from the grave beside his at West Point and be re-buried in New York City.[22]

* * *

Confederate Major General Matthew Calbraith Butler commanded some of the troops who surprised Kilpatrick that March morning at Monroe's Crossroads. Like Kilpatrick, he was a man who admired a good-looking woman.

In 1858, Butler had married Maria Pickens, daughter of Francis Pickens, who became governor of South Carolina. Although they had two children by the time Butler rode off to war in 1861, the pair's relationship was frequently rocky. Maria was a child of privilege who enjoyed spending money and disliked mundane wifely duties. Butler was a bit of a rounder with a roving eye.[23]

He probably began having affairs while serving in J.E.B. Stuart's cavalry; at least one letter to Maria from that period could be read as a confession of sorts.[24]

When he lost a leg at the battle of Brandy Station, the limb was stored in the attic of his South Carolina home so that it could later be buried with him. The injury did not dampen his libido, however. During his recovery, the general formed an unusually close acquaintance with a twenty-year-old neighbor girl. Years later, the woman wrote to Butler asking his help in obtaining a government job. Butler responded enthusiastically to the request until it became clear the woman was actually looking for work and not a renewal of their romance.[25]

Despite these difficulties and periods of separation, Butler and his wife had a total of seven children. He also, however, helped financially support a child he had fathered with another woman and there may have been others as well. His bedroom was at the opposite end of the house from Maria's. It had its own outside door raised high so the one-legged man could conveniently slide onto his horse and slip away unnoticed for nocturnal visits.[26]

Though even friends and neighbors denounced General Butler's promiscuous lifestyle, it did not affect his political career. He served three terms in the United States Senate and, when the Spanish-American War began, the old Confederate became a major general of U.S. Volunteers.

Maria died in 1900. As he headed toward his eighth decade of life, Butler remarried in 1905, this time to a forty-six-year-old widow who was the same age as one of his sons.

* * *

Butler's war-time commander, James Ewell Brown Stuart, had a reputation as a ladies' man. The epitome of the dashing cavalier with his plumed hat and red-lined cape, Stuart made Southern women swoon wherever he went. John Esten Cooke recalled how female admirers would gather around the blue-eyed general to present him with flowers and receive a kiss in return. Passing through Middleburg, Virginia, in the autumn of 1862, Stuart was waylaid by fifty or sixty ladies of various ages who kissed his glove and the skirt of his coat. Stuart told them that the "kisses would be more acceptable...if given on the cheek." After brief hesitation, the females charged forward and delivered a heavy volley of smooches.[27]

Stuart's wartime letters and the recollections of his staff make the man appear as if he was something of a "kissing bandit"— except that the kisses were not stolen but given willingly. Maybe what made him so irresistible was his untrimmed red-brown beard which, as of 1861, Stuart had not touched with a razor in seven years.[28]

Stuart's festive camp life added greatly to the "moonlight and magnolia" mystique of the Civil War. He gave memorable parties, such as the one at the female academy in Urbana during the Maryland campaign of September 1862. While his horsemen were providing a screen for the movements of Lee's army, Stuart decorated a large room with battle flags and hosted a gala ball. The fun was interrupted when unchivalrous Yankees made a late-night run upon his outposts. A month later, while trying to escape after a raid into Pennsylvania, Stuart briefly left his command and wandered off for a late-night visit to the "New York Rebel," one of the attractive women whom he had met during the party in Urbana.[29]

That same fall, Stuart made his headquarters at "The Bower," a private estate near Shepherdstown, West Virginia. He described it as "a charming place, full of pretty girls, all dear friends of mine." That made for a memorable series of evening socials, enlivened by party games and the merry sounds of Sam Sweeny's banjo. Colonel Tom Rosser of the 5th Virginia had a flirtation with one or more of the young ladies. He was somewhat embarrassed to encounter these same girls when the cavalry returned to the area a few months later. In the meantime, Rosser had married someone else.[30]

J.E.B. Stuart's oversized personality and showy behavior grated on some observers. An anonymous Culpeper, Virginia, woman wrote Jefferson Davis that Stuart's cavalry reviews of June 1863 were "apparently a monkey show" with Stuart as the monkey. She complained that the foppish, flower-decked general was "devoting his whole time to his lady friends' company." The president's aide, Custis Lee, forwarded the letter to Stuart with the advice that he either "cease his attentions to the ladies or make them more general."[31]

Stuart's wife, Flora, did occasionally object to the many female admirers seeking her husband's favor. After she had visited his camp, a carte-de-visite photo of one of the general's woman friends was mysteriously missing. Stuart believed that Flora had taken it. In 1864, he wrote her to defend his fondness for "the society of ladies," saying that she was better off than if he preferred some other things.[32]

In fact, Flora probably did not have much to worry about. While Stuart's numerous detractors tried to cast the endearing attentions he received in the worst possible light, there is no true evidence of sexual misconduct on the general's part. The tender kisses taken in public were simply a perk of being, as a staff member put it, one of the "heroes of romance fresh from the fields of glory."[33]

Stuart's military family greatly enjoyed the female companionship that proximity to the general provided. Fair-haired John Pelham of Alabama, who commanded Stuart's horse artillery, liked the ladies as much as they liked him. When the gallant Major Pelham died after being mortally wounded in action at Kelly's Ford, Virginia, on March 17, 1863, three women reportedly donned mourning dresses. The twenty-five-year-old officer's personal effects included a Bible in which the legendary Confederate spy Belle Boyd had written, "I know that thou art loved by another now. I know thou will never be mine."[34]

Belle Boyd, however, did not stay lonely long. Captured in May 1864 while aboard a Bermuda-bound blockade runner, she fell in love with a Yankee naval officer. Ensign Samuel Hardinge of Brooklyn wooed his lady prisoner with pieces of poetry from Shakespeare and Byron. After they arrived in New York, the Northern authorities banished Belle to Canada and cashiered Hardinge for his dalliance with an infamous Rebel spy. The two lovers met up in England and, on August 25, 1864, they married at St. James' Church not far from London's Picadilly Circus. Curiously, her new husband then returned to America while Belle remained in Britain. The Federals arrested Hardinge on suspicion of espionage and he marked time in jail until the war was nearly over.[35]

Accounts vary as to what eventually happened to Belle's husband. In one version, the unlucky ensign returned to England

and was briefly reunited with his bride before dying from prison-induced ailments. Another version has Hardinge drowning at sea. Even Belle's memoirs, published in May 1865, give no true clue to his fate.[36]

In any event, after the Confederacy collapsed, Belle was a twenty-one-year-old widow with an infant daughter. Traveling back to America, she married an Englishman who had served as an officer in the 7th Massachusetts Infantry. That marriage ended in divorce in 1884, and Belle married for a third and final time the following year.[37]

Belle was not the only Confederate lady to fall for a handsome boy in blue. One of J.E.B. Stuart's favorites, attractive Antonia Ford of Fairfax Court House, received an honorary commission naming her as a member of his staff. Stuart's gift helped land Antonia in the Old Capitol Prison. She carelessly showed it to a female informant whom the Yankees had sent to befriend her. Antonia had come under suspicion of helping raider John Mosby capture Union General Edwin Stoughton, and Stuart's document was proof enough that she was a spy. In the end, all turned out well, for Antonia married Major Joseph Willard, one of the officers who had arrested her! [38]

When it came to matrimony, however, it was hard to beat Ginnie and Lottie Moon, two secessionist sisters who hailed from southwestern Ohio. Ginnie was reportedly engaged to sixteen men at one time during the war while Lottie had a pre-war suitor in the form of future Union General Ambrose Burnside. Burnside supposedly got Lottie to agree to marry him but was embarrassingly jilted at the altar. Nevertheless Ambrose kept up his pursuit of the young lovely until Lottie's mother finally informed him that her daughter had gotten hitched to someone else.

With a twist worthy of pulp fiction, in 1863, General Burnside commanded the Department of Ohio at Cincinnati when two Rebel smugglers were apprehended. Despite the passage of some thirteen years, Burnside immediately recognized the mother and younger sister of his runaway fiancée. The pair had been caught heading down to Dixie with quantities of opium, morphine and other contraband. There were documents as well though Ginnie managed to swallow the most important of these.

The reunion must have brought back bittersweet memoirs for the man Ginnie knew by the unwar-like nickname of "Buttons." Burnside asked the girl, who was to have been his sister-in-law, why she had not come to him for a pass through the lines. She replied that she could not do so, knowing she would violate his trust.

However Burnside's trip down memory lane had not ended. A short time later, his former lover, Lottie, was hauled into headquarters. Although she tried to pass herself off as an English-woman, she did not fool her old flame for an instant. Burnside sent her to join her mother and sister, and the trio remained in custody for several weeks before being released. Though all is fair in love and war, Burnside remained the gallant beau.[39]

* * *

"Stonewall" Jackson's sister reportedly had a romance or two with the dreaded Yankees. Laura Jackson Arnold lived in Beverly, West Virginia, and was married to a man who in 1863 was arrested for his Southern sympathies. Despite these family connections, Laura backed the Federal government and nursed sick and wounded bluecoat soldiers in her home. Local gossip had it that Laura gave her body to one or more of the Northern officers. She had once been close to her now-famous brother but the pair had become estranged and she publicly accused him of having cheated on his West Point entrance exam. No one mentioned Laura when Jackson was present and she insisted that his name never be spoken in front of her. Nevertheless, she did write to her sister-in-law, Anna, in November 1862. Almost two years later, in September 1864, the widowed Anna sent through the lines a long and heartfelt letter to tell Laura the details of "Stonewall's" final hours.[40]

Winnie Davis, daughter of Confederate President Jefferson Davis, disappointed many an unreconstructed Rebel when she became engaged to marry a New Yorker named Alfred Wilkinson in 1889. Born during the war in the Richmond White House, Winnie was nicknamed the "daughter of the Confederacy." The thought of that child being betrothed to a Yankee—and that Jeff Davis had actually agreed to the match—upset many an old unreconstructed Rebel.[41]

One such die-hard Southerner was Jubal Early, whose bitter-end attitude may have been an effort to make amends for his military failures in the war's final year. Early received a letter from Varina Davis, asking for his opinion on her daughter's proposed marriage. No record of his response exists. Early's unreconstructed postwar attitude, however, is a bit ironic considering he had originally opposed Virginia's secession from the Union.[42]

Early comes down to us in history as a crusty old bachelor who had little patience with women, especially the camp-following wife of his subordinate, John B. Gordon. Blunt and direct to the men under his command, Early was somewhat shy around the fairer sex. When General Ewell directed him to make an impromptu address to the women of Winchester, he could only stammer, "I can't speak to ladies. Excuse me."[43]

Supposedly Early soured on females after falling in love with a Quaker lass from Pennsylvania during a pre-war visit to the summer resort of White Sulphur Springs. When he later received a "Dear Jube" letter telling of his beloved's marriage to another, he resolved to forever live the single life. Perhaps the fact that the faithless female hailed from above the Mason-Dixon line also influenced his latter view of Northerners.[44]

But Early's late nights were not as lonely as legend might have us believe. It is known that, without benefit of ceremony, the general sired children, possibly to both white and black mothers. The white woman was Julia McNealy, who had four of Early's children before she ended the relationship in 1871 and married another fellow. Robert E. Lee may have called the hard-cussing, whiskey-drinking, tobacco-spitting Early "my bad old man" for more reasons than one.[45]

* * *

When Judge Charles Sherman of Lancaster, Ohio, died in 1829, he left behind a wife, eleven children, insufficient income and substantial debt. Family friend Thomas Ewing volunteered to raise one of the children as his own and that is how William Tecumseh Sherman met his wife. He and Ellen Ewing grew up together virtually as brother and sister and then married in 1850 when "Cump" was an army captain.

Their marriage produced eight children and survived frequent separations as Sherman struggled to develop a successful civilian career after resigning his military commission. Then the war came and, by its end, Sherman was a Northern hero second only to U. S. Grant. Even in peacetime, Sherman's married life was interrupted by his ongoing duties as general in chief of the army and an increasing number of veteran reunions and other social invitations. In 1871–1872, the general took a ten-month trip to Europe, unaccompanied by his wife.

None of these activities particularly interested Ellen, who was increasingly devoted to the Catholic Church. Sherman, unfortunately, did not share his wife's religious enthusiasm. He was aghast when their son, Tom, decided to become a Jesuit priest instead of an attorney.[46]

The couple also had periods of separation because they were no longer getting along with one another. Sherman, despite his well-known "if elected, I would not serve" disavowal of the presidency, enjoyed the public acclaim brought by his wartime accomplishments. He was seduced by fame and by the women it drew to him.

Vinnie Ream was the first female and youngest artist ever to win a commission from the U.S. Congress. In 1866, at age eighteen, she was offered the chance to sculpt a statue of Abraham Lincoln for the Capitol rotunda. Mark Twain called her "the shrewdest politician of all" with a "mild talent for sculpture." In his book *The Guilded Age*, he sarcastically described her statue of a "petrified" Lincoln holding the Emancipation Proclamation as if it was a "folded napkin" in which he has found "fault with the washing." Regardless of Twain's opinion, Vinnie was quite talented and had studied for a time in Italy. She was even more gifted at meeting and getting her way with influential people.[47]

During the impeachment trial of Andrew Johnson, Senator Edmund Ross of Kansas was a lodger in the home of Vinnie's mother. The night before the ballot, radical Republicans were rounding up the votes to ensure the president's conviction. Though Ross was one of their party, they were concerned that he might waver. One-legged General Dan Sickles was sent out to the Ream household to lock in Ross' critical vote. From outside, Sickles could see the light burning in Ross' room but the general was waylaid at the downstairs door by Vinnie Ream. Vinnie, a Johnson supporter, told the "hero of Gettysburg" that the senator was not home. Without invitation, Sickles stumped his way inside and sat down to await Ross' return. Certain that Ross was upstairs, Sickles remained in place until 4 a.m. He finally admitted defeat after Vinnie told him that Ross planned to support the president. Johnson was acquitted by that single vote.[48]

William Sherman met Miss Ream in 1873 when she was competing for a $20,000 commission for a memorial statue of the recently deceased Admiral David Farragut. The fifty-six-year-old general was smitten with the young artist and she enlisted his influence in helping her win the project. Today the ten-foot statue stands in Washington's Farragut Square.

The two became lovers soon after their meeting as evidenced by contemporary gossip and surviving letters; Vinnie did not destroy Sherman's correspondence as he had requested. The relationship continued until Sherman left Washington in the fall of 1874 with occasional meetings afterward. Author Michael Fellman, who researched the general's extra-marital love life for his book, *Citizen Sherman*, hypothesizes that Vinnie Ream appealed to the grizzled war hero because she was both a sexy little girl and brave independent woman.[49]

Vinnie apparently liked military men. Another of her favorite male friends was Albert Pike, the Boston-born Confederate general and noted Freemason. Pike had abandoned his wife in Arkansas after the close of the war. Nearly forty years Vinnie's senior, he wrote impassioned letters to her which he signed only with an asterisk to mask his identity. When the sculptress finally did marry, it was to West Pointer Richard Hoxie then working his way up the ranks to brigadier general.[50]

Sherman went on to more extra-marital romance. Colonel J. C. Audenried was a West Point graduate from the class of 1861 who had served as Sherman's aide during and after the war. In his memoirs, the general wrote of Audenried that "a more honorable, chivalrous, and courteous gentleman never lived."[51]

Sherman also thought highly of his subordinate's wife and, when Colonel Audenried passed away in 1880, the general called to pay his respects. Thus began the most serious of Sherman's affairs, one that continued for almost a decade. A favorite Sherman rendezvous was to take his lover for a ride through the country in a closed carriage. There they could enjoy themselves unobserved by either the driver or the public.

When Sherman retired from the army in 1883, his family moved from Washington to Saint Louis. Sherman tried to break off his affair with Mary Audenried but the temptation was too strong. Instead their meetings were restricted by whenever his travel plans brought the pair to within a convenient distance of one another.

On one occasion, Sherman actually asked his lover to be a guest at the family home in Saint Louis. This ended badly, for Mary and Ellen had a terrible argument. The disagreement centered not on the general but on the Catholic Church. Ever afterward Mrs. Audenried was persona non grata to Ellen, a view totally confirmed when she discovered one of the love letters that this woman had written to her husband!

A passage in one of Sherman's own surviving love letters is a Freudian delight. He describes a dream in which his daughter, Rachael, is in bed with Mary Audenried. He kisses Rachael good night and then turns to Mary who embraces him passionately. In today's world, a few thousand dollars worth of psychoanalysis might have helped explain some things to the old soldier.[52]

In 1888, Ellen Sherman passed from this mortal coil. Despite their estrangement of later years, Sherman was overcome with emotion by the loss of his life-long companion and mother of his children. Learning that his wife was in her final moments, he rushed to her room shouting, "Wait for me, Ellen! No one ever loved you as I loved you."[53]

The death did not create an opening for Mrs. Audenried. Her romance with Sherman was now a guttering flame. The aged war hero, less than three years from his own demise, lacked the spirit to enter into the confines of a new marriage.

Shown here at the height of her power as a Washington society belle, Kate Chase Sprague spent her final years in poverty.

CHAPTER FOUR
POLITICS AND LOVE

During the Civil War years, young Kate Chase rivaled first lady Mary Lincoln in her hold on Washington society. Born in 1840, Kate was the enchanting daughter of Salmon Chase, a former U.S. senator from Ohio and secretary of the treasury in Lincoln's cabinet.

A widower who had buried three wives and four children, Salmon Chase had an unusually close relationship with his daughter. Given her natural charm and finishing school manners, Kate made an excellent hostess for her ambitious father. In his diary, Secretary of the Navy Gideon Welles described her as "beautiful, or, perhaps more properly, interesting and impressive."[1]

There were rumors about a flirtation with a married man back when her father was governor of Ohio, but people always liked to gossip about Kate. Everybody wondered whom she would marry.

The answer came on November 12, 1863, when she wed handsome William Sprague, a United States senator and Rhode Island's former "boy governor." Sprague was the heir to a textile fortune and had served with the army in the early part of the war. As a wedding present for his new bride, he visited Tiffany's and purchased a diamond-and-pearl tiara, bracelet and earring set which cost over $6,000.

The pair made an interesting match. Some felt that Kate could have done better and that she was simply marrying for money. The Chases had position but no wealth. Much of Sprague's success had come thanks to his family name and inherited fortune. He was overly fond of drink; Kate and her father supported temperance. William could be gruff and slovenly; Kate was socially refined and dressed fashionably. While it would not be generally known until later, Sprague also had ties to shady dealings in which Confederate cotton was smuggled north for the family textile mills.[2]

Sprague was a womanizer. Before meeting Kate, he had fathered a child out of wedlock with Mary Eliza Viall of Providence. The expectant mother was married off to a man named Anderson but she secretly continued her affair with Sprague even after his marriage. Sprague also bedded chambermaids and visited houses of ill repute with a regularity to which his wife eventually became resigned.[3]

Kate's dream was the same as that of her father: that Salmon Chase would become president of the United States and that Kate would reign as hostess in the White House. Chase had tried and failed to get the Republican nomination in 1860. Four years later, radical Republicans promoted his candidacy over that of the president whom he served. The subsequent embarrassment eventually led to Chase's resignation from the cabinet.

Lincoln, however, was not a vindictive man and he still liked his former treasury secretary well enough to name him chief justice of the Supreme Court in December 1864. Kate did not approve of the appointment for she felt it meant the end of her father's presidential hopes. When Senator Charles Sumner brought news of her father's confirmation, she asked him accusingly, "You, too, in this business of shelving Papa?"[4]

Though their union produced four children, the Spragues' married life did not improve in the postwar era; instead, the couple endured a series of separations and reconciliations. In a curious move, Senator Sprague actually provided the one-vote margin needed to reduce the size of a much-desired salary increase for his father-in-law, the chief justice.

Salmon Chase died in 1873 and that same year a financial panic significantly diminished Sprague's fortune. Reduced circumstances did not improve the troubled couple's relationship. Matters worsened even more when a drunken Sprague was arrested in Massachusetts after being caught *in flagrante delicto* with his old girlfriend, Mary Eliza Viall Anderson. For her part, Viall had never accepted Sprague's marriage and even privately published a book that was a thinly veiled attack upon her rival.[5]

The Spragues led increasingly separate lives. Kate sought companionship in the form of Senator Roscoe Conkling of New York, known both for his prominence as a radical Republican and his reputation as a ladies' man. Washington society matrons clucked over how Kate would watch adoringly from the Senate gallery as Conkling delivered his speeches and of the special attentions that he gave her at social gatherings.

It was Conkling who brought about the final collapse of the Spragues' shaky marriage in 1879. William Sprague returned unexpectedly to their summer home in Narragansett, Rhode Island, and discovered Conkling was his wife's guest. According to one version, only a servant's warning prevented the New Yorker from being caught in Kate's bed. A terrific row ensued as Sprague waved a shotgun and ordered the distinguished gentleman out of his house. Conkling left but Sprague followed, reportedly packing a pistol. The argument continued outside a local café until the wronged husband had finished venting. Conkling then took the train to Providence.[6]

The newspapers played up the story in a series of conflicting sensational articles. Conkling used friends to get his version of events to reporters and Kate issued her own statement—neither account flattered William Sprague. A messy divorce ended their messy marriage.[7]

Kate nursed her emotional wounds in Europe until financial concerns dictated that she return to America. She still owned her father's Washington estate, Edgewood, where she actually tried to earn a living as a produce farmer, peddling milk and vegetables to the society matrons whom she had once lorded over.[8]

William Sprague was equally impoverished. He remained at the Narragansett house with Willie Junior, the only son that he and Kate had. When the house was sold at a sheriff's auction, Sprague refused to vacate the premises. He actually occupied the property until the new owner died and then he bought it back. Sprague also remarried and, in a bizarre twist, Willie Junior then married his new stepmother's sister, so that he became his own uncle as well as his father's brother-in-law. Junior's marriage ended a year later and he drifted from job to job until he committed suicide in Seattle at age twenty-five.[9]

Kate continued to struggle against poverty, selling whatever valuables she had left and barely managing to hang on to Edgewood. She died on July 31, 1899. It was a sad end for the woman who had been the reigning belle of Civil War Washington.[10]

As for William Sprague, he made an ill-conceived attempt to reenter Rhode Island politics and reclaim his old post as governor. Given his scandalous reputation, this effort ended in failure and ridicule. When his Narragansett house burned to the ground, Sprague decamped to France where he died September 11, 1915.[11]

* * *

Another United States senator had his own postwar marital woes. Charles Sumner of Massachusetts was a leading figure in the pre-war abolitionist movement and is best remembered today for being beaten with a cane on the floor of the Senate by South Carolinian Preston Brooks. Sumner later helped lead the radical Republicans in taking a harsh stance against the rebellious Southern states.

Throughout his life, the New Englander had been a confirmed bachelor, more interested in collecting autographs and mediocre paintings than he was in romancing women. When his mother died, leaving him a reasonably large inheritance, the fifty-five-year-old statesman felt he was financially and emotionally ready to settle down.

His choice of a bride was Alice Mason Hoops, a widow with a seven-year-old child whose husband had been killed while serving with the Union army in 1863. Mrs. Hoops was in her twenties, almost three decades younger than the man she wed on October 17, 1866.

All went well—at least briefly. Then the good senator learned that his wife had a temper and was not afraid to use rough language when riled. Her husband, never much of a participant in the Washington social scene, grew weary of the numerous parties that his young mate found so exciting. He wanted to leave early; she liked to stay late. The bride complained of being left alone as her husband was "always reading, writing and snoring."

It was well known in Washington that Sumner tended to be overly serious and self-important, not qualities that many lively young women find attractive. Told that Sumner had little belief in the Bible, U. S. Grant replied, "Well, he didn't write it." Asked if he had ever conversed with Sumner, Grant joked that no, he had only heard him lecture.

Then there was the expense of married life. During his bachelor Senate career, Sumner had lived a simple existence in rented rooms. Now as a family man, he needed a house—and not just any house but a mansion that would befit his social position. The couple found one being constructed near the White House. The cost was $30,000—exactly ten times the $3,000 Sumner earned each year in the Senate. Plus there were the costs of entertaining plus servants and running a carriage. Sumner's inheritance no longer looked as large as it once had.

Just a few months after the wedding, the young bride was increasingly seen in the company of a handsome Prussian attaché, Baron Friedrich von Holstein. Rumors began to fly. Sharp-eyed observers noted that the husband turned his back and pretended not to notice his wife if she was accompanied by her European friend. When von Holstein was recalled to Berlin, many, including Mrs. Sumner, were sure that the distinguished senator, who chaired the powerful Foreign Relations Committee, had something to do with it. This he denied.

Less than a year after they married, Charles and Alice quietly separated. As news of the rift spread so did a supposed reason for it: Charles Sumner was unable to perform sexually. Questionable stories circulated that, as a student at Harvard, he had been humorously nicknamed "The Stag" due to this problem. Political enemies took to calling him "The Great Impotent."[12]

No outsider would ever know for sure what really went on in the Sumner bedroom. Perhaps with a half century of pent-up desire, the senator was truly a tiger between the sheets. At its most straightforward, the Sumner marriage was simply the age-old story of a mature man attracted to a woman many years too young for him. As Mary Lincoln commented of her friend, "It was a great mistake he made in marrying so late in life!!"[13]

* * *

Like his father before him, Henry Ward Beecher was one of the most famous ministers of his age. His Plymouth Church, located in Brooklyn, seated some 2,500 persons and it was always packed with worshipers eager to hear the renowned clergyman expound upon morality.

Like his sister, Harriet Beecher Stowe of *Uncle Tom's Cabin* fame, the good reverend abhorred slavery and was a persistent agitator against it. In the 1850s, he encouraged free staters to settle in the disputed Kansas Territory and raised funds to purchase Sharps carbines—known as "Beecher's Bible"—so that the settlers could defend themselves. He called the South "a great scowling slave state." After John Brown's raid on the Harpers Ferry Arsenal, he urged that no prayers be offered to spare the abolitionist from the scaffold; Beecher knew that Brown would serve the anti-slavery cause far better if he was moldering in a martyr's grave.[14]

There was some quiet gossip about the Reverend Beecher. For example, he could deliver a wonderful temperance sermon and then go home and drink a beer with his lunch. There were also rumors about his marriage and whether it was truly a happy one. Henry and his wife, Eunice, seemed to have grown apart and, as early as 1857, he may have begun an affair with Lucy Maria Bowen, the wife of a close friend. Lucy's husband would later testify that he learned the reverend was a "libertine" and an "adulterer" sometime around 1860.[15]

In 1866, Beecher began paying special attention to Elizabeth Tilton and the pair eventually began a sexual relationship. Elizabeth and her husband, Theodore, were members of Beecher's Plymouth Church and had been married by him in October 1855. Later Theodore worked on a religious newspaper, the *Independent*, and had served as a ghostwriter for articles under Beecher's byline.

In 1870, Elizabeth told her husband of the illicit relationship and the couple tried to mend their damaged marriage. Some months later, Henry Bowen, the husband of Beecher's earlier lover, learned of Beecher's second act of adultery. He persuaded Theodore to write a letter to Beecher demanding Beecher's resignation as minister at Plymouth Church. Learning of this and hoping to save himself, Beecher convinced Elizabeth Tilton to write her own letter denying any immoral activity; Beecher actually dictated what his former lover should write, but the gambit didn't work. The next day Beecher surrendered Elizabeth's denial when confronted by one of Theodore's friends.

By this time, rumors of the scandal were spreading in the reverend's social circle. However, it was not until October 1872 that *Woodhull and Claflin's Weekly* published an exposé about it. The publication was the platform of Victoria Woodhull, who had gained notoriety for her views on women's liberation and free love.[16]

As a contemporary of Elizabeth Cady Stanton and Susan B. Anthony, Victoria Woodhull had mounted her own long-shot campaign for the presidency. In fact calling it a "long shot" is being polite; the "Equal Rights Party" had no chance at all in the contest between incumbent Republican U. S. Grant and Democrat Horace Greeley. Frederick Douglass, who was nominated to be Victoria's vice-presidential running mate, simply ignored the entire campaign.[17]

Woodhull was upset that Henry Beecher's sisters, Catherine and Harriet, had ridiculed her candidacy. She also felt that Henry was a hypocrite who secretly believed in the concept of free love but would not say so publicly.

Woodhull's exposé of the reverend's adultery created a sensation which Beecher and the Tiltons tried to ignore. Despite his silence, the following year, Theodore Tilton was expelled from the Plymouth Church for his "slander" of the good reverend. Nevertheless Tilton kept quiet until a derogatory series of articles about him appeared in his former newspaper, the *Independent*. The wronged husband fired back in a long statement that he sent to the New York newspapers.

Now the scandal blazed anew. Public indignation rose to fever pitch and Beecher himself was forced to act. He asked six friends to form an investigating committee to take testimony and offer a verdict on the matter. Despite much evidence to the contrary, the friendly committee absolved Beecher of any wrongdoing.

Enraged by the charade, Theodore Tilton filed suit against the seducer of his wife. The case took six months to try—from January to June of 1875—and the newspapers gave it prominent play. The trial ended in a hung jury and Beecher trumpeted this as a triumph. In celebration, his congregation gave him a $100,000 raise to cover legal costs. A second church investigating council was formed and once again Beecher was exonerated. Some of those who testified against him, including Elizabeth Tilton, were banished from the church.

Elizabeth Tilton died in 1897, blind and living in her daughter's Brooklyn home. Her former husband, Theodore, was unable to find employment in America; he moved to France and lived in poverty. The Reverend Beecher continued in the pulpit though his reputation was tarnished.

As for Victoria Woodhull, who helped bring the scandal to light—well, she moved beyond her radical free love views and married a wealthy English lord.

* * *

Frederick Douglass, the escaped slave who rose to national prominence as an abolitionist and political leader, kept some sexual skeletons in his closet, too. He apparently had several extramarital affairs, including one with an unstable German writer, Ottilia Assing, which lasted for twenty-eight years. When Assing first met Douglass, she mistook his wife, Anna, for a household servant. Before long, Assing had moved in with the family, ostensibly to help prepare a German translation of Douglass' autobiography. She went with Douglass on speaking tours, vacationed with him and told people that she was Douglass' "natural wife"—a statement that must have come as a shock to Anna Douglass. Not surprisingly, the two women had a difficult time getting along with one another.[18]

Anna Douglass was a free woman in Baltimore when she met her future husband, then a slave from the eastern shore of Maryland who went by the name Frederick Bailey. She helped Frederick escape north where he became increasingly influential in the abolitionist movement. He had natural skills as a writer and orator. Anna, on the other hand, remained illiterate her entire life. Frederick's speaking tours, including lengthy visits to the British Isles, meant that he was frequently absent from his family. It would not be surprising that Anna and her famous husband found themselves with less and less in common.

However, by the time Anna died, the relationship between Assing and Douglass had also cooled, in part due to the German woman's increasingly erratic temperament. Even so, she was devastated when Douglass married his secretary, Helen Pitts, in 1884. A few months later, Assing left her Paris hotel and walked to the Bois de Boulogne where she committed suicide by drinking a vial of poison. In her will, she left a $13,000 trust fund to Douglass and requested that her letters be destroyed.[19]

The second Mrs. Douglass was white and nearly twenty years younger than her new husband. The union provoked criticism from enemies and allies alike. Hoping to minimize the furor, Douglass kept the ceremony low key, informing only a few friends until after it was over. Helen Pitts' father had been a strong abolitionist but he refused to accept the interracial couple. Her uncle, who was Douglass' neighbor, also ended all contact. Even Douglass' children felt that their father's marriage to a red-headed white woman was to some degree a repudiation of his own race. Nevertheless, the couple honeymooned at Niagara Falls and later made a grand tour of Europe, living happily together until Douglass died of a heart attack in 1895.[20]

* * *

Pennsylvania Representative Thaddeus Stevens, the "great commoner" who championed public education, minority rights and the impeachment of Andrew Johnson, never married. It was widely whispered that he had a sexual relationship with his housekeeper, Lydia Hamilton Smith, a mulatto widow and mother of two children. Smith worked for Stevens from the 1840s until his death in 1868. Their close friendship even survived the trauma of Stevens' evicting Smith's son, Issac, from the home that they shared in Lancaster, Pennsylvania. Historian Fawn Brodie, author of *Thaddeus Stevens, Scourge of the South*, is convinced that the pair were lovers while Hans Trefousse, author of *Thaddeus Stevens, Nineteen-Century Egalitarian*, believes the affair can be neither proved nor disproved from the available evidence. In any event, Stevens' political enemies used the gossip against him. When he died, Stevens left Smith $500 a year or a lump sum of $5,000, plus the opportunity to decide what household furniture belonged to her.[21]

As a final note, there is the story of a female abolitionist who greatly admired Stevens and asked for a lock of his hair as a keepsake. Bald-headed Thad promptly pulled off his dark wig and offered it to her.[22]

* * *

Confederate President Jefferson Davis began his romantic life with tragedy and ended it years later with a hint of scandal. As a young officer just about to leave the army in 1835, Davis married Sarah Knox Taylor, the daughter of General Zachary Taylor. That union ended sadly less than three months later when they both contracted malaria at Davis' rustic Mississippi plantation. Jefferson Davis recovered. His young bride did not. The young widower subsequently plunged into one of the darkest periods of his life, for a time becoming a virtual recluse.[23]

In 1843, the thirty-five-year-old Davis met eighteen-year-old Varina Howell, whom he married two years later. This marriage lasted until Davis' death in 1889 and it is fair to say that the two were devoted to each other. When the Confederacy collapsed in the spring of 1865, Davis might have escaped the Union dragnet had he not detoured to confirm the safety of Varina and their children. During Davis' subsequent imprisonment, Varina campaigned tirelessly for her husband's freedom.

That does not mean that the Davis marriage did not have its moments of disharmony. Given their age difference, there was something of a "father-daughter" aspect to the relationship. Davis expected his orders to be obeyed and his young wife was not always willing to do so.

Confederate insider John Wise wrote unflatteringly of Varina, "Physically, she was large and looked well fed." With her dark complexion, one Union officer likened her to an Indian squaw. As the years passed, the former first lady of the Confederacy found it increasingly difficult to keep her weight under control. Davis meanwhile remained slim, giving the two the appearance of Mr. Lean and Mrs. Stout. Possibly this disparity, coupled with frequent long separations from his wife, encouraged Jefferson Davis to flirt.[24]

In July 1871, Varina was in Baltimore where their sons were going to school while Davis lived in Memphis, struggling to make a living as the president of an insurance company. The *Louisville Commercial* newspaper, no friend to Southern interests, reported a juicy item about a train trip Davis had supposedly made to Sewanee, Tennessee.

According to the story, Davis left Memphis' Peabody Hotel and boarded a Pullman sleeping car. Later he met up with a woman who boarded at the Overton Hotel. About 8:15 p.m., Davis asked for their berths to be prepared and he retired to the upper while his female friend took the lower. Shortly thereafter, fellow passengers were surprised to see the former president slipping under the curtains into the lower berth. The conductor was called to investigate and he is said to have found the illicit pair sharing the same bed.

It was an awkward moment to be sure. The conductor told Davis that his behavior was not acceptable. Davis protested that they had paid for the space and could use it as they wished. The woman in question was suitably embarrassed and tried to hide her face. A senior conductor was called and Davis retreated back to the upper level.

Who was the woman with Jefferson Davis that evening? Rumor said it was Virginia Clay, wife of former Confederate Commissioner Clement Clay, who was experiencing her own marital strife at the time. Certainly Jeff and Ginny were known to be friendly, the question is just how friendly? In any event, neither party honored the salacious newspaper story with a denial.[25]

Davis never regained a firm financial footing after the war. His venture in the insurance business failed, leaving him with little career except as the controversial figurehead of a lost cause. He decided to prepare his memoirs which became a lengthy justification of the South's struggle. Needing a place to write, he accepted the generous offer of Mrs. Sarah Dorsey to use a cottage on the grounds of Beauvoir, her home in Biloxi, Mississippi.

Though the widow Dorsey was her longtime friend, Varina Davis was not pleased with this arrangement. She stubbornly refused to join her husband, saying she had no desire to ever see her friend's house. She became even more upset when she learned that Davis was dictating his manuscript to Mrs. Dorsey, a function Varina had generally fulfilled.

As of April 1878, Jefferson Davis and his wife had spent just ten days of the previous seventeen months together. Finally Varina conceded defeat and joined her husband in Biloxi. She exploded into an emotional tantrum just before a party to celebrate her arrival. The kindhearted Mrs. Dorsey played the diplomat and managed to calm her friend before the guests appeared.

Afterward, Varina once again began taking her husband's dictation and put aside her fears about Mrs. Dorsey. In truth, her worries were probably groundless; Mrs. Dorsey simply enjoyed being a benefactor to the tragic hero in his time of need. When she died, her entire estate, including Beauvoir, went to Jefferson Davis.[26]

Jefferson Davis, incidentally, is believed to have had an unusual middle name: *Finis*. He was the tenth child born to his parents and, according to legend, they gave him that middle name as their declaration that he would be their last. Davis' mother at the time was almost forty-seven years old. While the story is generally accepted as fact, there is no conclusive evidence for it. Until the mid-1830s, Davis would occasionally use the initial "F" in his signature and official documents. After that, it disappears.[27]

* * *

Homosexuality was no more or less common in the general population of the 1860s than it was during any other period of mankind's history. However, it was certainly less publicized than it is today. When J.E.B. Stuart wrote to his wife in 1864 that the people of Charlottesville were "very gay," he was not referring to their sexual preference but using the word in its original meaning. "Gay" was a very popular word in the nineteenth century; it is equally popular now but, of course, in a very different context.

Walt Whitman is the most famous homosexual of the Civil War era. His love life has been carefully examined by both historians and students of literature and there can be little doubt that the celebrated poet was gay. Though he was not "out-of-the-closet," Whitman did crack the door open a bit. His Civil War-era notebooks list liaisons with numerous working-class and military men. He routinely hugged and kissed the soldier-patients at the Washington army hospital where he worked as a nurse, and some of those relationships may have gone further.[28]

Critics then and now believe some of his poetry, such as *Calamus*, concerns manly love. He was fired from a post in the Interior Department due to the nature of his published writings. Whenever he felt that his preferences had become too obvious, Whitman would backtrack. Of *Calamus*, he said it was "terrible" that such interpretations had been made. He also boasted that he had sired six illegitimate children, a claim his friends found amusing.[29]

In 1882, the flamboyant English playwright Oscar Wilde met with the aging American poet in Camden, New Jersey, where they sipped homemade elderberry wine and discussed their craft. Wilde put his hand on the old man's knee and later boasted that "the kiss of Walt Whitman is still upon my lips." Whitman remarked that Wilde "had the good sense to take a fancy to me!"[30]

The four years that Abraham Lincoln spent rooming with Springfield, Illinois, shopkeeper Joshua Speed have been pointed to by sensation seekers as proof that the sixteenth president was bisexual. Without any other evidence, the charge simply does not hold up. Lincoln and Speed did share a bed but such arrangements were common on the frontier. Strangers of the same sex routinely "spooned" together on the same hotel room mattresses and these most assuredly were not orgies. As Dr. Thomas Lowry points out in his book, *The Story the Soldiers*

Wouldn't Tell, Lincoln's law partner, William Herndon, and one of Speed's store clerks also occasionally bunked in the same room with Lincoln and Speed. Many people, like young Abe, were simply desperately poor, and sharing sleeping quarters was a matter of necessity.[31]

Later, while Lincoln was away from home trying cases in the circuit courts, his wife, Mary, became frightened because her maid sometimes permitted a lover to sneak in after dark. Mary wrote to a neighbor, James Gourley: "do come and stay with me all night—You can sleep in the bed with Bob and I." This was not an invitation to a sexual romp. It was a worried woman asking a male friend to come protect her and her child. The Lincoln household at the time had only one full-size bed.[32]

Even after he won the presidency, Abraham Lincoln enjoyed the companionship of male sleepovers. In September 1862, Companies D and K of the 150th Pennsylvania Volunteers, part of the famous "Pennsylvania Bucktails," were assigned to the Soldiers' Home in Washington, D.C. Lincoln used the home as a quiet retreat when he wished to get away from the White House during the warm weather months. As recounted in the unit's official history, Lincoln frequently visited with the soldiers and established friendly relations with their officers. The regimental historian noted that the commander in chief grew particularly fond of Captain David Derickson. The captain "advanced so far in the President's confidence and esteem that, in Mrs. Lincoln's absence, he frequently spent the night at his cottage, sleeping in the same bed with him, and—it is said—making use of His Excellency's nightshirts!"[33]

When cold weather ended use of the cottage at the Soldiers' Home, Lincoln sent the following note to the War Department:

Executive Mansion,
  Washington, November 1, 1862

Whom It May Concern:

  Captain Derickson, with his Company, has been for some time keeping guard at my residence, now at the

*Soldiers' Retreat. He and his Company are very agree-
able to me, and, while it is deemed proper any guard to
remain, none would be more satisfactory to me than
Captain D. and his Company.*

   A. Lincoln

Company K moved its camp to the White House lawn. Captain Derickson's friendship with the president continued until
the following spring when Derickson was appointed provost marshal of the 19th Pennsylvania District, headquartered in
Meadville.[34]

* * *

The sexuality of Lincoln's White House predecessor, James
Buchanan, has long been a topic of discussion. The closest personal relationship that the bachelor president had outside of his
family was with his longtime roommate, Senator William Rufus
de Vane King of Alabama.

Buchanan, the last chief executive to have been alive at the
same time as George Washington, was born in 1791 in a log cabin
at Cove Gap, Pennsylvania. His Irish immigrant father owned a
successful trading post frequented by travelers headed west across
the Allegheny Mountains. Buchanan's mother and sisters doted
upon him as he was the household's only male child for most of
his early life. Sent off to Dickinson College in Carlisle, Buchanan
was a good student but also enough of a hell-raiser to be dismissed from the school after his first year. Only special pleading
by an influential family friend returned him to academia.

After graduation, Buchanan pursued a career in law and
moved to Lancaster, which was then Pennsylvania's capital. In his
off-hours, he would hang out at the local barroom and occasionally
embarrass himself by getting drunk and dancing on the tables.

In 1818, Buchanan began what is traditionally depicted as
the major love affair of his life. He became smitten with twenty-
two-year-old Ann Coleman, described by Buchanan biographer
Phillip Shriver Klein as "the belle of the town" and possibly "emotionally unstable" as evidenced by her rapidly changing moods.

Her family was also very rich. Ann's father, Robert Coleman, had emigrated from Ireland. He rose to wealth by marrying the owner's daughter of the iron-making business where he worked. When James began courting Ann, Robert Coleman owned a string of six iron furnaces and was a millionaire in an era when millionaires were rare indeed.

Robert Coleman was highly protective of both his family and his finance. Neither he nor his wife believed that young James Buchanan was the right man for their daughter. Coleman had been a trustee of Dickinson College and no doubt knew the story of Buchanan's dismissal. He probably also heard of the six-footer's propensity for table dancing at the tavern. What's more, did this struggling ambitious lawyer really want Ann or was he using her to get to her family's money?

It did not particularly please the Colemans when the two young lovers became engaged in the summer of 1819, but her parents did not specifically prohibit Ann from marrying her beau. After all, being in her early twenties, she was rapidly approaching that era's matrimonial sell-by date.

What happened next is a bit unclear. That autumn James' career kept him occupied with several important cases. Ann felt neglected and, encouraged by her parents, wrote James a pouting letter questioning his motives in marrying her. Shortly thereafter, James made an apparently innocent social call at a house where another attractive young woman was visiting. Ann learned of this and fired off a new note ending their engagement. Buchanan was mortified.

Perhaps the breach could have been repaired. On the other hand, Buchanan might have been lucky to have escaped marriage to the temperamental heiress. However, subsequent events were to scar him forever.

Mr. and Mrs. Coleman knew how distressed Ann was over this turn of events and shipped her off to visit a sister in Philadelphia. It was early December and Ann caught a cold en route but otherwise seemed quite healthy. Nevertheless, while in Philadelphia, she developed hysterical convulsions and died.

The circumstances of her demise being curious, unsubstantiated rumors of suicide circulated around Lancaster.

To Buchanan, the death was a black thunderbolt. He wrote Ann's parents requesting permission to visit the corpse and walk in the procession as a mourner. The letter came back to him unopened. The Colemans felt that the young lawyer somehow bore responsibility for their daughter's tragic end. Years afterward, Buchanan still preserved Ann's letters and even purchased and, for a time, lived in her old family home.

The scandal had no lasting impact on "Buck's" career. Buchanan rose through the political ranks, serving first in the Pennsylvania General Assembly and then in the U.S. Congress at Washington. There he began a close and long-lasting friendship with Senator King. The pair lived together and were so inseparable on Washington's social scene that they were known as the "Siamese twins." King seems to have come in for particular ridicule from wags, being given nicknames such as "Aunt Fancy" and "Buchanan's wife." Andrew Jackson called him "Miss Nancy."

Nevertheless, the affable and even-tempered King enjoyed the respect of his fellow politicos—though he was neither an accomplished public speaker nor particularly brilliant. The Southern moderate first came to Congress in 1811 as a North Carolina representative and served three terms. After a diplomatic tour in Naples and St. Petersburg, he moved to Alabama and, in 1819, came back to Washington as senator from that state. He remained in the Senate until 1852 except for a stint as ambassador to France during President John Tyler's administration.[35]

With his appointment to Paris, King wrote Buchanan that he was "selfish enough to hope you will not be able to procure an associate who will cause you to feel no regret" at the separation. For his part, Buchanan admitted feeling "solitary and lonely" at King's departure. Though he had "gone a wooing to several gentlemen," he had "not succeeded with any one of them." He anticipated finding "some old maid" to nurse him when sick and provide good dinners without expecting "any very ardent or romantic affection."

That "old maid" description echoes an earlier episode which was Buchanan's only other known brush with marriage. Biographer Philip Klein called it more mystery than story. In 1837, Buchanan was apparently engaged to Mary Kittera Snyder of Philadelphia and some scraps of written evidence indicate his intention to be married. Klein believes it was possibly a marriage of convenience with a family friend. In any event, no wedding ever took place and Buchanan remained a bachelor.

Buchanan did seem to enjoy the company of women in a social setting. For a time, he was enamored with Anna Payne, the niece of Dolly Madison, and later he thought highly of Dan Sickles' wife, Teresa, until she disgraced herself in an adulterous affair. Clever banter and some dancing were about as far as Buchanan's intimacy with females seemed to go.

Whatever their sexual preference, both King and Buchanan went on to higher honors. King was elected vice president of the United States in 1852. Unfortunately, he had by then contracted tuberculosis and journeyed to Cuba in hope of recovery. When it became obvious that King was dying, Congress passed special legislation that allowed him to take the oath of office outside the United States, the only such episode in our nation's history. The sixty-seven-year-old statesman passed away on April 18, 1853, just one day after returning to his Alabama plantation.[36]

Four years later, James Buchanan entered the White House where his niece, Harriet Lane, acted as hostess. "Old Buck" had already served as U.S. Senator, ambassador to both Russia and England as well as secretary of state. His single term as president was not a success, ending as it did with the election of Lincoln and the secession of the Southern states.

Whatever animosity was directed toward Buchanan came about not as a result of his sexuality but his perceived pro-Southern leaning. Perhaps the long friendship with King influenced him in that regard. During King's career, he had been similarly assailed by Southern fire-eaters for being too cordial with the North.

When the war came, public opinion blamed Buchanan for not dealing more forcefully with the crisis. Union General Ben Butler, a fellow Democrat, declared publicly that Buchanan had handled South Carolina's secession as if "it was but a riot; and, as there were no civil authorities there to call out the militia, Fort Sumter must be given over to the rioters."[37]

Anonymous notes were posted to the back door of Buchanan's Lancaster home, Wheatland, warning that the residence would be burned to the ground some evening. Each day's mail brought a new selection of angry, threatening letters. In the United States Congress, a resolution condemning the elderly former chief executive was introduced but failed to pass. Radical Republicans did, however, revoke the ex-president's franking privileges and Buchanan's portrait was removed from the Capitol to prevent it from being vandalized by an angry public. The *New York Daily Tribune* published a blurb headlined "Buchanan Yet in Rebel Service" because, as a Democrat, he did not back Republican radical Congressman Thad Stevens for reelection.[38]

In June 1863, Robert E. Lee's Rebels invaded south-central Pennsylvania and came within ten miles of Wheatland. Some of the refugees fleeing the invaders shouted curses as they passed the stately red-brick residence, feeling that its owner had been responsible for their current plight.

Even the family of Union Major General John Reynolds harbored resentment for Buchanan. Reynolds, a Lancaster native and West Point graduate, died from a Rebel bullet at Gettysburg on July 1. Though the Reynolds family had been friendly with Buchanan for almost fifty years, in their grief, they turned their backs upon their renowned neighbor.[39]

Reynold's demise, incidentally, left its own romantic tragedy. Unbeknownst to his family, the forty-year-old career army officer had fallen in love with a twenty-four-year-old woman while returning from California just before the war. Catherine Hewitt

and John Reynolds decided that they would wed after the conflict ended. They kept their engagement secret. This may have
been because she was Catholic and he was Protestant. As tokens
of their love, she wore his West Point ring while he cherished a
gold band that was inscribed "Dear Kate."

After Reynolds fell at Gettysburg, his body was returned to
his sister's house in Philadelphia, reaching there in the wee hours
of July 3 after a circuitous journey. That morning a distraught
Kate Hewitt arrived and met her beloved's family for the first
time. From her, they learned of the marriage that was to be.
Kate withdrew from life, entering a Catholic convent at
Emmitsburg, Maryland, just a few miles from where her general
had died. She disappeared from the historical record in 1868.[40]

Following the war, former Confederate raider John S. Mosby allowed his hair-trigger temper to lead him toward the dueling grounds.

CHAPTER FIVE
DUELS AND OTHER DUSTUPS

Through centuries past, man has preserved and participated in the ritualized concept of fighting known as the duel. Its origins might be traced to the chivalric tournaments of the Middle Ages, but the real roots go back to homo erectus's earliest aggressive instincts. When one caveman clubbed another caveman in order to get the best-looking cavewoman, you have the essentials of the duel—if not necessarily all the formalities. One evolutionary theory holds that this is how homo erectus developed his thick forehead.[1]

In France, during the thirteenth century, dueling could be used to resolve criminal cases, such as rape, incendiarism, assassination and burglary. Much like the concept of trial-by-fire, the surviving party was accepted as having prevailed in the dispute. Louis IX liked the idea so much that he allowed it to be used even in civil cases.[2]

As an example of how this worked, consider the plight of Sieur de Carronges. Returning to Paris from the Holy Land in the fifteenth century, he learned that his wife had been violated by the Sieur Legris. Legris then compounded the offense by maintaining that the lady had been a most willing partner. To settle the issue, a duel was arranged with King Charles VI himself in attendance. When the lady in question arrived to watch the battle for her virtue, the king directed that she stand upon a scaffold as a sort of purgatory until the matter was decided. The duel began and Carronges defeated the villainous Legris, who admitted to both rape and slander. This confession did not save the guilty man's life; he was taken up to the scaffold and hung. Carronges, however, had successfully redeemed and avenged the honor of his wife.[3]

By the reign of Louis XIII, dueling had become such a mania that it was a routine topic of daily conversation. "Did you hear who fought who?" was lumped in with such pleasantries as "How are you?" and "What's new?" France was not alone in its acceptance of duels; they were popular throughout Europe, despite efforts to curtail the practice as civilization progressed. Naturally enough the custom of dueling came to America along with European colonization.

The code duello regulated how such contests should be conducted. Though it varied from region to region, the code basically consisted of twenty-five or so rules for gentlemen to use in avenging insults to their honor. Such insults could be almost anything from the trivial—"I don't like your coat"— to the more serious— "You are a lying coward and your wife is a diseased whore."

In many cases, the code became almost a set piece where preening male peacocks could demonstrate their bravery and willingness to fight without sustaining any injury. Oftentimes, either before or after a harmless exchange of shots, the parties agreed to a face-saving settlement arranged by their friends who served as seconds.

Many duels though did lead to injury and death. For example, Button Gwinnett, a signer of the Declaration of Independence, was killed at age forty-four on a "field of honor" near Savannah, Georgia. As a result of his early demise, Gwinnett's signature is very scarce and commands a premium among autograph collectors.

In 1802, New Yorkers DeWitt Clinton and John Swartwout fought a duel over their political disagreements. Each man fired three shots without injuring the other. After every round, the seconds suggested that they call it a draw but Swartwout insisted on continuing. With the fourth round, Swartwout was hit in the left leg and Clinton agreed to shake hands to end the contest. Swartwout would not leave without a signed apology, which Clinton refused to offer. Pistols were loaded a fifth time and Swartwout suffered yet another wound in his left leg. Despite his injuries, he still demanded a signed apology before the shooting could stop. In disgust, Clinton walked off the field, leaving behind his sputtering, bloody opponent.[4]

Probably the most famous duel in American history took place in July 1804 when Alexander Hamilton met Aaron Burr on a New Jersey hillside overlooking the Hudson River. Burr, who was then vice president of the United States, fatally shot the Revolutionary War hero and former United States treasurer. Though indicted by both New York and New Jersey, Burr escaped the law and even managed to return to his chair presiding over the United States Senate.[5]

Andrew Jackson, who stared down South Carolina's threats of secession during the "Nullification Crisis" of 1832, fought numerous duels throughout his life and carried two bullets in his body as souvenirs. These wounds caused pain for "Old Hickory" until his death in 1845.[6]

Being an expert marksman was no guarantee of success in a gunfight. Cassius Marcellus Clay, the well-known Kentucky abolitionist and one of the founders of the Republican Party, was a remarkable shot who could cut a string with a pistol bullet at ten paces. Nevertheless a duel was called off after he and his opponent had missed hitting each other three times. Asked how to reconcile his skilled target shooting with the day's sorry performance, Clay replied, "Oh, that darn string had no pistol in its hand."[7]

Cassius Clay, however, did not miss with his very last shot. In 1903, the old man lay dying while a horsefly buzzed about the ceiling of his sickroom. Clay called for his rifle, took careful aim and blasted the insect into eternity.

* * *

By the eve of the Civil War, eighteen states had passed legislation prohibiting duels and Congress had outlawed it in the District of Columbia. The latter restriction, however, was easily circumvented thanks to the availability of the Bladensburg dueling grounds, just across the Maryland line, where the practice was still permitted. This prohibition in the national capital played a role in the famous incident between Senator Charles Sumner of Massachusetts and Representative Preston Brooks of South Carolina.

Sumner was an outspoken abolitionist. On May 19 and 20, 1856, he gave a fiery and impassioned speech on the Senate floor. Entitled "Crime Against Kansas," portions of Sumner's address crossed the line from the purely political to the personally insulting. He portrayed South Carolina Senator Andrew Pickens Butler as slavery's Don Quixote with "a mistress...who though ugly to others, is always lovely to him." Later he assailed Butler as "incoherent" and making every possible deviation from the truth. He declared that Butler could not "open his mouth but out flies a blunder."

Other Senate members received a similar lashing. Stephen Douglas of Illinois was labeled "the squire of slavery, its very Sancho Panza." Sumner addressed his colleague, James Mason, as coming from Virginia "where human beings are bred as cattle for the shambles."

All and all, it was strong stuff, particularly in an era and city where the wrong look could result in a trip to the dueling grounds. After the speech finally ended, Stephen Douglas fumed "that damn fool will get himself killed by some other damn fool." Sumner's friends offered to make up a bodyguard to escort him safely home.

Senator Andrew Butler, elderly and unwell, was not present for the tongue-lashing from a man he had once befriended. His kinsman, Congressman Preston Brooks, however, had heard some of Sumner's speech in person and he had read the rest of it. Given the insult to his state and his family, Brooks took it upon himself to personally address the matter.

One might assume this meant an early morning excursion across the Maryland line to the bloody grounds of Bladensburg. Butler was not afraid of such a fight and had once been wounded in a duel with future Confederate Senator Louis T. Wigfall. Butler, however, assumed that Sumner would refuse to fight and report him to the district authorities for issuing an illegal challenge. Beyond that, a duel suggested an affair of honor between two gentlemen and Brooks did not see the loud-mouthed abolitionist as any kind of gentleman. Instead, the South Carolinian would take his satisfaction with a gold-headed gutta-percha cane. He would beat the Massachusetts senator much like one might beat an ill-mannered servant.[8]

On May 21, Brooks hunted but failed to find Sumner on the grounds of the national Capitol. The following day, he located his prey on the Senate floor, shortly after its noon adjournment. Brooks waited impatiently for the chamber to clear, in particular for some ladies to leave. Sumner sat preoccupied at his desk, putting his postal frank upon copies of the offending "Crime of Kansas" speech.

Brooks approached the unsuspecting senator. Had Sumner been aware of what was about to happen, he was large and powerful enough that he may have been able to restrain his attacker. Instead, he was taken by surprise.

Shouting "a libel on South Carolina and Mr. Butler," Brooks quickly laid thirty blows in less than a minute on the startled speechmaker. Sumner struggled to get up from the desk and Brooks recalled that his victim "bellowed like a calf."

A melee ensued as surprised solons rushed to break up the one-sided battle. Stephen Douglas considered intervening but feared that observers might think that he was actually part of the attack on Sumner. Brooks was pulled away with his elegant walking stick shattered into pieces. As a memento, he retained the gold head. A short time later, district authorities placed the congressman under arrest and he was released from jail on a five-hundred-dollar bond.[9]

Sumner lay bleeding and in shock, propped up against a chair on the Senate floor. His wounds were serious but far from fatal. To the North, he became a symbolic hero and his reelection chances improved dramatically in his home state. The South, on the other hand, firmly applauded Brooks' action in what they saw as a defense of home, family and friends.

The district court found Brooks guilty of assault and slapped him with a three-hundred-dollar fine. The House of Representatives voted 121 to 95 to expel him but the motion failed because the tally came below the two-thirds majority required. Afterward, Brooks gave a speech in his defense, drawing both cheers and hisses. At the conclusion, he announced his resignation from Congress. The voters of his district returned Brooks to his old seat in a special election but he died a few months later in January 1857.[10]

During the controversy, Brooks had issued a challenge to Anson Burlingame, a friend of Sumner, in response to some insulting remarks that had been made. Burlingame agreed to fight but chose the Canadian side of Niagara Falls as the location. To reach the site, Brooks would have had to risk life and limb by traveling through the outraged North.[11]

* * *

Jefferson Davis became embroiled in the code duello on several occasions but none of the incidents concluded with actual bloodshed. Without question, the most dangerous situation arose when Davis was colonel of the 1st Mississippi Rifles during the Mexican War. Davis and his second-in-command, Lieutenant Colonel Alexander Keith McClung, engaged in a feud over the amount of credit each deserved for the victory at Monterrey.

McClung was not a man with whom you wished to trifle. Nicknamed the "Black Knight of the South," he was a handsome red-haired nephew of Chief Justice John Marshall and he had a reputation as a ladies man. Given to fits of melancholy, he would ride his horse, "Rob Roy," to the cemetery, lie down on a grave and stare at the stars. His primary claim to fame, though, was as a duelist.[12]

In one encounter, he used a pistol to shoot his opponent through the mouth at a distance of more than one hundred feet. In another, he fought John Menefee, commander of the Vicksburg Rifles militia. With their first shots, Menefee missed while McClung's gun misfired. With the second round, McClung's shot struck the lock of Menefee's weapon, driving a piece of metal into the man's brain and killing him. McClung dropped to his knees, kissed his gun and offered a prayer of thanksgiving. McClung was particularly hard on the Menefee clan; he reportedly killed seven of their menfolk in duels.

McClung's reputation was widespread. When one fool flung his card in McClung's face as a challenge to a duel, the man immediately recanted upon discovering McClung's identity and meekly requested to have his card returned. When a hotel guest objected because McClung stuck his eating knife in the butter dish, McClung slapped the butter against the complainer's face. He then called, "Waiter! Remove the butter. This man has stuck his nose in it." The fellow fled when he learned McClung's name.

In the victory at Monterrey, McClung had received a serious wound which sent him home from the war. Back in Mississippi, he spent his recovery collecting statements to justify his own heroic account of the action and bad-mouthing Jefferson Davis. Davis, who received a wound of his own in the later battle of Buena Vista, tried to defend his report of the Monterrey fighting without actually contradicting the volatile McClung. The prolonged bickering got into the press and McClung told friends that he wanted to fight his former commander "because the United States will be better off without him." Davis, well aware of McClung's deadly record, somehow managed to avoid a formal challenge. In a November 1846 speech given in Vicksburg, Mississippi, Davis went out of his way to describe McClung at Monterrey as "brave," "glorious" and having "military judgment that mark him made by heaven for the soldier."[13]

McClung lived until 1855, drinking heavily and haunted by the spirits of the men whom he had killed. One day, he pinned a poem entitled "Ode to Death" on the front of his shirt. Then he picked up his pistol and claimed himself as his own final victim.[14]

Jefferson Davis went on to a stint as secretary of war under Franklin Pierce, after which Mississippi voters elected him to the United States Senate. In that distinguished body, he served with Judah Benjamin of Louisiana. In 1858, the two tangled on the Senate floor over whether an appropriations bill included a provision for the purchase of breech-loading rifles.

It was a trifling disagreement, made serious only by the tone of voice which Davis used. Benjamin took offense to the "sneering reply to what was a respectful inquiry."

Davis haughtily responded, "I consider it an attempt to misrepresent a very plain remark." The pudgy Louisiana senator retorted that Davis' manner was "not agreeable at all" and Davis told him to "keep it to himself."

As the verbal clash ended, Davis muttered that he had no idea that he was to be met with "the arguments of a paid attorney in the Senate chamber." Benjamin asked if he had understood Davis correctly and Davis said that he had.

Shortly thereafter, Benjamin sent a written challenge to the Mississippian in the Senate cloakroom. By then, the future Confederate president had cooled down and, when he read the note, he said, "I will make this all right at once. I have been wholly wrong."

Returning to the Senate floor, Davis apologized before his fellow solons and Benjamin agreed to forget the incident. Davis later remarked, "When I am aroused in a matter, I lose control of my feeling and become personal"—a statement which could have applied to many of the young hot bloods who found themselves facing pistols at dawn.

In the Confederate government, Davis appointed Benjamin first as attorney general, then secretary of war and finally and most importantly secretary of state. In Richmond, their offices were in the same building and the two conferred on a regular basis, earning Benjamin his reputation as the "brains of the Confederacy." With the Rebel capital's fall to the Northern army in

1865, Benjamin accompanied Davis on his dangerous flight south. After the war, the two met cordially in England where Benjamin had rebuilt his career and become a highly respected Queen's Counsel. The long-ago argument on the floor of the U.S. Senate was truly forgotten.

Or was it? Despite their extremely close wartime relationship, when an elderly Jefferson Davis penned his *Rise and Fall of the Confederate Government*, Judah Benjamin received but a passing mention in the lengthy two-volume text.[15]

* * *

Abraham Lincoln found himself sucked into a trip to the dueling grounds. In 1842, he and his politically astute fiancée, Mary Todd, authored a series of anonymous articles in the *Sangamon Journal* satirizing the Illinois state auditor, Democrat James Shields. As was the fashion, the humor crossed the line to the personal with a send-up of Shields' vanity and purported romances. Shields, learning of Lincoln's involvement, first demanded a retraction and then demanded satisfaction.

By custom, the challenged party had the choice of weapons, and the long-armed Lincoln selected broadswords. The dueling party traveled across the state line to Missouri for the fight. Fortunately, in the nick of time, the seconds reached an amicable settlement before the contestants came to blows. Lincoln was embarrassed by the entire affair and disliked being reminded of it. Shields, who had been born in Ireland, went on to a remarkable political career that included representing three states, Illinois, Minnesota and Missouri, in the United States Senate. A brevet major general during the Mexican War, he received a general's commission from his old friend, Abraham Lincoln, in 1861.[16]

* * *

In 1852, during his first year as a professor at the Virginia Military Institute, Thomas Jackson—still nine years away from being dubbed "Stonewall"—and Cadet James Walker disagreed over the correct answer to a classroom exercise. Walker, it seems, was using a different edition textbook which gave another solution to the problem. This minor incident became major as the student, who was just weeks away from graduation, argued heatedly with Jackson and refused a direct order to sit down and be quiet. Jackson had Walker placed under arrest and the cadet was expelled from V.M.I.

Infuriated and disgraced, Walker sent Jackson a note specifying the time and place for a duel and warning that, if the instructor did not appear, Walker would track him down and shoot him on sight. A court restraining order was obtained and Walker's father arrived to take his humiliated son home.

All was forgiven in the fullness of time. When the war came, Walker served with distinction under Jackson's command. The old professor recommended his former student for promotion to brigadier general and Walker became commander of the legendary "Stonewall" Brigade.[17]

* * *

John Singleton Mosby, who earned a reputation for cunning as a Confederate partisan, shot his first man while he was still a student at the University of Virginia in March 1853. George Turpin, the son of a Charlottesville tavern owner, served as the town bully. He had already assaulted one student with a knife and beaten another so badly that the victim nearly died.

Turpin and Mosby came into conflict when they both planned parties for the same night. Each wanted the same musicians for entertainment. When the musicians accepted Mosby's invitation, Turpin made some angry comments which were relayed to Mosby. Another more romantic version of the story says that Mosby was defending the "good name of a young lady."

Turpin was a much larger man than the diminutive Mosby but that did not stop the future Rebel raider from writing a letter demanding an explanation of Turpin's remarks. Reading the note, Turpin roared that the next time he encountered the writer, he would "eat him up, blood raw."

The antagonists met just after lunch on the back porch of the Cabell House where Mosby boarded. "I understand you have been making some assertions," Mosby said by way of opening. Then Turpin rushed at Mosby who wasted no time pulling out a pepperbox pistol and firing at his attacker.

Turpin fell with a bullet in his neck. He survived the wound and eventually left the area for Alabama. He must have continued his aggressive ways, for a later enemy fatally poisoned him.

Mosby was arrested on the evening of the shooting and locked up without bail in Albemarle County Jail. His parents hired three lawyers who made a strong case for self-defense and Mosby's trial nearly resulted in a hung jury. The judge explained that the lack of a decision would result in the young defendant being held in custody for another six months until the next court session. The jurors reconsidered and found Mosby guilty of unlawful shooting. He received a twelve-month sentence and a five hundred-dollar fine. He was also kicked out of the University of Virginia.

Mosby spent the summer and fall in prison before being pardoned by the governor in December. Mosby never publicly regretted the affair. Writing to a friend nearly fifty years later, he declared, "I have never done anything that I so cordially approve as shooting Turpin." Mosby even became friendly with both the judge and prosecutor from his trial; the latter helped the young prisoner begin his law studies while still incarcerated. In Mosby's twilight years, when the University of Virginia offered honors to its former student, he rarely missed an opportunity to mention how the school had tossed him out. He did not, however, mention the incident in his memoirs, possibly for fear that readers would believe he was indeed the blood-thirsty brigand depicted by his enemies.[18]

Even four years of horrific civil war failed to dampen Mosby's fighting spirit. After Lee's surrender, he simply disbanded his raiders when negotiations with the bluecoat invaders fell through. For a time, he was a hunted man with a five thousand-dollar reward on his head. He finally accepted parole more than two months after Appomattox. Even so Mosby continued to find himself in trouble with the federal authorities until his wife personally obtained a handwritten order from U. S. Grant exempting Mosby from arrest and giving him freedom to travel.

He took up the practice of law in Warrenton, Virginia, near the heart of his wartime stomping grounds. Being an authentic Confederate hero, Mosby should have spent the rest of his life as a prosperous pillar of the community. That did not happen. Part of the raider's nature was to always be on the outside of whatever side there was.

He became active in politics as a member of the Conservative Democratic Party and waged war on Fauquier County Sheriff William Boyd whom he considered a financially irresponsible carpetbagger. When Mosby heard that Boyd had called him a highway robber, he challenged the sheriff to a duel. Instead, Boyd resigned from office and left town for healthier climes.

By 1872, Mosby had become friends with President U. S. Grant and actively supported the Republican's reelection to the White House. That, of course, was not a popular stand for a former Rebel to take, particularly one of Mosby's stature. Two years later Mosby made an abortive run for the U.S. Congress which ended when he and a former state senator began flailing each other with a buggy whip and a cane on a public street.

Mosby dropped out of that race but convinced a friend of his to run instead. Even as a non-candidate, however, Mosby could not stay out of trouble. When a Warrenton attorney and former officer of the Black Horse Cavalry, Captain Alexander Payne, circulated a document that accused Mosby of duplicity and deceit in the campaign, Mosby challenged Payne to a duel. Since dueling was illegal in Virginia, Mosby went to Washington, leaving word for Payne to meet him in Maryland. Payne accepted the challenge and chose squirrel rifles at forty paces; however, law or no law, Payne wanted to fight in Virginia. Word of the contest spread around town and arrest warrants were issued for both men. Once the would-be duelists were taken into custody, satisfactory apologies were arranged and the crisis passed.[19]

When Rutherford B. Hayes ran for president in the autumn of 1876, Mosby again backed the Republican candidate and he again challenged a political opponent to a duel. This time the circumstances were almost laughable. One of Mosby's young sons was heard cheering for Hayes by a passerby, Littleton Helm, who responded with his own cheers, "Hurrah for all traitors to their country" and "Hurrah for Alex Payne." The easily riled Mosby took offense and demanded satisfaction. Helm agreed and made a deadly choice of double-barreled shotguns at twenty paces. However, Helm diffused the situation by writing a letter clarifying his remarks and Mosby accepted the explanation.

Mosby's support of Grant and Hayes and his penchant for personalizing politics made him an outcast among his fellow Southerners. Income from his law practice shrank and people avoided him on the street. One evening in 1877, someone shot at him as he disembarked from a train in Warrenton. Previously he had always refused any political office in the Grant administration, fearing it would appear to be a quid pro quo. This time he quietly but actively sought a post under President Hayes. Ex-Confederates were still difficult for a Republican to appoint to any prominent position. When offered the post of U.S. consul in faraway Hong Kong, Mosby accepted and began a decades long exile from his native state. The daring and dramatic style that made Mosby famous as the "Grey Ghost" did not serve him nearly as well in his latter life as a private citizen.[20]

* * *

In 1852, future Confederate General John Bankhead Magruder visited San Diego, California, while serving as a colonel of the 3rd United States Artillery. Magruder was the guest of honor during a dinner party at Harry Monrie's restaurant where copious amounts of alcoholic refreshments were served.

Most of those present were probably well into their cups when Magruder casually remarked that "Andrew Jackson was the greatest man who ever trod in shoe leather." Another officer nominated Henry Clay and a third guest suggested Daniel Webster.

Then a local physician loudly declared, "My father who was sheriff of Cayuga County was the greatest of all Americans!"

Magruder was not amused by the comment and retorted icily, "Doctor, you are a damned fool."

A challenge was quickly issued and accepted with the two combatants agreeing to settle the matter right then and there. The pair faced off across the dining table, each armed with a Derringer-style pistol and instructions to open fire at the count of three.

The doctor, however, fired early and completely missed his target. This left Magruder with the only loaded gun. He rose and advanced upon his opponent, thrusting the pistol into the man's face. The doctor backed away and began circling the table, closely pursued by Magruder. Finally the medicine man dropped to his knees and pled for mercy.

Magruder kicked the doctor and declared, "Damn you! I'll spare you for the hangman." The terrified physician ran from the room as the remaining guests resumed their party.[21]

* * *

In 1859, David S. Terry was defeated in his run for reelection as chief justice of the California Supreme Court. Terry made a speech blaming the loss on those who were "the personal chattels of a single individual" and belonged "heart and soul, body and breeches to David C. Broderick." Broderick, a United States senator, responded that he had considered Terry "the only honest man on the supreme bench, but I now take it all back."

Terry, who hailed from Tennessee and supported slavery, learned of the comment and demanded satisfaction. Unlike so many other affairs of this ilk, this one amounted to more than mere posturing. The two actually wanted to fight. A first effort to stage the duel was interrupted by police but the offended parties met again on September 13 at Laguna de la Merced, about eleven miles from San Francisco. A hair trigger apparently caused

Broderick's gun to misfire and its bullet plowed into the earth about two-thirds of the way toward its intended victim. Then Terry returned fire and Broderick fell mortally wounded from a .58-caliber pistol ball.

It took the senator three days to die. He reportedly said, "They have killed me because I was opposed to the extension of slavery and the corruption of justice." His body was put on view in the Union Hotel and thousands attended the funeral of the "martyr to the slaveocracy." Terry, who had fled from San Francisco to the more remote reaches of Stockton, was brought to trial but acquitted. The affair ruined him politically and Southern influence in the state declined. A coda to the incident came thirty years later; a deputy marshal shot and killed David Terry when he attacked Judge Stephen Field in a railroad lunchroom at Lathrop, California.

In 1998, the cased single-shot Belgian pistols used by Broderick and Terry were sold at auction for $34,500.[22]

* * *

Littleton Quinton Washington, a bona fide member of George Washington's clan, also lived in San Francisco during that raucous pre-war era. Littleton worked as deputy collector at the U.S. Customs House, where so many former residents of the Old Dominion were political appointees that it was nicknamed the "Virginia Poor House."

Then in his early thirties, Washington was an unusual sort of fellow: single, politically connected and always in search of but never quite reaching the next rung on the ladder of success. He did, however, find his way into an impressive number of scrapes in which a gentleman's honor had to be satisfied.

The first of Littleton's conflicts came about in August 1857 when William Ross, an inspector at the customs house, stopped by his desk with another man. Littleton said that he was too busy to see visitors and Ross said that he merely wanted to introduce Mr. Herbert. Littleton remarked that he was pleased to meet the fellow and the men left.

Two days later, Washington was chatting with a friend on a street corner when Ross came up and asked to speak with him privately. Littleton agreed. The pair walked off together and Ross accused Littleton of treating him in "a damned in-courteous way." Littleton denied any intent to offend, but Ross continued arguing, so Littleton tried to apologize once more. Ross still rambled on about the perceived slight and Littleton disengaged himself from the conversation.

Suddenly Ross began pummeling Littleton with his fists and then grabbed Littleton's cane. Littleton tried to draw a pistol but was knocked to the ground where Ross continued to beat him using the cane. A crowd gathered, Littleton was rescued and his wounds were treated in a nearby barbershop.

It took the injured Littleton more than a week to recover during which he plotted his revenge. He planned to challenge Ross to a duel but none of Littleton's friends agreed to serve as his second, suggesting that he should wait until he was feeling better. In the meantime, Ross sent a letter of apology which Littleton accepted at the urging of his comrades. There the episode ended.

A few weeks later, Littleton lost his post as deputy at the customs house. This was probably a result of his feud with a fellow Democrat, Dr. William Gwin, who controlled much of the patronage in the state. Littleton's lukewarm support for the recently elected president, Democrat James Buchanan, also probably played a role in his ouster.[23]

Doctor Gwin's colorful career deserves a brief mention here. It included stints in the U.S. Congress representing both Mississippi and California. On June 1, 1853, he fought a duel with Congressman J. W. McCorkle while his wife waited at home to learn the result. A messenger brought word that the first round of shots had been fired and neither party was injured. Mrs. Gwin received the news with great joy. A short time later, another messenger arrived and said the second round had resulted in no casualties either. Again Mrs. Gwin expressed great relief. Finally a third messenger came with news that one more round had been fired, no one was hurt and the duel had been called off. Mrs. Gwin's reaction this time was more subdued and an observer asked her if this was not wonderful news.

"Yes, but there's been some mighty poor shooting today," she replied.[24]

Doctor Gwin's term representing California in the U.S. Senate ended just as the War Between the States began. The Federals accused him of disloyalty and expelled him to the Confederacy. In 1863, he sailed to France, hoping to find a role in Napoleon III's plan to conquer Mexico. At the end of the war, the Federals arrested the former senator after he crossed the border back into Texas and he was jailed for eight months. He died in New York in 1885.[25]

In any event, with no thanks to Gwin, Littleton Washington was out of a job. He made the long journey home to the District of Columbia where he struggled to earn his living as a lobbyist. Littleton still nursed a grudge over losing his San Francisco post, and, in chatting with friends, he made offensive remarks about his successor, John Wise. That man, of course, was three thousand miles away, but his family lived in the district.

John Wise's mother encountered Littleton on the street and took him to task for his comments. She also informed him that her other son, George, was very upset about the language that Littleton had used. Littleton replied that he "could not converse with her on the subject" and excused himself.

Shortly thereafter, a note arrived from George Wise, asking if Littleton had indeed made offensive remarks about his brother. Littleton wrote back declining to give any specifics until he was told the source of George's information. George, in turn, called Littleton "cowardly."

Littleton was ready to reach for his pistols and wrote a note to that effect. However, after conferring with several friends, he changed the wording to merely call for a withdrawal of the offensive language. George Wise's reply arrived the next day. Littleton found it unsatisfactory and issued his challenge for a duel, dating the letter as coming from Prince Georges County, Maryland, to skirt the law against dueling in the district. Littleton then packed a bag and told everyone he was leaving for Baltimore as a ruse to escape the sheriff's deputies if they learned of the proposed contest. Instead of Baltimore, however, he hid out in the room of General Joseph Lane who represented Oregon in the U.S. Senate and who, in the 1860 presidential contest, would be John Breckinridge's running mate.

For the next two days, Littleton laid low in Lane's room. George Wise, though, was arrested by the district marshal, having been turned in by his own mother who was determined to stop any gunplay. The affair ended there with Littleton content that he had come out of it "handsomely."[26]

The growing crisis between the North and South did not keep Littleton away from the dueling field. When the war came, he traveled to Montgomery, Alabama, where he conferred with Jefferson Davis and received a lieutenant's commission in the Confederate army. He served with the quartermaster corps at First Bull Run and then resigned when promised a higher position in the adjutant general's office. That post never materialized and he ended up at loose ends in the Confederate capital where he was befriended by John Moncure Daniel, the outrageous editor of the Richmond *Examiner*.[27]

Daniel was truly a piece of work. He first became editor of the *Examiner* in 1847 at the tender age of twenty-two. His outspoken opinions on politics and nearly everything else made him a force to be reckoned with in the capital. Edgar Allan Poe took offense at some of Daniel's remarks and planned a challenge. Poe backed away when he found Daniel sitting at his work desk with two waiting pistols at hand.

In 1852, the editor fought a bloodless duel with Edward Johnston of the Richmond *Whig* when they disagreed over the merits of a nude statue, *The Greek Slave*. President Franklin Pierce appointed Daniel U.S. chargé d'affaires in Sardinia but he returned to the *Examiner* just as the secession crisis reached its boiling point. In the spring of 1861, his acid pen editorials offended attorney Marmaduke John and the two traded potshots at each other on Richmond's Franklin Street. To preserve order, Mayor Joseph Mayo placed both parties under a peace bond.[28]

Littleton Washington agreed to act as editor of the *Examiner* while Daniel went off on a military expedition in western Virginia. Washington's brief residency at the paper provided the fodder for "the code" to be evoked on several occasions.

The first came when Littleton spotted an anonymous article signed "Cassius" in the Richmond *Whig* which he felt personally insulted him. Littleton responded with his own article in the *Examiner* and was rewarded with the delivery of a challenge from Alexander Mosely, the editor of the *Whig*. The seconds met to arrange terms but came out instead with a proposal for both parties to disavow their respective writings and the affair concluded. Littleton later learned that Mosely had not actually written the offending article.

The next incident concerned an editorial about Virginia Governor John Letcher which John Moncure Daniel had asked Littleton to write. The tone was so offensive that the governor's brother, Sam Houston Letcher, took it upon himself to even the score by placing a notice in the *Whig* calling Daniel a "slanderer and coward." Under normal circumstances, this would have resulted in pistols at dawn but Daniel remained under the peace bond from the Franklin Street shootings, so the two sides simply continued to insult each other.

The final controversy spawned by Littleton's brief tenure at the newspaper took longer to be resolved. Littleton had authored some editorials which were critical of Confederate Vice President Alexander Stephens. These were answered by the Atlanta *Confederacy*, a newspaper friendly to "Little Aleck." Littleton felt that the response written by "Sigma" assailed him with the "coarsest invective and calumny" and was "vulgar and unprovoked." Since he could not then travel to Atlanta and settle the matter, Littleton stored the Georgia newspaper in a trunk for future reference.

More than two years later, in December 1863, J. Henly Smith, editor of the *Confederacy*, checked into Richmond's

Spottswood Hotel. Littleton, then serving as the chief clerk to Confederate Secretary of State Judah Benjamin, learned of this and sent Smith a note, inquiring if he was the author of the long-ago article. Henly wrote back stating that the actual correspondent was dead but Henly was responsible for the publication. Littleton answered with a demand for a retraction.

Six days later, Smith, probably trying to end the dispute, replied that two expressions in the article were unjust to Littleton and that "Sigma" had misapprehended Littleton's character. This did not mollify Littleton and he wrote again with a sterner request for a more specific apology. Smith, no doubt wishing that he had remained in Atlanta, sent a letter requesting details on who had authored the Stephens comments in the *Examiner* that started the entire mess. Washington replied by challenging Smith to a duel.

Smith, however, was having none of it and refused to fight. In response, Littleton published an ad in the December 29 Richmond *Enquirer* denouncing Smith as a coward. This satisfied Littleton's honor and one can imagine that J. Henly Smith looked forward to having no further correspondence with the easily irritated State Department clerk.[29]

Littleton was involved in still another wartime duel. On September 30, 1863, Lewis E. Harvie, president of the Richmond and Danville Railroad, approached Littleton and several other gentlemen with a letter from his son, Major John B. Harvie, a quartermaster serving in southwestern Virginia. Major Harvie wrote that Colonel William Peters of the 21st Virginia Cavalry had accosted him while he was both unarmed and undressed and struck him without provocation. Harvie immediately went to get his pistol to exact retribution but was restrained by friends. Peters departed from the area with his regiment shortly thereafter.

Lewis Harvie requested that Littleton and Dr. R. F. Taylor visit his son in camp at Glade Springs and act as seconds in setting up a challenge. The two men agreed and left on the afternoon train after Littleton had obtained leave from the State

Department and picked up his rifle and a pair of dueling pistols. At Powhatan Station, another man, E. G. Leigh, joined the party.

They reached Glade Springs the following evening. The initial plan was that Major Harvie would board the train and they would continue traveling to Bristol where Colonel Peters was thought to be. Major Harvie could not leave immediately, however, and the trip was delayed until the next evening.

General Sam Jones telegraphed permission for the three civilians—but not Major Harvie—to journey on through the military district. Harvie went anyway, using his general permit to travel on army business.

Arriving in Bristol on the evening of October 3, the party spent the night and pushed on the next day toward Jonesboro where the 21st Virginia Cavalry was camped as part of Wharton's Brigade. Reaching Carter's Depot, they found the bridge over the Watauga River destroyed and they were unable to proceed. This became a moot point when the men learned that the object of their trip, Colonel Peters, was on his way to Richmond for a session of the Virginia State Senate.

Leaving Major Harvie at Glade Springs, the disappointed dueling party made the long journey back to the Confederate capital, spending a bitterly cold night on a train car with broken windows and no working stove. They reached town on the evening of October 5. The very next day, Littleton tracked down Colonel Peters and explained their interest in seeing him. The colonel gave no comment.

Major Harvie came to Richmond on October 15 and that evening Littleton delivered a written challenge to Colonel Peters. The officer said that he would need to ask a friend from the country to serve as his second and that would require some time. Ten days passed with no further word, so Littleton delivered another note to the colonel. Peters responded that Harvie and Washington had taken their own time in sending the challenge, so he would take his time in delivering a reply. Anyway he was busy with his duties in the Virginia State Senate. Littleton pondered whether this response was personally offensive and grounds for yet another challenge, but his friends convinced him that it was not. Instead, Littleton wrote to Peters that he would accept his word to give satisfaction after the close of the Senate session on November 2.

On that day, Littleton received a note from a Mr. Clendine, acting on behalf of Colonel Peters, and terms were agreed upon. The offending parties would meet at sunrise on Monday, November 9 in Bristol. The weapons would be rifles at sixty yards.

Once again the international affairs of the Confederacy could wait as Littleton took leave from the State Department and headed back to southwestern Virginia. Part of the trip this time was made in the comfortable private car of Robert Owen, president of the Virginia and Tennessee Railroad.

The two Confederate officers did not meet until Tuesday due to an absence of one of Colonel Peter's seconds. The dueling party spent most of Monday playing cards and Littleton read Charles Dickens' *Great Expectations*. The next morning, after preliminary discussions on the field, a first round of shots was exchanged but both men escaped unscathed.

Littleton requested a reduction of the distance to forty yards but this was refused. Instead Colonel Peters offered a conditional apology. Major Harvie did not accept but withdrew his challenge. Colonel Peters, in turn, offered a full and unconditional apology which was followed by Major Harvie stating that he had never meant to insult Peters. Littleton drew up a statement of what had happened, which representatives of both parties signed. Everyone could then go home happy with reputations intact.

Littleton and company arrived back in Richmond on November 12; the clerk noted in his diary that Judah Benjamin had made no objection to him being gone. In the meantime, Colonel Peters was belatedly arrested but released when it was learned that the duel already had been concluded. Peters, incidentally, would be arrested once again in July 1864 when he refused a direct order from General John McCausland to burn the town of Chambersburg, Pennsylvania.

Littleton Washington continued with the Confederate State Department to the very end, fleeing the capital when it fell in April 1865. It is interesting to note that for all the "affairs of honor" in which he was involved, not one resulted in any blood shed.[30]

That logical thinker U. S. Grant never understood the rationale behind this kind of folderol. He wrote, "If any man should wrong me to the extent of my being willing to kill him, I would not be willing to give him the choice of weapons with which it should be done, and of the time, place and distance separating us, when I executed him." Grant believed that "a majority of the duels fought have been for want of moral courage on the part of those engaged to decline."[31]

Union General Jefferson C. Davis was never even brought to trial after he publicly murdered a fellow officer at a Louisville hotel.

CHAPTER SIX
MORE DUELS

Charleston, South Carolina, was noted for its Southern chivalry which, naturally enough, included a strong interest in the code duello. In fact, in the early 1800s, the city actually had its own dueling society with officers chosen according to the number of men each member had killed or injured. The society disbanded at the request of its president after he was mortally wounded in a contest with a visiting English sea captain.[1]

The ubiquitous Civil War diarist Mary Chesnut wrote of "manly specimens" who would fight "a duel or two if kept too long sweltering in a Charleston sun." Discussing "South Carolina ethics," she mentioned that men may be "dishonest, immoral, cruel, black with every crime" but with one "defamatory word" spoken, "pistols come at once to the fore."[2]

As an example, consider Captain W. Ransom Calhoun and Lieutenant Alfred Rhett of the 1st South Carolina Artillery Battalion. Both came from prominent South Carolina families. When the pair served together during the Civil War's opening bombardment of Fort Sumter in Charleston Harbor, they also began a personal conflict that would end in death.

Rhett became irked when Calhoun was appointed second-in-command at Fort Moultrie by Lieutenant Colonel Roswell Ripley. Rhett saw this as Ripley taking care of his fellow West Point graduate Calhoun. The situation worsened when Calhoun skipped the chain of command during the shelling of Fort Sumter and gave orders directly to Rhett's soldiers. Rhett responded by openly cursing Calhoun; for some time afterward, he continued to make insulting comments about his superior in the hope of being challenged to a duel.

Calhoun ignored the insolent officer and the situation temporarily resolved itself when Calhoun was transferred to Virginia. A few months later, however, he returned to Charleston and was placed in charge of Fort Sumter. His number two officer was none other than Alfred Rhett.

Having drinks at the Charleston Club with Captain Arnoldus Vanderhorst, Rhett remarked that many West Point graduates were "not worth a damn" and that Calhoun was "a damned puppy." Vanderhorst felt personally insulted and challenged Rhett to a duel. The pair fired two shots in a bloodless confrontation which allowed both gentlemen to walk away satisfied. The public knowledge of Rhett's derogatory comments, however, now made it impossible for Calhoun to continue to ignore the man's offensive behavior any longer.

They met late on the afternoon of September 15, 1862, with pistols at ten paces. Each man fired and Calhoun fell mortally wounded. The Charleston *Mercury*, which the Rhett family owned, was strangely quiet about the incident and calls for prosecution of Alfred Rhett went nowhere. In fact, he was promoted to colonel and assumed Calhoun's former place in command of Fort Sumter.[3]

These incidents were in violation of Number 25 of the Confederate Articles of War which prohibited dueling under threat of court-martial. Officers could be cashiered and enlisted men sentenced to corporal punishment for any offense. Obviously, the regulation was selectively enforced.[4]

* * *

William Nelson spent twenty-one years in the United States Navy, rising to the rank of lieutenant. However, when Fort Sumter was fired upon, he was commissioned as a brigadier general of army volunteers, thanks to the influence of his brother who had political ties to Abraham Lincoln. Nicknamed "Bull" due to his impressive size and sometimes gruff demeanor, William Nelson took command of the home guard in his native Kentucky and worked to keep that state from joining the Confederacy.

In late summer of 1862, Confederate General Braxton Bragg led his Rebel army on an impressive campaign of maneuver into the Bluegrass State. Nelson marshaled the Union forces against the grey invaders in battle at Richmond, Kentucky. In the fighting, Nelson was wounded and his soldiers fell back to Louisville.

Making his headquarters at the prominent Galt House Hotel, Nelson prepared the city's defenses for the anticipated Rebel attack. A career army officer with an ironic name, Brigadier General Jefferson Davis, came off sick leave in his native Indiana to help meet the emergency.

Unfortunately, Nelson and Davis did not get along. Perhaps Davis, who had been in the army since the Mexican War and was inside Fort Sumter when it was fired upon, resented having a former navy lieutenant as his superior. Perhaps "Bull" was in one of his irritable moods, which would have been understandable given the critical situation that he faced.

For whatever reason, "Bull" found fault with Davis and, after just two days, relieved him from command. On the morning of September 29, 1862, Davis, accompanied by his friend, Indiana Governor Oliver Morton, and a Captain Gibson, met up with Nelson in the vestibule of the Galt House.

"Sir, you seemed to take advantage of your authority the other day," Davis declared.

Nelson did not understand and Davis repeated the statement.

"I don't know that I did, sir," Nelson protested.

"You threatened to arrest me and send me out of the state under a provost guard!" Davis replied. He crumpled a card and threw it at Nelson's face in a traditional form of challenge.

Nelson responded by slapping Davis with the back of his hand and shouting, "There, damn you, take that!" Nelson looked at Governor Morton and asked why the prominent politico was in the company of Davis. He then headed back the hall toward his room.

In a rage, Davis borrowed a pistol from Captain Gibson and stalked after Nelson. "Bull" turned around to meet him and Davis shot the general in the chest, inflicting a mortal wound. Nelson died shortly thereafter. Twelve thousand troops turned out for his funeral.

Davis was placed under arrest and, given the unsettled military situation, a request went off to the War Department to provide officers for a court-martial. But Davis' friend, Governor Morton, intervened and Davis was released to stand trial before a civil court. The civil trial, however, never happened. Jefferson Columbus Davis literally got away with murdering an unarmed superior officer.[5]

Davis earned a distinguished record in later campaigns through Tennessee and Georgia but, toward the end of the war, he again found himself mired in controversy. As William Sherman's Yankees approached Savannah in December 1864, they were accompanied by a large population of black slaves who had fled their masters in the hope of finding freedom. The refugees became a growing nuisance and slowed the army's march. What's more, since Sherman's bummers were living off the land, it was more and more difficult to feed these extra mouths as the army entered the swampy, less fertile section of southeast Georgia.

Davis commanded the XIV Corps, which reached the icy waters of Ebenezer Creek about twenty-five miles north of Savannah on December 3. Pontoon bridges were thrown over the 165-foot waterway and the bluecoats marched across. Davis ordered the blacks held back for their own safety, citing the possibility of fighting on the other side of the bridge. When the soldiers were across, instructions were given to take up the pontoons, and an estimated five thousand refugees were stranded on the wrong side of the flooded creek.

"Fighting Joe" Wheeler's grey horsemen, who had been harassing the rear of the Union column, rushed in. Some of the frightened slaves drowned trying to escape across the water while others were killed by the angry Southerners. The survivors were returned to captivity.

Word of the ugly episode reached Washington and Secretary of War Edwin Stanton sailed down to Sherman's army to investigate. As a Democrat, Davis might have made an easy target for the rising power of radical Republicans, but his luck held. The unfortunate affair at Ebenezer Creek was deemed a military necessity.[6]

Still Davis' career was tarnished. After these two incidents, his only promotion through a long military career came in the form of a brevet. He died of pneumonia in 1879 and was buried in Indianapolis.

* * *

Nathan Bedford Forrest and Earl Van Dorn were two Southern cavalry leaders who nearly came to blows in the spring of 1863. Forrest was an unschooled Memphis slave trader who seemed to have a natural genius for military matters. Van Dorn was a West Point graduate who had won renown in the Mexican War. Both men had fiery personalities and Forrest had been transferred to Van Dorn's command after he refused to serve any longer under "Fighting Joe" Wheeler.

The trouble started when Forrest appropriated some captured Federal supplies for the use of his command. Van Dorn, who viewed Forrest as a potential rival, was instructed by the commanding general, Braxton Bragg, to get the enemy spoils back from Forrest and forward them to army headquarters.

The meeting at Spring Hill, Tennessee, between the two generals began badly and quickly got worse. Accounts vary as to what was actually said. Van Dorn apparently accused Forrest of having laudatory articles published in the press and of making false claims to the army higher-ups. The arguments grew louder and neither man was afraid of a fight. Forrest threatened to run his saber through whoever was making these accusations.

Nathan Bedford Forrest was not a man to be trifled with. Even before the war, he had demonstrated his unwillingness to back away from trouble. In 1845, four men attacked his uncle in Hernando, Mississippi. Though his uncle was killed, Forrest gunned down two of the attackers before running out of ammunition. He chased after the remaining two with a Bowie knife.[7]

But, on this day in Spring Hill, both Forrest and Van Dorn uncharacteristically avoided the flash point. Van Dorn agreed when a staff officer suggested that Forrest had nothing to do with the press reports. Forrest agreed that both of them had enough Yankees to fight without fighting each other. The matter was smoothed over and Van Dorn sent Forrest off to chase Abel Streight's marauding Union cavalry.[8]

Van Dorn remained at his Spring Hill headquarters, enjoying the pleasures of camp life which included the attractive young wife of a prominent local doctor. Though Van Dorn was married, his fondness for whiskey and women had been the source of much gossip and even attracted unfavorable comments in the press.

Despite owning slaves and having two sons in Confederate grey, Dr. George B. Peters was a Union man. In 1863, he was about fifty years old and married to his third wife, Jessie, a woman half his age and quite pretty. She did not go unnoticed by Earl Van Dorn and the general began keeping company with the young woman when her husband was away on business. Rumors of an improper relationship soon reached the doctor's ears.

The suspicious husband became convinced that the stories were true and he intercepted a servant carrying a note to his wife from Van Dorn. He threatened to kill Van Dorn if that officer ever set foot in the Peters' house again.

Shortly thereafter, the doctor crossed through the army lines and spent several days in Union-occupied Nashville. Van Dorn took advantage of the husband's absence to visit Jessie Peters every night. Upon his return, the doctor learned of this and decided to catch Van Dorn in the act. He announced that he was leaving on another business trip but instead he secreted himself near his house and kept watch for the Rebel Romeo. Two days later, at 2:30 a.m., he claimed to have caught Van Dorn with Mrs. Peters.

According to the good doctor's account, he was ready to shoot Van Dorn but instead agreed not to kill him in exchange for a statement admitting the illicit affair. Eager to make his escape, Van Dorn agreed.

On the morning of May 7, Peters went to Van Dorn's office to collect the statement. Van Dorn had not prepared anything. Peters said he would return in thirty minutes for it. When he came back, Van Dorn handed him a weakly worded document that did not meet the doctor's demands. Sharp words ensued and the doctor drew his pistol and fired. The bullet struck Van Dorn on the left side of the head, just above the ear.

Or at least that is the offended husband's account of the shooting. It is also possible that the doctor never accosted the general in the early morning at the Peters household. It may be that Peters merely made up the written statement episode in order to help justify his shooting of Van Dorn.

Another account by a Rebel cavalryman who was camped near the general's office said that Van Dorn found Peters waiting there to request a pass through the lines. Van Dorn agreed and wrote out the necessary paper. While the general's back was turned, Peters shot him in the head, grabbed the pass and fled to the Union army.

Peters later fell into the hands of the Confederates and stood trial for the murder in a Mississippi courtroom. The cuckolded husband was acquitted.

The strangest part of the story comes at the end. Dr. Peters divorced Jessie but, after the war, they reconciled and remarried. When her husband died in 1879, the grieving widow reportedly put on a black veil for the funeral with the remark, "I never cared much for George, but I guess I owe him this much."[9]

Nathan Bedford Forrest, too, found himself the victim of an assassination attempt shortly thereafter. In Forrest's case, the assailant was not a wronged husband but a disgruntled subordinate.

When Forrest pursued Streight's Yankees across Alabama and Georgia, Lieutenant Andrew Gould had abandoned two pieces of artillery in a battle at Sand Mountain on April 30. Forrest was enraged at losing these guns and openly questioned the lieutenant's valor. Afterward, he decided to have Gould transferred to another command.

Gould felt that his reputation had been smeared and he arranged to meet with Forrest on June 13 at the Masonic Building in Columbia, Tennessee. Gould challenged the circumstances of his transfer but Forrest refused to reconsider it.

"Damn you! What right have you to put the brand of a coward on me when I fought as long as I could?" Gould demanded.

"You abandoned my guns," Forrest charged. "That makes you everything I said about you and worse."

Gould shouted, "It's false." He attempted to draw a pistol from his linen duster but it caught in the fabric. Forrest pulled out a pocketknife and unfolded the knife blade with his teeth as he reached with his other hand to grab Gould. Then Gould's pistol roared and a ball struck Forrest in the hip. Gould's gun was out of his coat now but Forrest pushed the barrel of the weapon into the air. With his free hand, Forrest sank the knife deep into his assailant's right side.

Gould ran out into the street. Forrest tried to follow but was waylaid by some officers who persuaded him to have his wound examined. Taken to a doctor's office, the general learned that his injury might be fatal.

"No damned man shall kill me and live!" Forrest vowed, heading back out into the street and pausing only to grab a revolver from the saddle of a nearby horse.

Gould's wounds were being examined at a tailor shop. In a sputtering rage, Forrest burst through the doorway and chased Gould out into a back alley. Forrest fired a shot that missed Gould but hit another soldier. Gould fell into some weeds and Forrest nudged him with his foot to see if he was dead. Then the general went off to find medical attention, taking with him the two doctors who had come to attend Gould.

Forrest's wound proved not to be nearly as serious as first thought. Learning that he would survive and, in fact, would soon be back in the saddle, Forrest had a change of heart toward his assailant. He ordered that Gould be taken to the Nelson House

Hotel for treatment. But it was no use. Forrest's knife had done its deadly work well and the lieutenant's wound was fatal. According to one account, Forrest was carried to Gould's deathbed where the two men forgave each other.[10]

A few months later Nathan Bedford Forrest was embroiled in another quarrel which under most circumstances would have brought about a duel. Forrest had became so infuriated with army commander Braxton Bragg that he burst into the general's tent, refused to shake Bragg's outstretched hand and launched into a scathing tirade.

"I have stood your meanness as long as I intend to," Forrest thundered as he worked through his spiel. "You have played the part of a damned scoundrel and are a coward, and, if you were any part of a man, I would slap your jaws and force you to resent it. You may as well not issue any orders to me, for I will not obey them, and I will hold you personally responsible for any further indignities you endeavor to inflict upon me. You have threatened to arrest me for not obeying your orders promptly. I dare you to do it, and I say to you that if you ever again try to interfere with me or cross my path it will be at the peril of your life."

Few superiors have ever received such a severe dressing down from a subordinate. Many Southern officers would have put propriety aside and settled the matter with pistols. Forrest though knew his man well. As he rode away from Bragg's tent, a member of his staff told him, "Now you are in for it."

Forrest disagreed, "No, he'll never say a word about it. He'll be the last man to mention it and, mark my word, he'll take no action in the matter. I will ask to be relieved and transferred to a different field, and he will not oppose it."

A short time later, after a visit to the army from President Jefferson Davis, Forrest was moved off to Mississippi with Bragg regretting to lose the services of "that distinguished soldier."[11]

A hot temper must have run in the Forrest family. The general's second oldest brother, John, had been paralyzed below the waist by a musket ball in the Mexican War and was forced to remain at home in Memphis when the fighting began in 1861.

After Union troops occupied that city, his mother complained to him about the rudeness of a particular Union officer. John tracked the man down and a heated argument ensued. When John tried to hit the Yankee, the officer kicked away the invalid's supporting crutch and he fell to the ground. John pulled out a pocket pistol and shot the Northerner. Fortunately, the wounded man lived, which made it easier for John to be acquitted at his subsequent trial.[12]

* * *

Englishman Francis Dawson came to America in 1862 and briefly served in the Confederate navy before receiving a lieutenant's commission and joining the staff of General James Longstreet. There he encountered Major Thomas Walton, a Mississippian whose strong opinions made him no favorite of many of the other officers. In the fall of 1863, as the Confederates attempted to lay siege to Chattanooga, Walton undiplomatically informed Dawson that Southerners enjoyed their own government and that they did not intend to have any "damned foreigners" in their country. Dawson asked what should become of soldiers like himself who had come to help the struggling new nation. Walton gave a curt reply and Dawson followed with an angry comment. Walton tried to strike Dawson but the Englishman parried the blow and managed to slap Walton's face.

The next day Dawson sent Walton a challenge via Captain Fitzgerald Ross, an Englishman visiting the Confederacy as an observer for the Austrian army. Walton said that he did not want to fight but would send an apology in writing. No apology, however, was forthcoming and Dawson sent Ross again to see the major. Walton had decided that he preferred not to apologize and would not do so unless he had actually promised that he would. Ross tactfully told Dawson to forget everything that had happened since his first visit and they would begin again with a challenge being presented. The Mississippian saw that his only options were to either write or fight and so he sent Dawson the apology.[13]

* * *

On March 18, 1865, two privates in the South Carolina horse artillery got into an argument, the specifics of which have been lost to history. Thomas Chew and Marx Cohen, Jr., agreed to settle their differences the next day with pistols at dawn. Chew, Cohen and their seconds gathered a little distance from camp and began blazing away at each other with revolvers.

As if a miracle had occurred, neither of the battle-hardened veterans was injured even after they had emptied all six rounds of their handguns. The principals left the field puzzled until Cohen realized that their seconds had loaded the weapons with blanks. By this stage of the war, the seconds had seen too many of their brothers in grey die on the field of battle; they would not allow any more senseless loss of life. The hot-headed Cohen turned accusingly to his second and declared, "I understand now. I shall hold you to account for this."

At the moment, however, duty called. The cannoneers went off to fight that day at Bentonville in a last-ditch effort to halt William Sherman's march through North Carolina. During the action, Chew was killed by an enemy shell. Cohen fell mortally wounded a short time later. It seemed as if fate had intervened in what was, in all likelihood, the last duel of the Confederacy.[14]

* * *

On March 30, 1865, shortly before the fall of Richmond, firebrand editor John Moncure Daniel died—not as the result of a duel but from tubercular fever. After the Union occupation of the city, his newspaper, the *Examiner*, resumed publication under the leadership of the Pollard brothers, Edward and Henry. Both men had served on the editorial staff during the war. Like their predecessor, John Daniel, these men were experienced with a caustic pen and neither shrank from using it.

To keep the struggling newspaper afloat, the *Examiner* pursued some government printing contracts. A rival publication, the *Enquirer,* took note and wrote that the *Examiner* was well qualified because it had "a man who knows how to make public printer's accounts so that a dollar of real service will produce ten dollars in pay." This infuriated Henry Pollard and he sought satisfaction.

On the afternoon of January 5, 1866, Pollard accompanied his employee, the English Confederate Francis Dawson, to the rotunda of the Virginia state house. There they encountered the publishers of the *Enquirer*, Nathaniel Tyler and William Coleman, coming out of the House of Representatives. Pollard went after the two waving his cane but he was restrained before he could strike them. Breaking free, Pollard raced around Houdon's statue of George Washington in the center of the rotunda and pulled out a pistol. Tyler and Coleman drew their handguns. Shots were exchanged but the only injury was to the marble George Washington who had the tassel blown off his cane. The three men were taken in custody and Pollard received a reprimand.[15]

A short time later, E. P. Brooks of *The New York Times* wrote an article from Richmond which spoke in unflattering terms of Pollard. Francis Dawson went out to track down the Yankee reporter and, after a long search, found him in the billiard room of the Spottswood Hotel. Word was sent to Henry Pollard, who arrived at the establishment "armed to the teeth" and ready for a fight. The unsuspecting Brooks walked into the hotel lobby where he was jumped by the Richmond editor. The two tussled about in the public area as Dawson aimed a pistol at anyone who tried to stop the melee. Pollard jammed Brooks' head into a glass partition and Brooks ripped out part of Pollard's beard. Richmond society, which generally did not approve of the Pollards, nevertheless took delight in the Yankee's thrashing.

Henry Pollard's brother, Edward, did his part as well to maintain the family's fighting tradition. During an 1867 visit to Baltimore, he was wounded in a duel with John Wise for offensive remarks Edward made about John's father, former Virginia governor and ex-Confederate general Henry Wise.[16]

The very next year, Henry Pollard came to an untimely end. By then, the two brothers had started a new newspaper, *Southern Opinion*, which published a sensational account about a reported elopement of a young woman named Mary Grant. Miss Grant's family published a rebuttal in the Richmond *Daily Dispatch* but the matter did not end there. On November 24, 1868, near the corner of Fourteenth and Main Streets, Henry Rives Pollard was en route to his office when he fell dead from a shotgun blast fired out a third-story window. The assassin was James Grant, brother of the maligned Mary.

Though public opinion felt Grant should have confronted Pollard face-to-face instead of shooting him from ambush, he was acquitted by a jury after only forty minutes of deliberation.

Meanwhile, Pollard's employee, Englishman Francis Dawson, had moved on to South Carolina where he edited the Charleston *News and Courier.* He became opposed to dueling and refused to fight them for religious reasons. His editorials on the subject helped mobilize support for legislation that finally outlawed the practice in the Palmetto State. Ironically, Dawson was later gunned down in an argument over improper advances that a neighbor had made to Dawson's Swiss housekeeper.[17]

According to historian Ashley Halsey, Jr., eight Confederate generals of the 318 who made it through the fighting later fell as victims of postwar personal vendettas. These included Lieutenant General Thomas Hindman, who was killed in 1868 at Clarkton, Missouri; Brigadier General James Clanton, who was shot by a former Union officer in 1871; Brigadier General William Adams, who was shot during a Jackson, Mississippi, street fight in 1888; and Major General Byran Grimes, shot down near his North Carolina plantation in 1880.[18]

There were also many of lesser rank who died violently after Appomattox; for example, William McKaig, Jr., ended the war as a first lieutenant in the 2nd Maryland Confederate Cavalry and then rose to colonel in the Maryland National Guard. He was gunned down on the streets of Cumberland, Maryland, by Crawford Black. McKaig had been romantically involved with Black's sister and family honor had to be avenged when she became pregnant.[19]

*Confederate Secretary of War Judah Benjamin compen-
sated for a failed marriage by spending his nights in
Richmond's gambling dens.*

Joyce Yost

CHAPTER SEVEN
OFF DUTY IN CAMP AND TOWN

Confederate Secretary of State Judah Benjamin had always been something of an unusual bird in the upper strata of Southern leadership. For one thing, he was a Jew—not a particularly observant one perhaps, but a Jew nevertheless—in an era when antisemitism was open and commonplace. Those in the know also gossiped about the curious circumstances of Benjamin's abrupt departure from college when he was a student at Yale. Could it really be true that he was responsible for a series of thefts on campus?

And then there was his marriage! He had wed Natalie St. Martin of an aristocratic New Orleans Catholic family. But in 1844, Natalie had packed up their daughter and moved to live a separate life in Paris, France. While serving as a U.S. senator in the 1850s, Benjamin briefly lured his wife to Washington by spending lavishly to outfit the Decatur Mansion in the finest style. Natalie, however, did not stay long in America but hurried back to France where she remained for the rest of her days. She left behind lively stories of her European lifestyle which scandalized strait-laced Washington society. Admitting defeat in his efforts to re-woo his wife, Benjamin dejectedly put the mansion's furnishings up for auction.[1]

But as people talked behind his back, Judah Benjamin seemingly ignored his troubles and kept a smiling face turned to all. With his "keg-like form and over-deferential manner," he was a man who had made his own way in the world, rising from nothing to the United States Senate and then becoming successively the attorney general, secretary of war and finally secretary of state in the Confederate president's cabinet.[2]

At the State Department, he would arrive at nine in the morning and work until three in the afternoon. These hours ensured plenty of time for social visits and other matters, including his regular pastime of haunting Richmond's gambling halls. There his calm smile and unchanging demeanor allowed him to win large sums playing poker and faro.

Even before the war, elegantly furnished gambling saloons had been popular in the city, and the laws against them were laxly enforced. As soldiers arrived in the new Confederate capital, the number of these establishments multiplied. One estimate is that there were more than one hundred gambling parlors in wartime Richmond, and all of them were illegal. Many were located on the upper floors of Main Street shops where the proprietors furnished food, whiskey and willing women to high-rolling patrons. The District of Columbia was filled with similar establishments as were other large cities, North and South.

A Richmond newspaper noted the proliferation of the illegal joints in a satirical article entitled "Stranger's Guide": *"The very large number of houses on Main, and other streets, which have numbers painted in large gilt figures over the door, and illuminated at night are* Faro Banks. *The fact is not known to the public."*[3]

In an effort to suppress the trade, ax-wielding Richmond police raided several gambling halls in the autumn of 1861. The gambling tables and other equipment were seized and set ablaze on Broad Street on December 27 as some sort of post-Christmas warning. Richmond City Council passed legislation imposing fines, imprisonment and thirty-nine lashes upon those operating the joints. They also ordered the barrooms closed at 10 p.m.[4]

Nevertheless the fun continued. When Union Colonel Abel Streight escaped from Libby Prison, the military police raided a gambling den in search of him. Startled gentlemen of high position raced through a trap door on the roof of the building to avoid detection, much to the amusement of the crowd standing in the street below. Judah Benjamin may have been among those on the roof; he reportedly made at least one similar "out-the-back-window" maneuver when his evening game was interrupted.[5]

Gambling was not restricted to cities but started up wherever soldiers had time on their hands. At the beginning of the war, Confederate recruits stationed north of Richmond at Ashland found themselves quartered at a race course. This provided a convenient venue for both their love of fine horses and wagering.[6]

In June 1863, Union artillery commander Colonel Charles Wainwright encountered a "large gambling saloon of at least a couple acres" set up in a shaded grove near White Oak Church, Virginia. Wainwright estimated that there were a thousand men, some holding large stacks of greenbacks, clustered around checkered cloths and ring boards.

Wainwright thought gambling had become increasingly popular; even the black "contrabands" were at it when they were supposed to have been working for their bluecoat patrons. He opined that since women were scarce and whiskey was tough to get, the enlisted men were driven to gambling as the sole remaining source of illicit amusement.[7]

Some of the games could go for high stakes with successful players sending home as much as a thousand dollars at one time. Confederate Thomas Walton of Longstreet's staff won two thousand dollars from an army surgeon named Maury. Walton was so ill-mannered as to send for his winnings before the good doctor got out of bed the next morning.[8]

Longstreet himself was an old army poker player who early on also enjoyed a little hell-raising in camp. One festive evening, the general is said to have mounted the back of a staff officer and ridden him around the headquarters tent. However, after three of his children succumbed to scarlet fever in January and

February 1862, Longstreet put the cards aside and his manner became more reserved.[9]

One of Longstreet's division commanders, the sad-eyed John Bell Hood, earned his reputation as a reckless gambler while serving in Texas with the pre-war army. One time a flat-broke Hood borrowed six hundred dollars, put it all on a single card in a faro game and won his bet. On another occasion he supposedly put one thousand dollars on one card and again managed to win. Another story purports that Hood wagered $2,500 in a poker game with "nary a pair in his hand." The same "go-for-broke" philosophy characterized Hood's military career but his luck did not last through the war. He emerged from the fighting without the use of an arm and missing a leg. What's more, he had devastated his once-proud Army of Tennessee in disastrous battles at Franklin and Nashville.[10]

Robert E. Lee strongly disapproved of his soldiers' gambling. While visiting the camps of Longstreet's command, he spied men gathered about shooting dice. Lee asked his subordinate to end the practice and "Old Pete" replied evasively that he would see about it. Longstreet knew that nothing would stop soldiers from gambling and he took no further action.[11]

In November 1862, Lee sounded much like a scolding father when he issued this order to his troops:

> *The general commanding is pained to learn that the vice of gambling exists, and is becoming common in this army. The regulations expressly prohibit one class of officers from indulging in this evil practice, and it was not supposed that a habit so pernicious and demoralizing would be found among men engaged in a cause, of all others, demanding the highest virtue and purest morality in its supporters. He regards it as wholly inconsistent with the character of a Southern soldier and subversive of good order and discipline in the army. All officers are earnestly enjoined to use every effort to suppress this vice, and the assistance of every soldier having the true interests of the army and of*

the country at heart is invoked to put an end to a practice
which cannot fail to produce those deplorable results
which have ever attended its indulgence in any society."[12]

Robert E. Lee's august presence could put a bit of a damper
on the fun and games of his subordinate officers. Just before the
Gettysburg campaign, when Lee was to be away in Richmond,
some of Brigadier General Richard Garnett's staff took the occasion for a dinner party which continued through the evening with
loud singing and general hilarity. One song had the titillating
title "Rum tum ta, touchie fol la." The next morning, the officers
were shocked to see Lee had not left camp after all. He greeted
them with the understatement, "You had a lively crowd in your
tent last night."[13]

As a career army officer, Lee no doubt had already heard
the ribald lyrics to some of the songs that the party-goers were
singing. Perhaps in the privacy of his tent, he allowed himself an
amused smile. Douglas Southall Freeman, however, stated that
in all the years of research he conducted for his landmark four-
volume biography of the general, he found not one instance where
Lee used an obscene word or phrase. Confederate officer John S.
Wise recalled that Lee was "never censorious touching the mode
of life of his inferiors when they discharged the duties assigned
to them."[14]

Gambling was both widely popular and widely seen as immoral. In 1862, the Richmond *Whig* published a pamphlet containing the arguments of "Erskine" and "W.M." over the
practicality of suppressing gambling. "Erskine" put forth that
men have always gambled and always will, so it should be legal-
ized in licensed establishments; "W.M." built a moral case against
it. Both arguments read very much like the modern day advocates on each side of this issue.[15]

The Reverend J. B. Jeter of Richmond wrote a tract entitled
The Evils of Gaming: A Letter to a Friend in the Army. He described gambling as "a sinful practice" and "seductive vice" where
"the path that leads to this dangerous precipice is strewed with
flowers." He warned ominously, "Over the door of the gambler's

retreat might be appropriately described, in letters of lurid flame, 'This is the way to hell; going down to the chambers of death.'"[16]

Even some of the players harbored inner doubts and hedged their bets just to be safe. Before embarking on Pickett's Charge, Major Edmund Berkeley buried the deck of cards that he had used in games all through the previous winter's camp. Many other soldiers did the same, fearing their chances of salvation would be reduced if they were killed while carrying playthings of the devil. But when the battle ended, new cards were found and the fun began again.[17]

* * *

In late 1862, complaints reached the U.S. War Department of "drunkenness, gambling, fighting and even murder" at the Annapolis, Maryland, camp set up to handle paroled Union soldiers recently returned from Confederate prisons. A board of inquiry learned that gambling was "so open, so universal and so near headquarters" that one soldier, perhaps disingenuously, assumed it was permitted. To ward off thirst, the players could purchase liquor in close-by "whiskey shanties" or from roving vendors, carrying canteens and jugs of rot-gut. A crackdown the week before the investigators began their work netted sixty gamblers.[18]

Captain Albert Hunter of the 1st Maryland Potomac Home Brigade was awaiting exchange at the Annapolis camp about this time. Hunter had been paid but his men had not. He loaned one of them a dollar and shortly thereafter saw the soldier staggering along the street. Hunter asked the man how he was. The fellow replied, "Oh, first rate! I have a pound of tobacco, pretty drunk and ten cents left."[19]

Wagering was popular with Confederate prisoners at Point Lookout, Maryland, in the fall of 1863. On the pen's main thoroughfare, "The Change," Rebs could be found playing cards, keno and sweat-cloth for money or rations. At Camp Douglas, Illinois, Southerner John Copley recalled that his fellow prisoners would gamble for "little chews of tobacco, about the size of buck-shot, and thirds of bread." Copley himself valued his "grub too highly to fool it away on a game of cards." He did play euchre in which the wager was that the losers would haul water from the hydrant for the whole mess. Copley and his partner never carried any water, not due to their superior playing ability but thanks to their skill in padding the score with unearned points.[20]

Through the winter of 1864, the regimental historian of the 150th Pennsylvania Volunteers recalled that "poker—more or less indulged in at all times—suddenly became an absorbing occupation." Even at headquarters, the game grew into an epidemic and staff officers won or, more frequently, lost months of pay in a single evening. Lieutenant Miles Rose of Company I, a battle-hardened veteran who had been wounded during the first day at Gettysburg, fell victim to the gambling mania. Disregarding regulations, he engaged in play with the enlisted men of his command. One night, long after the bugler had played "Taps," a loud argument broke out and awoke the sleeping camp. It was Rose engaged in fisticuffs over the results of a poker game. Under normal circumstances, the lieutenant's violation of the regulations might have been discreetly dealt with by a reprimand. This incident though was too public and a subsequent court-martial dismissed the man from service.[21]

Cheaters could suffer even more serious consequences. Confederate Sam Watkins wrote the classic memoir *Company Aytch*, detailing his experience as a "high private" in the Army of Tennessee. There was one story which Sam did not include in the original printing of his humorous and entertaining book. It concerned the time a gambler came to the army's 1864 winter camp in Dalton, Georgia. Watkins called the fellow a "blackleg" who worked his way through the ranks, winning large stakes at the poker table.

One day the gambler got into a game with Watkins' friend, Tom Tuck. As the cards were being shuffled, Tuck placed a Bowie knife and a pistol on the table and warned his opponent that he believed the man's extraordinarily good luck was a result of

cheating. If Tuck caught him at it during this game, he would
stick the blade between his ribs.

The "blackleg" promised to play fair and square and so the
game began. Large stakes moved back and forth between the
players as whiskey flowed freely. Watkins watched the action
and noticed that the "blackleg" occasionally would throw up his
hand and not bet, even when he was holding four aces. Then Tom
Tuck hit a bad streak, losing hand after hand to the stranger
until all of Tuck's money was gone.

Watkins suspected something funny. He grabbed the playing cards and showed Tuck that the deck was marked. Tuck looked
at the cards and swore that he would keep his promise of killing
the "blackleg" if he cheated. The stranger made it out the cabin
door but Tuck was right behind him. In the company street, Tuck
fired two times. The gambler screamed and fell dead. The *Chattanooga Rebel* later reported that a man's body was found near
the Dalton train depot; the victim had been shot twice and his
throat slashed.

Watkins had helped Tuck dispose of the corpse. He did not
reveal his part in the gambler's demise until he wrote a brief
account of it for the November 1909 edition of *Confederate Veteran* magazine.[22]

Watkins' friend, Tom Tuck, enjoyed all sorts of gambling,
including waging on cockfights. Tuck's champion pet rooster was
named "Southern Confederacy" which was later abbreviated to
"Confed" and finally just "Fed." During the siege of Atlanta in
the summer of 1864, the Confederates entertained themselves
by building a cock-fighting ring just out-of-range of the Yankee
artillery. It was here that Fed met his match. While the bets
were being placed, the combatant roosters were outfitted with
deadly steel spurs called gaffs and the battle began. Shortly thereafter Fed fell dead. Tom Tuck mourned the loss of his pet but put
sentiment aside to cut his losses by cooking the bird for that
evening's dinner.[23]

Company G of the 3rd Ohio and Company G of the 10th
Ohio each had their own champion fighting cocks. When they

were pitted against each other, the waging and the cheering were intense. General Ormsby Mitchell happened to pass the event and acknowledged the ovation, mistakenly believing it was for him.[24]

A variation on cock fighting involved humans. Two soldiers would be trussed up so that they could not move their arms and then try to head-butt each other into submission. The victor was the man left standing—perhaps bloodied but unbowed.

* * *

Gambling continued through the end of the war and after. As the Army of Tennessee waited for Joe Johnston to conclude surrender negotiations, the roadsides around its final camp filled with chuck-a-luck and other games of chance. Corn whiskey and apple jack were consumed in quantity, leading to frequent brawls among the players. What valuables these worn-down veterans of Franklin and Nashville had to wager at this stage of the war is anybody's guess. They had already won their biggest bet by surviving the conflict.[25]

The Northern armies celebrated their ultimate victory by gambling for weeks after the fighting ended. Two months after Appomattox, the commander of the United States Armies ordered a crackdown:

> *Confidential Circular Washington, June 22, 1865*
>
> *All department commanders commanding in States where martial law prevails will immediately put detectives upon the watch for gambling houses, especially faro banks, and at the appropriate time make a descent upon them all simultaneously, arresting all disbursing officers of the Government who may be found gambling in them or visitants therein at the time, and who, it can be proven, had previously gambled at such places. The gambling institutions will be completely broken up, and their money and stock confiscated, and the owners or proprietors of such gambling institutions be made to disgorge and refund all money they have won from*

United States disbursing officers. The officer so taken will be imprisoned and tried immediately.

The same proceeding will be taken by department commanders in the North, within their respective commands in the cities where disbursing officers may be located, except that instead of confiscating the money and stock of the gambling establishments or compelling, by military action, the owners and proprietors of the same to disgorge or refund any moneys they may have won from disbursing officers of the Government, they will be immediately reported to the civil authorities for their action.

This will be kept strictly confidential except so far as it may be necessary to communicate it to those who are to carry it into execution.

    U. S. Grant
    Lieutenant-General[26]

* * *

Holidays were an excuse to break the boredom of camp life with special celebrations. Some were officers-only events, while others included the rank-and-file.

In the winter of 1862, while stationed near Williamsburg, Virginia, Louisianans under the command of Major General John Magruder decided to stage a Mardi Gras celebration. The soldiers scrounged to improvise costumes and some two hundred participated in a New Orleans-style procession through camp. One fresh-faced young soldier wore female clothing and make-up so effectively as to pass for the genuine article.

The parade was followed by a reception for the general and his staff at a local inn. The cross-dresser was escorted to the party and introduced to Magruder as "Miss Campbell" visiting her brother in the army. The ever-gallant "Prince John" took charge of the "lady" as she freely enjoyed the refreshments, especially the liquor.

Meanwhile, upstairs, some of the soldiers had ripped apart a hotel mattress. Through an opening in the ceiling, they dumped the feathers onto the party-goers in the dining room and shouted, "This is Louisiana snow!" "Miss Campbell" took that as her opportunity to suddenly depart, leaving behind a rather disappointed general.[27]

* * *

The flamboyant General Dan Sickles staged a New Year's Day 1863 party for his officers that was long remembered. Colonel Philippe Regis de Trobriand of the 55th New York noted that "the champagne and whiskey ran in streams" and that no moderation was shown in its use. He wrote that the subaltern officers partook so freely that "it was not to the honor of the uniform nor to the profit of discipline."

Colonel Robert McAllister of the 11th New Jersey was a teetotaler who declined his invitation to the memorable Sickles' celebration. He wrote his wife that Colonel William Sewell of the 5th New Jersey got so drunk at the general's reception that he tumbled from his horse while returning to quarters. This greatly amused the enlisted men who came out to see the inebriated officer. Brigadier General Gersham Mott, who accompanied Sewell, quickly rode away to avoid being connected with the embarrassing ruckus. Sewell's remaining companions tried and failed to get their man back into the saddle, and finally an ambulance was called to haul the colonel home. McAllister wrote that Sewell believed that "officers ought to have a little," sarcastically observing that the man would probably someday get promoted to general. McAllister's snide prediction was correct; Sewell not only became a brevet major general by the war's end but also received the Medal of Honor for his services on the battlefield of Chancellorsville where his friend, General Mott, was wounded.[28]

A number of units in the Union Army of the Potomac celebrated Saint Patrick's Day 1863 in high style at their camps around Falmouth, Virginia. It had been a long and depressing winter following the lopsided defeat at Fredericksburg, and the boys in blue were ready to have some fun. The 9th Massachusetts hosted members of the 62nd Pennsylvania in a day-long frolic that included barrels of beer and a greased pole contest. Atop the pole was a fifteen-day pass which would belong to the first man who could grab it. Unfortunately the pole was too slippery and no climber got within arm's reach. Horse races were also on the program with competition so fierce that two horses and a regimental quartermaster were killed.[29]

Naturally the Irish Brigade had its own party that March 17, and General Joe Hooker and his staff attended as the honored guests. The horse races included a steeplechase event with jockeys decked out in real riding silks. The Irish Brigade's greased pole was crowned with both a furlough and a twenty-dollar gold piece. There were also foot races and amateur theatrics. These festivities were momentarily interrupted when the long roll sounded, and the men raced for their muskets. It was a false alarm, occasioned by the distant drifting cannon fire from a cavalry battle at Kelly's Ford. While some men partied, other men died.

That evening brought a standing-room-only banquet at which the exceptionally strong punch proved very popular. Irish Brigade commander Thomas Meagher drank so deeply that he got into a sloppy argument with his command's surgeon. An agreement to settle the matter with dueling pistols was forgotten after they both sobered up. Before the war, the colorful Meagher had worked for independence in his native Ireland. He narrowly escaped the hangman before being exiled to Tasmania by the British. Eventually Meagher made his way to New York City where he became a political leader. In 1867, while serving as territorial secretary of Montana, he fell from a steamboat and drowned in the Missouri River. Reportedly, alcohol was involved in the accident.[30]

Meanwhile, down in Suffolk, Virginia, the Corcoran Legion had an 1863 Saint Patrick's celebration that got out of control after the whiskey ration was issued. A few of Corcoran's soldiers kidnaped a large African-American cook from the 13th New Hampshire. They hauled the man back to their camp, stripped him down and painted his body with every color they had available in order to create a "rainbow nigger." When they turned him loose, the terrified victim ran for dear life back to the safety of his own quarters.[31]

* * *

Many soldiers helped break up the boredom of camp life through reading. Not all of them, however, were immersed in the Bible or the latest novel of Charles Dickens. Some preferred the pornographic publications which were shipped to them via mail. Tame by contemporary standards, these racy cartes de visite and cheap pulp periodicals were hot stuff for lonesome lads at the front. In June 1863, Army of the Potomac provost Marsena Patrick confiscated and burned some of the offending imprints as they made their way through the army postal system.

Postmaster General Montgomery Blair asked for congressional action to stop the flow of naughty books that the soldiers enjoyed so much. The war was nearly over but, in March 1865, it became illegal for an obscene book, pamphlet or picture to be sent through the U.S. mail, with a $500 fine for each offense. Postal inspectors could not, however, open envelopes or tamper with the seal of suspect packages. Thus we may fairly credit the Civil War for the birth of the infamous "plain brown wrapper" that allowed sexy tomes to travel unimpeded by censors.[32]

While lurid literature might be enjoyable to some, it is no substitute for the real thing. For an enlisted man in camp, finding a willing female could be difficult. Nevertheless a surprising number succeeded in doing so. Naturally most of this activity never made it into letters home and many of the missives that did mention it were later destroyed to preserve Papa's reputation. The regimental historians remain silent, too. Still the first-hand accounts that survive are revealing.

For example, Private Tabor Parcher of the 10th Vermont wrote this gossipy letter to his wife, Sarah, from a camp near Culpeper, Virginia, in April 1864:

> *You wanted to know why I doant say who is going*
> *to have baby wall there is three girls that is goin to have*

babies that I know Hon John Minor Botts[33] *girl is going to have one she is a nice pretty girl about 20 years of age the safe guard knock her up I wish it had been me she was one of the first girls in this vacinity before she got fucked & it doant make much difference now well another is Sarah France she lives near the picket line at Poney Mountain She is about 3 ½ months along so she told me last time that I see her & the other is Alis Poland she lives near the right of this divisions Picket line she I am not much acquainted with but I have seen her I guess it is about as you say they fuck so much that they cant have babies but thare is three girls that I know near hear that wont fuck for money or love nor anything else & such a thing as the clap they are pretty much all free from it thare is not half so meny of them got the clap hear as thare wer at Conrads ferry or Rockville or eaven Brattleboro that was the rottenest hole that ever was & so it was at Poolesville.*[34]

Even the president of the United States found himself drawn into the procreation problems of his soldiers. In April 1864, Abraham Lincoln received a letter from a young woman with a special concern. Her fiancé, a private in the 140th Pennsylvania, had been home on leave and the lovers wanted to get married but her father refused permission. Unfortunately, the couple had "very foolishly indulged too freely in matrimonial affairs" and the girl was now pregnant. Not surprisingly, given this development, her father had changed his mind on the marriage. Her boyfriend urgently needed another furlough to make things legal before the baby was born. Lincoln graciously ordered the soldier sent home for the ceremony.[35]

If sexual favors could not be had for love, there was always money. The world's oldest profession flourished before, during and after the American Civil War. War always creates a boom in the business of prostitution as thousands of men leave the restraints of home and march off to engage in deadly combat.

Even before the fighting began, an estimated five hundred prostitutes worked in Washington, D.C. It was, after all, the seat of national government, where a ready market already existed for a frisky girl's charms. Business really took off when the soldiers arrived. In 1862, the district's provost marshal had four hundred fifty bawdyhouses registered on its books. A year later, the *Washington Star* estimated that there were five thousand "daughters of Eve" plying their trade in the city with another twenty-five hundred in neighboring Georgetown and Alexandria. According to one calculation, 10 percent of Washington's residents earned their living as prostitutes. The combined efforts of the district police, the army's provost guard and Lafayette Baker's detectives were required to keep the trade at least somewhat under control.[36]

In the spring of 1863, two "notorious prostitutes" were somehow included in a group of citizen prisoners taken from the Old Capitol Prison and sent to Richmond for exchange. This prompted a heated protest from the Confederate commissioner, Robert Ould, who until 1861 had served as the U.S. district attorney in Washington.

City Point, Va., May 14, 1863.

Lieutenant-Colonel Ludlow, Agent of Exchange.

Sir; I send back to you two strumpets who were landed at this place yesterday in company with honorable and virtuous women. If after arriving here they had behaved themselves I should have stood the transaction, though with hard thoughts. A state of war even does not allow any outrage to be perpetrated upon the sanctity of a pure woman's character and last of all where a flag of truce is the vehicle. We are husbands and fathers and brothers and no form of war should stifle or subdue the holy feelings that spring from those relations. If I did not believe you were imposed upon I would be justified in taking this matter as a personal affront. These women since their arrival at City Point have descended to a depth of infamy that I hardly thought could be reached by the sex. They have delighted themselves with the foulest billingsgate that ever disgraced a fish-woman, courting prostitution at every turn and making themselves loud-mouthed in their denunciation of everything cherished and beloved by our people. Their conduct for one night has been so outrageous as to attract the attention of the press and engage the gossip of the streets. Though I cannot charge myself with blame in the affair I feel a deep sense of mortification that so infamous a proceeding should have had the countenance of the purity of a flag of truce. I have written strongly about this matter not only because every sensibility of my nature has been aroused but because of the further reason that I have a jealous regard for a flag whose honor and purity it is our special mission to uphold.

Very respectfully, your obedient servant,
Ro. Ould,

Lieutenant Colonel William Ludlow forwarded the letter to Colonel William Hoffman, the commissary general of prisoners. He noted that "the description of these women as given by Mr. Ould is fully sustained by the officer in charge of them." He was certain that "the character of these women was of course not known to you, and they were probably sent by some mistake on a flag-of-truce boat instead of to a penitentiary."[37]

Richmond had its own share of working girls, known as "Cary Street women." Their open flaunting of their profession even in respectable areas such as Capitol Square greatly annoyed the townfolk. One house of ill repute opened on Tenth Street, directly across from the YMCA hospital where there was a steady customer base of soldier-patients who were nevertheless well enough for a little "horizontal drill."[38]

Any city with a sizable soldier population attracted the tarts. One Confederate officer called Atlanta a "modern Sodom"where "vice and immorality seek not the cover of night." In Chicago, home to Camp Douglas, an estimated two thousand prostitutes walked the streets in 1864 and 1865.[39]

Lydia Bixby is best remembered in history as the recipient of a touching letter from Abraham Lincoln comforting her over the loss of five sons in battle. Lesser known is that she allegedly earned her living by running a Boston whorehouse. What's more, Mrs. Bixby was reportedly a Southern sympathizer who lied about her sons; only two—not five—died in the war.[40]

The bawdyhouse business boomed in Norfolk, Virginia, during the 1864 siege of Petersburg. That was about as close as the "working girls" could get to the boys in blue serving in the front lines. Department commander Ben Butler complained of "officers habitually drunk in the streets" of the city. To combat the problem, Butler issued the following instructions:[41]

August 6, 1864.

Colonel Sanders:

I have assigned you to duty in Norfolk as provost-marshal because I have confidence in your judgment, integrity, and personal habits to correct abuses which exist there. The great vices of the officers are whoring and drinking, neither of which can be interfered with, of course, unless they interfere with duties or are open and public. Officers seen riding in the streets with notorious women will be arrested at once whatever may be their rank. Drunkenness in public will be at once arrested, no matter what are the staggering insignia of officer. I will support and sustain you, rest assured. I doubt not you have a kind heart, but in dealing with offenders it is the worst quality a man can have. Another matter which is suffered to go unchecked is brawling and talking in public places against the Government and its officers. That is not permissible in a garrison. There is hardly a person who has a permit to sell liquor who does not violate it. Get the general order and

make the retailers live up to it, specially innholder and
restaurants.

> Yours, truly,
> Benj. F. Butler
> Major-General, Commanding[42]

In the western theater, Nashville, Tennessee, was con-
tinuously occupied by Union troops from early 1862 through
the end of the war. It became an important base for Northern
efforts farther south. With so many soldiers present, there was
a correspondingly large demand for female companionship. It
could be found on "Smokey Row," a three-quarter-mile-long
street, lined with ladies of the evening plying their trade. Hoping to suppress this activity and the incidence of venereal disease affecting the troops, authorities rounded up as many of
the women as they could and shipped them north by boat to
Louisville and Cincinnati. Not surprisingly, those cities did
not welcome the new arrivals and sent angry protests back to
Tennessee.

Lieutenant Colonel George Spaulding, who served as
Nashville's provost marshal, finally recognized the impossibil-
ity of eliminating the trade, given so many willing buyers and
sellers. He decided to try another tact. In August 1863,
Spaulding announced a program for licensing prostitutes at a
cost of five dollars each. They would be inspected for disease
every ten days and pay a fifty cent tax for upkeep of the hospitals where infected women would be treated. By June 1864, there
were one thousand such cases. Memphis, suffering the same
problem, also implemented Nashville's program which continued through the end of the war.[43]

Perhaps such a program should have been instituted back
east as well. In the spring of 1864, the medical director of the
Army of the Potomac, Thomas McParlin, noted in a report that
venereal disease was "extremely prevalent among the veterans
returning from furlough." Approximately 8 percent of all Union

soldiers received the era's ineffective treatment for venereal disease. How many more cases went unreported and untreated is anybody's guess.[44]

One Union soldier had taken drastic measures to avoid the temptation of prostitutes. Prior to the war, English immigrant Boston Corbett struggled to reconcile his religious convictions with his carnal desire to visit houses of ill repute. In 1858, he solved the problem by castrating himself with a pair of scissors. Corbett later became famous as the cavalryman who killed John Wilkes Booth.[45]

As Lincoln's first secretary of war, Pennsylvania's Simon Cameron was hampered by a reputation for questionable business dealings.

CHAPTER EIGHT
THE RICH MAN'S WAR

Politician and business tycoon Simon Cameron had a reputation for shady dealings that followed him to Washington during his short run as Lincoln's first secretary of war. Cameron, born in 1799, was one of six children sired by a poor Scotch-Irish tailor and barkeeper. At age eleven, after his father died, young Simon was sent to live with a neighborhood physician who helped educate the boy. Pursuing a career in journalism, Cameron borrowed money to buy part interest in a Harrisburg newspaper and then had the good fortune to marry a wealthy woman. He increased his riches through railroads, canal-building, banking and real estate ventures. For the last fifty years of his long life, he drank a glass of champagne every morning at eleven.

Cameron acquired political power, but generally avoided any office where he would be directly elected by the masses. He was more of a backroom operator; courting favor of the great unwashed was not his style. Even Cameron's service in the United States Senate came in an era when those seats were filled not through a general election but by horse-trading statehouse legislative votes. At the 1860 Republican convention, Cameron provided vital support to help Abraham Lincoln capture the party's presidential nomination. When the Illinois "log splitter" won the general election, he rewarded the Pennsylvanian with the position of secretary of war.

The appointment caused controversy due to Cameron's questionable ethics. According to popular legend, the new secretary coined the saying, "An honest politician is one who, when he is bought, stays bought." Fellow Keystone Stater and fellow Republican Thaddeus Stevens reportedly once said that the only thing Cameron would not steal was a hot stove. When Cameron demanded an apology, Stevens cleverly agreed that he was incorrect when he claimed that Cameron would not steal a hot stove.

A passionate practitioner of political patronage, Cameron added twenty-two Pennsylvanians to the War Department payroll in addition to the five who already worked there. Grumbling arose that too many military contracts were being awarded to the secretary's native state.[1]

Critics accused the secretary of buying obsolete weapons and overpaying for army livestock—some of which was blind or diseased. Military purchases were made through private negotiations and were not publicly advertised as required by law.

Given the rush to arm more than half a million men, Cameron's War Department turned to Europe. There they found Confederate agents already buying up many of the best weapons. What's more, the loyal states had sent their own purchasing agents overseas, and they bid up prices by competing against the national government. Free-lance profit-seeking middlemen also got government contracts and then headed abroad to fulfill them.

For foreign arms dealers, the American war became an opportunity to unload their outdated and second-rate inventory. A U.S. government commission subsequently said of these weapons that "a large portion of our troops were armed with guns of a very inferior quality...tens of thousands of the refuse arms of Europe are at this moment in our arsenals, and thousands more still to arrive, not one of which will outlast a single campaign..." Many of these unserviceable arms were paid for at rates which, "under a system of vigilance and obedience to law, would have procured improved rifles of the first class." In all, the Federal government purchased over one million arms overseas. Of these, 20 percent proved to be unserviceable.[2]

In the early part of the conflict, financier J. Pierpont Morgan acquired five hundred Hall carbines for $3.50 each. These firearms the army had already condemned. The demand for weapons was so great that Morgan resold them to General John Fremont in Missouri for $22 apiece. The higher price in no way improved the quality of these substandard weapons and they were again condemned as a danger to any soldier who was unfortunate enough to fire one.

Cornelius Vanderbilt saw the government's war-time spending spree as an opportunity to exit the steamship business and use the capital to purchase railroads. Many of Vanderbilt's old ships were sold to the Union navy. In one case, he outfitted a military expedition to New Orleans with unseaworthy vessels whose beams were so rotten that they could not hold a nail. Vanderbilt escaped prosecution by claiming ignorance and blaming his agents. According to one estimate, the government lost $25 million to contractors selling substandard vessels to the navy.[3]

In at least one instance, Secretary of War Cameron did save the government money. Instead of sending soldiers on the train from New York to Baltimore at a cost of $6 each, he re-routed them through Harrisburg for only $4. The change also put the troops on the Northern Central Railroad, a primary Cameron business interest, which saw its profits increase 44 percent that year. President Lincoln had refused when Cameron supposedly offered him an opportunity to invest in the rail line.[4]

Throughout the war, there were many abuses of government contracts. The dark blue caps issued to troops of the 1st Rhode Island turned quickly to brown because of the inexpensive non-fast color dyes used in their production. Profiteers produced overcoats of sieve-like felt, almost paper-thin and totally unsuited for active campaigning. The poor quality wool cloth was known as "shoddy," which has since become a synonym for cheap and inferior. One Pennsylvania contractor switched the mixture of Indian corn and oats in the army horse feed to fraudulently make a higher profit.[5]

In the autumn of 1861, Rhode Island gun dealer Caspar Schubarth hoped to get one of the many weapons contracts from the U.S. War Department. To assist in his bid, he enlisted the services of one of his state's senators, Republican James F. Simmons. The senator, who came from a manufacturing background himself, agreed to help—especially since Schubarth offered him a 5 percent commission on any deal that was made. Schubarth, a native of Norway, had been told by friends that was how such matters were done in America.

Schubarth's proposal was not initially viewed with favor by the ordnance chief, Brigadier General James Ripley. He believed that sufficient weapons were already on order and sent a note recommending against acceptance to Acting Secretary of War Tom Scott. The ordnance chief was apparently unaware that Schubarth had a powerful friend in the U.S. Senate.

The very next day, at the acting secretary's instruction, Ripley reversed course. He issued a contract to Schubarth, ordering 20,000 muskets. The following month, the order was increased by an additional 30,000 weapons, most likely due to senatorial influence.

All would have been right with the world except that the partners Schubarth had assembled to produce the firearms backed out of the deal. He now had a large government contract and no means to fulfill it. Luckily, he found two new partners. They were informed of the kickbacks that Senator Simmons was to receive and gave the senator two promissory notes of $10,000 each toward the $50,000 that he was due.

Unfortunately for Senator Simmons, the loose administration of Simon Cameron ended when Lincoln shipped the secretary off as minister to Russia in January 1862. A few months later, the House of Representatives censured the Pennsylvanian's handling of the War Department in a vote of 79 to 45. The congressional rebuke must have hurt Cameron's pride; he managed to have it reversed thirteen years later.[6]

The new secretary, Edwin Stanton, was a highly skilled attorney of national renown. Unlike Cameron, money was not a primary motivation for Stanton. To accept the $8,000 a year cabinet post, he had left a lucrative legal practice which brought him upwards of $50,000 a year in income.

Looking at the tangled mess of weapons contracts, Stanton appointed a commission to sort them out. Judge Joseph Holt, a former secretary of war, and Robert Owen, an arms dealer, were instructed "to audit and adjust all contracts, orders, and claims on the War Department in respect to ordnance, arms, and ammunition." They were to be assisted by Major P. V. Hagner, a weapons inspector.

In less than four months, the commission investigated 104 cases worth $50 million and rejected or modified enough contracts to save almost $17 million. The committee noted that many of the contractors were truly "public spirited citizens" but there were a few exceptions who "delude themselves" that "the country, as a whole, is a fair subject of plunder."[7]

During its investigation, the commissioners learned of Senator Simmons' financial interest in Schubarth's arms order. Surprisingly, under the narrowly drawn statutes of that time, the commission concluded that the arrangement technically conformed to the letter if not the spirit of the law and they signed off on the deal. Schubarth eventually delivered 9,500 Springfield rifle muskets to the army and received a payment of $189,305.10.[8]

His patron, James Simmons, did not fare as well. On July 2, 1862, a Unionist senator from Indiana, Joseph Wright, introduced a resolution to expel Simmons on charges of corruption. For once the wheels of government turned quickly. The matter went to the Judiciary Committee on July 8 and that committee delivered its findings on July 14. They reported that the charges of monetary kickbacks to Simmons were essentially true. Senator Simmons even acknowledged the arrangement but expressed amazement at the uproar it had caused, claiming he had merely acted in the interest of his constituents and the nation. He noted that the manufacturer's payments to him were not tied to any guarantee of a government contract—which would have made them illegal.

By this time, Congress had acted to close that ethical loop-hole, but Simmons could not be charged ex post facto. Neverthe-less, the threat of expulsion loomed. To avoid disgrace, Simmons resigned from the Senate on August 15, 1862, and returned to Rhode Island where he died two years later.

In 1863, the United States Congress passed the False Claims Act which contained both criminal and civil penalties for suppli-ers trying to defraud the government. It also offered an entice-ment for whistle blowers to come forward by offering them 50 percent of any damages. In support of the law, Lincoln stated, "Worse than traitors in arms are the men who pretend loyalty to the flag, feast and fatten on the misfortunes of the nation while patriotic blood is crimsoning the plains of the south and their countrymen are moldering in the dust."[9]

The amount of money the national government spent on the military was enormous. In just one year, from June 1863 to June 1864, the quartermaster paid out almost $285 million to pur-chase supplies, with another $221 million in accounts still due.[10]

Confederate soldiers may have suffered less from intentional fraud in the contracting for manufactured goods. Much of the substandard equipment they received was simply the result of the South's lack of production ability. The differences between Northern and Southern manufacturing skills can be seen by com-paring the common cavalry saber which both sides produced in large quantities. A Northern-made edged weapon from Ames or Roby is a precision piece with a fine brass hilt, leather-wrapped grip, straight blade and polished scabbard. The typical Confed-erate "Dog River" version of the same saber features a crudely cast hilt, oil-cloth wrapped grip and a wobbly blade that appears to have been beaten into shape by hand. The scabbards are pieces of overlapped sheet metal so crudely fashioned that in some cases they will fit only the individual sword for which they were fash-ioned. So much for the concept of interchangeable parts!

Nevertheless each "Dog River" has an individual character that today's relic collectors prize. Such swords would have been instantly rejected by any Yankee weapons inspector if they had been submitted to fulfill a U.S. contract. For the South, they were the best that could be produced. Grey horsemen were always eager to upgrade to a captured Yankee blade.

* * *

With the advent of the war, the Confederacy initially hoarded its cotton crop, hoping the impact upon Northern and European textile mills would force recognition of the Southern nation. This flawed strategy never achieved the hoped-for result as it encouraged competitors in Egypt and India to grab market share. The Rebel government could have exported much of its cotton before the Union naval blockade tightened. The proceeds would have financed overseas purchases of much-needed arms and equipment. Instead, bale upon bale of "King Cotton" sat waiting in the warehouses and on the docks of Dixie.

The situation was ripe for exploitation, and profiteers like Jim Fisk headed south. At the start of the war, Fisk had worked for Jordon, Marsh and Company of Boston, selling clothing of questionable quality to the Union army. He headquartered himself at Washington's Willard Hotel and boasted, "You can sell anything to the government at almost any price you've got the guts to ask."[11]

Looking for still bigger profits, Fisk headed to Memphis to deal in contraband cotton smuggled from behind Confederate lines. This son of a Vermont peddler reportedly purchased as much as $800,000 worth of cotton in one day, a tremendous amount by 1860 standards.

Fisk's illicit financial success attracted too much attention from the authorities. In 1864, Jordon, Marsh and Company fired their man, albeit with a very generous $65,000 in severance pay.[12]

Like Jim Fisk, Rhode Island Governor William Sprague was attracted by the profits in cotton. Sprague, who had served in the field with the Union army, put up $25,000 to own a quarter interest in ships taking arms and ammunition to Confederate Texas and bringing back loads of contraband cotton. Not coincidentally, Sprague's family owned textile mills. The operation continued until one of the ships was captured by the Union forces. William's cousin, Byron Sprague, and a close friend, William Reynolds, were found on board, so it was quite embarrassing when another of the smugglers confessed the details of the whole operation.

Inasmuch as William Sprague had become a U.S. senator and was married to the daughter of Salmon Chase—soon to be chief justice of the United States—the matter had to be handled most carefully. Adding to the embarrassment, Salmon Chase had been treasury secretary and was responsible for issuing the permits authorizing trade with the disloyal states. He had, however, not approved a permit for this operation, despite the urging of Sprague.[13]

Conveniently, the smuggler's confession disappeared and the entire matter was forgotten as the war ended. The scandal did resurface in 1870 during a Rhode Island political campaign. William Sprague admitted to some vague recollection of an effort to help the Union men of Texas and maintain employment in New England's textile mills. Unfortunately, he had forgotten any other details except to claim that his $25,000 investment had been totally lost. To maintain appearances, Sprague asked for the U.S. Senate to look into the matter, but this investigation, like the earlier one, went nowhere.[14]

In July 1862, Major General U. S. Grant, commanding in the District of West Tennessee, banned Northern speculators from paying in gold or silver for any cotton they purchased. Violators would be arrested and sent north with their property confiscated. Only U.S. Treasury notes could be used to buy cotton. The action came in response to complaints that this hard currency went directly to the Southern army and financed its war effort.[15]

In January 1863, Assistant Secretary of War Charles Dana formed a partnership with Congressman Roscoe Conkling to make some big money in cotton. Both men put $10,000 into the business. Armed with a letter of recommendation from Secretary of War Stanton, Dana traveled to Memphis and was appalled by what he saw. He felt that the cotton business had corrupted the army, with every colonel, captain and quartermaster secretly allied to a speculation scheme. Writing to Stanton, he urged that the trade be suppressed and replaced by a government-run system. On March 31, President Lincoln issued a proclamation banning the cotton business except when conducted under regulations proscribed by the secretary of the treasury. Secretary of War Stanton prohibited military personnel from any private participation.[16]

When one speculator approached Confederate authorities in the Trans-Mississippi for permission to engage in the cotton trade, they pulled together an estimate of his potential profits. The contractor planned to buy two thousand bales of cotton at $100 C.S. per four hundred-pound bale. He would then sell them in New York or New Orleans for $400 U.S. per bale. If shipped to Liverpool, he could get $300 per bale in gold. For his return trip, the speculator would purchase army supplies and deliver them back to the Confederates if he was guaranteed a 65 percent profit. The Confederates figured that the man stood to gain $4,928,000 on the deal. With fortunes like that ready to be made, what hope was there of halting the cotton trade?[17]

For that reason, sub rosa transactions continued throughout the war, sometimes sanctioned and sometimes not. The Northern mills needed cotton. The South had cotton but needed most everything else. Middlemen on both sides were eager to oblige.

Big money could be made by those with enough skill and daring to run the Yankee blockade and bring much-needed supplies into the South. In 1864, the shareholders of the Anglo-Confederate Trading Company received dividends of $1,000 and $1,500 on $100 par value stock. A captain willing to make the trip from Nassau to Wilmington, North Carolina, and back could earn 1,000 pounds sterling. A pilot could earn 750 and a chief engineer 500. In addition, the crews were often permitted to stow away goods of their own for additional profit.[18]

In Nassau, the war created a boom town atmosphere where momentarily wealthy sailors spent their earnings on wine, women and games of chance. Prosperity made the port so pro-Southern that U.S. Consul Sam Whitney became something of a pariah and was beaten up in a drunken fight at a local hotel. By June

1862, New York City customs officials required that a bond be posted for any Nassau-bound ship carrying cargo that was potentially useful to the Confederacy. The money would only be refunded upon certification that the merchandise had not been re-shipped to Dixie.[19]

Given the economy of scarcity, Southern speculators found opportunities everywhere. Blockade-run sugar might bring $4 a pound in Charleston but, by simply taking it on to Richmond, $11 a pound could be realized. When rumors of the capture of Vicksburg reached the Confederate capital in July 1863, skeptical residents first attributed the stories to conniving speculators trying to run up the price of sugar.[20]

In November 1863, Brigadier General John Imboden complained that his Shenandoah Valley command could not procure much-needed supplies because "speculators are in the market paying higher prices than those fixed by the government commissioners and sending such supplies out of the district to be sold again." Imboden tried without success to prohibit the practice.[21]

Some wartime speculators were too clever for their own good. In his memoir of Union soldier life, *Hardtack and Coffee*, John Billings mentions a failed attempt to corner the coffee market and force up the government's cost of this army staple. He also writes of Northern purchasing commissioner Amos Eaton being approached by a man named Sawyer who represented a prominent New York importer. The firm had recently bid on a coffee contract and now wished to enter another lower bid. Commissioner Eaton explained that the bids had been opened but not yet made public, so he was willing to entertain another offer. Sawyer gave his new price and Eaton replied that the man was the new low bidder. The government would take all the coffee that he could provide at that rate. Sawyer's pleasure turned to pain when Eaton informed him that he had also been the low bidder at his original higher price. Sawyer had underbid himself.[22]

The actor John Wilkes Booth in early 1864 joined three friends to speculate in the booming northwestern Pennsylvania oil business by buying land in Venango County. Booth lost about $6,000 when he sold out at the end of September to concentrate on his plot to kidnap Abraham Lincoln.[23]

John D. Rockefeller did much better. When the war began, he was engaged in a Cleveland mercantile business with contracts to supply foodstuff to the Union army. Rockefeller used those profits to start the company which eventually became Standard Oil and made his name synonymous with wealth.

Throughout the war, trading in the gold at the New York City exchange fluctuated with each new victory or defeat of the Northern armies; the gold speculators who made millions were called "General Lee's left wing." Money man Jay Gould even set up a private network of bribed telegraph clerks to ensure that he would be the first to obtain battle results.[24]

When President Lincoln asked Pennsylvania Governor Andrew Curtin what he thought of "those fellows in Wall Street who are gambling in gold at such a time," Curtin replied that they were "a set of sharks." Lincoln agreed, pounding the table with his fist and wishing that "every one of them had his devilish head shot off."[25]

In 1864, Congress passed and Lincoln signed legislation which made it illegal to buy or sell gold with delivery any later than the day the contract was signed. Gold also had to be in the possession of the seller at the time of the transaction. The intention of the law was to end the speculation that was causing the price of gold to rise higher and higher. Unfortunately the Gold Bill failed in its objectives and destabilized the market even more as prices swung manically higher and lower. The legislation was repealed only seventeen days after it had passed.[26]

When Philip Armour became confident of impending victory for the North, he sold short on pork futures. Armour anticipated that a demobilization of the army would significantly reduce government meat purchases and cause a corresponding drop in the market price. Armour's hunch proved correct. He made his first million dollars that way and went on to start his famous meat-packing company.[27]

After returning from his Memphis cotton trading days, big Jim Fisk developed a telegraph/steamship/courier communication system to the London financial markets. With the first news of Lee's surrender, Fisk sold short on Confederate bonds and once again pulled in big bucks. Fisk continued to concoct money-making schemes in the postwar era; at one point, he teamed with Jay Gould in an attempt to corner the gold market, which resulted in the Black Friday Crash of 1869. Three years later, this "Barnum of Wall Street" met his death at the Broadway Central Hotel where he was gunned down by a jealous rival for the attentions of a young actress.

* * *

When the U.S. army draft began, the wheeler-dealer money men did not worry. Under the law, anyone conscripted could either pay a commutation fee of $300 or hire a substitute to go in their stead. J. P. Morgan, John D. Rockefeller, Andrew Carnegie and Jay Gould all avoided the shooting war this way. Future president Grover Cleveland's name was drawn the first day of conscription. Cleveland did not have $300 but he managed to find a substitute willing to serve for only $150. Cleveland's political supporters later would maintain that since his two brothers were already in the army, Grover needed to remain at home and care for his mother. However, by the time Cleveland was called, one brother had already been mustered out and the other soon would be.[28]

The substitute idea was not a good way to increase military might. The Army of the Potomac noticed a marked decline in the quality and purpose of new men arriving to refill the battle-thinned ranks. Substitutes and bounty jumpers had signed up for profit, not patriotism, and many would slip away at the earliest opportunity. The Army of the Potomac's provost marshal reported that in one detachment of 625 men sent to reinforce a New Hampshire regiment, 137 deserted during the trip to the front, 82 went over to the enemy and 36 slipped off to go back north.[29]

It was not a good idea on the home front either. While $300 might be nothing to a financial speculator, it was a fortune to the average working man. As soon as the draft was implemented in July 1863, several days of bloody riots began in New York City. Blacks were lynched from lampposts and the Colored Orphan Asylum was set ablaze. Union troops had to be rushed from Gettysburg to quell the uprising. Smaller disturbances occurred in many other parts of the country, including Boston, Massachusetts; Newark, New Jersey; and Troy, New York.

In Pennsylvania, an editorial in the Harrisburg *Patriot and Union* declared: *"The odious $300 exemption clause which throws the whole burden upon the poor, while exempting the rich, should certainly be repealed; and we think the clause permitting substitutes to be taken is of the same character, and liable to even greater objections."*[30]

The draft aggravated civil unrest in the Keystone State's coal fields, where steady production was vital to the Union cause. In November 1863, a War Department official wrote to President Lincoln from the mining town of Mauch Chunk:

> *Since the commencement of the draft a large majority of the coal operatives have been law-defying, opposing the National Government in every possible way, and making unsafe the lives and property of Union men.*
>
> *They are so numerous that they have the whole community in terror of them. They dictate the prices for their work, and if their employers don't accede they destroy and burn coal breakers, houses, and prevent those disposed from working. They resist the draft, and are organized into societies for this purpose. The life of no Union man is secure among them, and the murder of such a citizen is almost a nightly occurrence.*
>
> *The civil authorities make no effort to arrest this state of things. They say they are powerless and that to attempt the arrest and punishment of these traitors and miscreants, without having the ability to do it successfully and*

effectually, would only add fuel to the flames. Besides all this our "civil authorities" here seem to have too much sympathy for these very men, and they know it and are not slow to take advantage of it. They have closed up several large collieries and threaten that all must suspend work until the National Government suspends the operations of the draft against them. These men are mostly Irish and call themselves "Buckshots."

They have caused the high price of coal more than any other thing. Many of them with the work they do make from one hundred to two hundred dollars per month.

Committees of these men have waited upon operators and have told them that they must stop work; that they intend to end the war by cutting off the supply of coal and thus embarrass the Government and create coal riots in the large cities. This is a part of the rebel programme. If they can have their own way a few weeks longer they will work serious mischief, set afoot a most damaging fire in the rear, and very successfully "embarrass" the Government.[31]

Troops were required to keep order in Pennsylvania's coal mines through the end of the war. Even in peacetime, the labor unrest continued through a suspected Irish secret society known as the "Molly Maguires."

Free black men living in the North were also subject to the draft—which is ironic considering the government's reluctance to enlist men of color during the early part of the war. One such fellow was George Morris of Salem, Massachusetts, who had served as cook for officers on the staff of General Birney. While boarding in Washington, D.C., Morris was arrested and placed in a regiment of "coarse, vulgar and indecent" men. The reluctant soldier petitioned the government that he was unjustly held and had never received any notice of being drafted. Morris asked that he either be released or allowed to procure a substitute.

Instead the government granted his request that he be transferred to the 54th Massachusetts. George Morris was later killed during the battle of Olustee, Florida, in February 1864.[32]

In the end, the Federal draft was hardly worth the fuss. Less than 3 percent of the men who served in the Northern army were actual draftees. Another 5 percent were substitutes, although how many of those stuck around very long before deserting is open to debate.

The Confederacy, too, implemented a conscription act which was widely resisted. A unique feature of the Southern draft was the so-called "Twenty Nigger Rule," providing for exemptions of men who owned that many slaves. This loophole created much dissatisfaction among the majority of white Southerners who owned no slaves and were more concerned with protecting their homeland than preserving the slavocracy.

Southern governors such as irascible Joe Brown of Georgia challenged the legality of the conscription act and created exempt government posts to keep supporters out of the army. In North Carolina, Tennessee, Mississippi and other parts of the South, there was open resistence to the authority of the central government.

* * *

Many Southerners proved their patriotism to the fledgling Confederacy by buying up large quantities of the new country's bonds. Sales of bonds continued to be brisk even as Rebel fortunes faltered. On August 7, 1863, one month after the defeat at Gettysburg and fall of Vicksburg, John Rutherford of Richmond wrote his son in Goochland, Virginia, to review their investments. The elder Rutherford had considered investing in land but instead believed that they should continue to hold on to their Confederate bonds which netted 5 percent after taxes. Little did father and son know that, in just twenty months, their Confederate bonds would be worthless.[33]

The French investment house of Erlanger et Cie saw an excellent chance to profit from the American war. In September

1862, Emile Erlanger approached John Slidell, the Confederate envoy to France, and suggested that his company underwrite an issue of Confederate bonds which would net the Southern government $25 million in gold. That in turn could be used to buy European-made guns, munitions and other equipment for the Southern armies.

The bonds would pay 8 percent and be backed by Southern cotton valued at twelve cents per pound. English and French textile mills were paying up to five times as much for their bales, which were in short supply due to the Union blockade of Southern ports. With a Confederate victory, an investor in these bonds might make a fortune.

Slidell and Erlanger had a close relationship; in fact, Slidell's daughter, Matilda, would soon marry Erlanger's son. Nevertheless, the Confederate diplomat had no authority to negotiate such financial matters. He suggested that Erlanger send emissaries to Richmond for discussions. In December, Erlanger, accompanied by Julius Bear and Lewis Ferdinand Floersheim, traveled to the Rebel capital and met with Secretary of State Judah Benjamin.[34]

Benjamin evidenced little enthusiasm for the thinly disguised cotton speculation. He did, however, see that such investment could increase the chances for French recognition of the new nation, especially given Erlanger's political connections. Benjamin agreed to the deal but reduced the issue from $25 to $15 million, cut the interest to 7 percent and raised the underwriter's discount from 70 to 77.[35]

The bond offering on March 18, 1863, created a sensation. Confederate fortunes were near their zenith and all over Europe investors wanted a chance to cash in on the new nation's success. The bond price rose as high as 95½, giving the House of Erlanger a handsome 18½ point spread above their cost.

Alas, it was not to last. Enthusiasm for the issue was short-lived and the price dropped, possibly due in part to the hidden hand of United States agents operating in Europe. For example, articles appeared in the financial press on how years earlier

Jefferson Davis had defended his home state of Mississippi when it defaulted on its bonds. Many of those had been sold in England.[36]

Concerned about the bonds and his company's own financial security, Emile Erlanger suggested that the Confederate government use some of the proceeds already collected to prop up the market. Erlanger painted a dire picture of the consequences if the Southerners refused. The Davis government put some $6 million into buying back its own securities. Unfortunately, the move failed to make a lasting improvement in the price. With the deadly debacles at Gettysburg and Vicksburg, Confederate cotton bonds plunged as low as 36.

This might have meant disaster for the House of Erlanger, given its base cost of 77. However, the firm had already sold its remaining stock of the securities. The buyer was the Confederate government with the funds they had authorized Erlanger to spend supporting the market. According to some estimates, the French bankers made a profit of $2,700,000 on the issue. After expenses, the Confederacy cleared about $2,500,000—two hundred thousand less than their underwriter. For that, they had pledged $15 million in cotton plus 7 percent annual interest.[37]

In September 1863, Erlanger sent an agent back to Richmond to suggest that another bond issue be floated. The French offered better terms this time but the idea went nowhere. For some Confederates, the proposal did briefly again spark the flickering hope of European recognition.[38]

The real losers of the whole saga were the Europeans left holding the cotton bonds. The securities could only be redeemed if the South won the war and that did not happen. The sole value that the Rebel notes had was as collector's items. In the 1980s, a large cache of the bonds was found in an overseas vault, where they had been stored for decades in the absurd hope that the United States government would someday assume responsibility for Rebel war debts. These bonds were shipped back to America. There they found a ready market of Civil War buffs eager to hang a piece of history on the walls of their family rooms.

* * *

Legends arise around any catastrophic event, particularly when large sums of money are involved. The rumors surrounding the great Confederate "treasure train" have endured ever since the boxcar carrying the Rebel treasury rolled out of Richmond in April 1865. Even today, fortune hunters go off in search of buried gold that is supposedly secreted somewhere in the South.

As the Confederate government fled to the temporary safety of Danville, Virginia, its treasury was guarded by navy midshipmen who were at loose ends after their ships had been scuttled in the James River. They protected some $327,000 in government funds, consisting of a bewildering array of gold and silver ingots, Mexican dollars and United States coins. They also had charge of approximately $450,000 taken from Richmond's financial institutions.

Fearing Yankee raiders, Jefferson Davis ordered the treasure train to continue south—first to Greensboro and then to Charlotte, still guarded by the midshipmen under the command of Captain William Parker. Thirty-nine thousand dollars in coin went to General P. G. T. Beauregard to pay Southern soldiers who were opposing Sherman's march through North Carolina.

Reaching Charlotte, the monies were stored in the vault of the old U.S. Mint, but rumors of a raid by George Stoneman's Yankee cavalry put the treasure back on the rails south. The midshipmen were accompanied part of the way by the Confederate president's wife, Varina Davis, and her children. In Chester, South Carolina, the sailors transferred everything to wagons and journeyed on to Newberry, where another train waited to take them to Abbeville. The heavy boxes of gold and silver were again moved to wagons before finally reaching Washington, Georgia, on April 19. The treasure was temporarily taken to a house in town.

The next day everything was once more loaded onto railcars and sent southeast to Augusta. Reaching that city, Captain Parker and his men learned of Lee's surrender at Appomattox. This news made for an unsettled situation in Augusta but the monies were transferred to the bank vault. With the Confederacy clearly collapsing, Parker pondered what he should do. After warnings to get the treasure out of Augusta for fear that the locals may storm the bank, Parker decided to take the treasure to Jefferson Davis—if the fugitive leader could be found. Everything was again loaded onto train cars and sent back to Washington on April 26. There the treasure went into wagons and the convoy retraced its steps to Abbeville, South Carolina. By now, with Parker's permission, some of the naval guards were slipping away—well aware that the war was over. At Abbeville, Parker found a warehouse to hold his valuables and went off to attend a May Day party. Nevertheless it was a nervous time with rumors of bandits and Yankees about. Concerned that the bluecoats were coming, Parker awoke his men in the middle of the night to load everything onto railcars. By daylight, they were once again ready to depart. Then along came Jefferson Davis.

At long last, Parker and his remaining sailors were freed from their burden. Brigadier General Basil Duke's Kentucky cavalry took charge of the Confederate treasury. Duke was not delighted by the assignment. Nobody knew for sure the exact total of what was there. What's more, Duke found the loot packed in a bewildering array of "money-belts, shot-bags, a few small iron chests and all sorts of boxes, some of them of the frailest description." Duke ordered the accumulation placed in wagons and, an hour later, the treasure hit the road again. Lieutenant John Cole chased after General Duke with a pine box across the pommel of his saddle. It contained two to three thousand dollars in gold that had been left behind.[39]

When the convoy reached the Savannah River, Jefferson Davis authorized some $108,000 in silver to be given to the soldiers as back pay. This action helped quiet a restlessness among some of the rank-and-file who questioned why they should continue to risk their lives for a lost cause. Officers and men alike received $32 each, according to Basil Duke's recollection. Many hours were spent counting out the coins and then the wagons rolled on again.[40]

In their wake, the Confederates left behind a box of jewelry which the women of Richmond had contributed to the Confederate government. This fell into the hands of a local family who tried to keep their windfall a secret. Federal cavalry confiscated the jewelry a short time later as they swept the area looking for Confederate gold. What happened to it after that is anyone's guess.

For the third time, the Rebel gold and silver rolled into Washington, Georgia, where Acting Confederate Treasurer Micajah H. Clark took charge of the remaining funds. The government was rapidly dissolving now and Clark accepted the difficult duty of dispersing approximately $180,000 which remained. This did not include the $450,000 from Richmond financial institutions; the responsibility for that was now dumped onto the bank representatives who had tagged along through the entire confusing journey.

On May 4, Clark distributed about $18,000 for soldiers' pay and other miscellaneous purposes. Another $40,000 was set aside to help feed the men of Joe Johnston's army as they made their way home from the surrender. All of that money later ended up in Union hands. James Semple, a C.S. naval officer, received $86,000 in gold with the understanding that it was to be taken abroad to continue the struggle. What eventually happened to this money remains unknown even today.

This left Treasurer Clark with about $36,000, which he placed in an ambulance and drove south later that night. Given the less-than-ideal circumstances and large amounts being handled, the distribution had been as carefully performed as possible. Still so much money could breed a casual contempt. According to Robert Toombs, General John Breckinridge rode past his house and casually tossed $5,000 worth of gold into the yard. Toombs had been one of the leaders of secession and was about to escape to England.

The treasury once again managed to catch up with Jefferson Davis and his small band of followers. A total of $10,000 went to several of Davis' aides and Confederate postmaster John Reagan. Davis took none of the money when he bade a final farewell to the treasure train, leaving the wagons behind in order to make better time on horseback.

Clark now had $26,000. Accompanied by a small guard under the command of Captain Watson Van Benthuysen, a distant cousin of Jefferson Davis, the remaining funds were hauled down to Florida. Near Gainesville on May 19, Clark learned that the Confederate president had been captured by the Northern cavalry. The "last ditch" had finally been reached; the question was what to do with the remaining money.

For his part, Clark wanted to pay the soldiers their due and get everything else to England where it might be useful in some further Confederate cause. Captain Van Benthuysen and his men had other ideas. They demanded that Clark reserve 25 percent of the fund, roughly $6,250, for the welfare of Varina Davis and her children. The rest was to be divided equally among themselves. Facing a united front against his own proposal, Acting Treasurer Clark reluctantly agreed.

Van Benthuysen took charge of the amount intended for Varina and the children. Unfortunately, this cousin of Jefferson Davis proved an untrustworthy custodian. Not until 1867, after repeated badgering, did Van Benthuysen send any money to the Davis family and then they received only $1,071.

Meanwhile, in Washington, Georgia, the Virginia bankers had obtained permission from the Federal troops now occupying the town to move their $450,000 back to Richmond. On May 24, the funds were loaded onto five wagons and the long journey began with a small escort of Northern cavalry. Rumors circulated that this was the Confederate gold being hauled off by the Yankees, and recently discharged Southern soldiers made plans to get back what they felt was rightfully theirs.

The convoy stopped for the night near the Savannah River at the home of a Reverend Chenault. There was a fenced horse corral where the wagons could be circled to defend against raiders. It was a good plan but not good enough. In the dead of night, a large body of horsemen stormed the camp and overwhelmed the Yankee guards. There was more gold than the bandits could possibly carry away but about $250,000 disappeared into the darkness.

The next day, the Virginia bankers persuaded some local residents to form a posse and a couple of the thieves were actually caught. Confederate Brigadier General E. P. Alexander gathered some of his reliable old soldiers and came from Washington to help. In all, between $80,000 and $110,000 was recovered. Alexander escorted the money back to Washington only to see it confiscated by the Yankees. Indeed, the raid set off a gold mania among the Union soldiers as they made a frenzied search of the area hoping to find more plunder. In 1893, the Bank of Virginia received less than $17,000 for the loss in an action by the U.S. Court of Claims. Some soldiers, however, came out of the war with a handsome discharge bonus of their own making.[41]

* * *

Jacob Thompson may be the man who gained the most money from the collapse of the Rebel government. A former secretary of the interior during the Buchanan administration, Thompson was the Confederate commissioner to Canada at the end of the war. During his time there he had been involved in a number of well-financed plots against the United States, including espionage, arson, destroying Great Lakes shipping and freeing Confederate prisoners from Northern camps. The end of the war found him the custodian of a great pile of cash—exactly how much no one is quite sure. Testimony at the trial of the Lincoln assassination conspirators alluded to $649,873.20 that had been withdrawn from the Bank of Ontario. This figure would have included funds captured during Rebel operations such as the October 1864 raid on Saint Albans, Vermont.

By any reckoning, Thompson had possession of enough money to make an honest man turn bad—an amount at least in the six figures. Therefore he did the only logical thing possible; he sailed to France and booked himself into Paris' Grand Hotel where he lived elegantly for the next several years. Other members of the Confederate Canadian mission, George Saunders and Beverly Tucker, complained bitterly about Thompson's perfidy.

John Breckinridge and Judah Benjamin were by that time in London where they hoped to liquidate any Confederate left-over assets and pay something of the Rebel war debt. Benjamin and John Slidell, the Confederacy's former envoy in Europe, conducted a stormy interview with Thompson in Paris. Thompson rationalized that the money was due to him as payment for his cotton crops which had been destroyed during the war. As a half-hearted compromise, he agreed to turn over 12,000 English pounds if $5,000 was returned to him, which he had contributed to the legal defense fund of Jefferson Davis. Lacking any leverage, this was the best deal that the skilled lawyer and the wily diplomat could get and so Thompson's embezzlement succeeded. Punished only by a loss of reputation, he eventually returned to America and died as a very wealthy man in 1885.[42]

* * *

There was still another sort of Confederate treasure missing in the years immediately after the Civil War. It came in the form of six large strongboxes filled with State Department archives.

These documents had been hustled away from Richmond at the end of March 1865 and eventually reached Charlotte, North Carolina. They were in the care of William J. Bromwell, a State Department clerk since May 1861. Bromwell was experienced in this kind of operation; he had previously hauled the Rebel records out of town when McClellan's army drew near the Confederate capital in 1862.[43]

Surprisingly, the Federals never located this trove of secret intelligence. Three years later, Bromwell still had possession of the boxes as well as the actual Great Seal of the Confederacy. The seal depicted the equestrian statue of Washington at Capitol Square in Richmond and bore the Latin slogan *Deo Vindice*— "God, Our Defender." It was quite an attractive piece of work, having been made by skilled English craftsmen and run through the Yankee naval blockade. The seal arrived in Richmond during the waning months of the rebellion, but the press required for its use remained in transit when the Confederacy collapsed. Years later, Bromwell's wife, Alice, claimed that, at the end of the war, she took charge of the seal and kept it safe beneath her skirt.[44]

With the Confederacy kaput, Bromwell decided that the time had come to unload these items and make some money. He was then practicing law in Washington, D.C., with Colonel John T. Pickett, a West Point graduate who had been the Confederacy's ambassador to Mexico. Pickett agreed to serve as the middleman in peddling the papers and approached the Federal government with an offer to sell them for $25,000. In doing so, he intimated that the documents were in Canada though they really remained close at hand. The government made a counteroffer which Bromwell and Pickett rejected. Several private individuals were also approached but without any success.

A few years later, however, the government realized that the Rebel records might be very valuable to them after all. Southerners who claimed to have remained loyal to the United States were filing for reimbursement of war-time damages to their property by Northern troops. If the State Department papers proved that these individuals had actually been disloyal, the claims could be denied and the Federal treasury might save substantial amounts.

Before an offer could be made, the papers had to be examined for authenticity. This meant a trip to Canada to maintain the fiction that the records were beyond the reach of Federal agents. Colonel Pickett and a U.S. Navy lieutenant, Thomas Selfridge, boarded a train for Hamilton, Ontario. Unbeknownst to Selfridge, the State Department records traveled on the same train as freight. In Canada, Selfridge found the papers to be as promised and agreed to recommend their purchase. In gratitude, Pickett gave the naval officer a splendid souvenir, the original Great Seal of the Confederacy.

On July 3, 1872, Pickett and Bromwell received $75,000 for the archives. Bromwell took his cut and boarded a boat to Britain, possibly to escape the outrage of ex-Confederates upset that he had profited from the leftovers of the "Lost Cause." The former clerk died in Chelsea on August 22, 1874.[45]

In 1873, Pickett borrowed the Great Seal from Lieutenant Selfridge and struck one thousand copies in gold, silver and bronze. These he tried to sell to Southern charities for use in fundraising. The copies were of sufficient quality to fool some people into thinking that they had purchased the actual Great Seal. Pickett suspended the sales when they, too, stirred a storm of controversy.

Over the years, the location of the authentic Great Seal remained a mystery to the general public. Jefferson Davis' black coachman, James Jones, claimed to have buried it during the fall of Richmond. Another rumor had it stashed in the cornerstone of a Confederate monument in Macon, Georgia.

Finally, in 1911, Thomas Selfridge, by then a retired admiral, confessed that he had the original and agreed to sell it for $3,000 if the relic would be placed in a suitable Richmond institution. The money was raised and the Great Seal came to the Museum of the Confederacy where it can be seen today. Colonel Pickett's restrikes of the seal are highly valued by collectors, as they are the singular examples of the only time that the original was ever used.

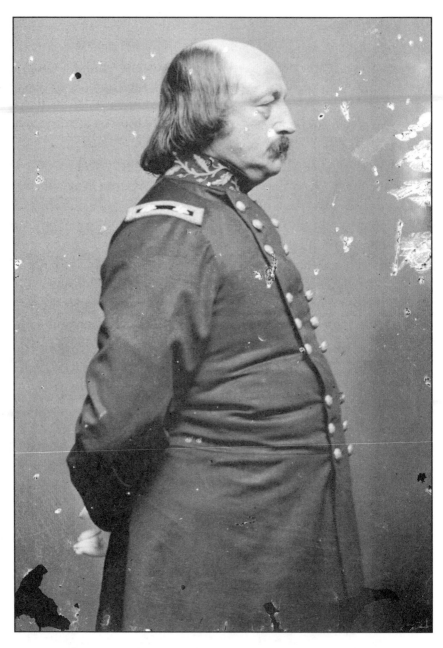

To many Northerners, Ben Butler was a hero. To many Southerners, he was fit only for hanging.

Chapter Nine
"Beast" Butler and the Spoons

Benjamin Franklin Butler was not a pretty man. He had a barrel-shaped body, a bald head, silly moustache and droopy crossed eyes. However, the Massachusetts lawyer possessed a razor-sharp mind and hard-driving work ethic that helped him rise to become a man of means and a powerful political leader in his home state.

Before the war, Butler served as a colonel in the state militia. Equally adept at being both ingratiating and obnoxious, he managed to alienate the commonwealth's governor, who took revenge by reorganizing the armed forces and eliminating Butler's position. Officers being elected by their men, Butler then ran for and won a brigadier generalship. His new commission came from the same chief executive who had tried to organize his ouster.[1]

With the outbreak of the War Between the States, Butler parried that militia position into a similar rank with the volunteer Union forces. Butler had never proven himself on a battlefield; his experience was more of a ceremonial and social nature. Nevertheless the Lincoln administration was eager to showcase prominent Democrats in the war effort in order to deflect charges that it was strictly a Republican affair.

Butler, in fact, had shown sympathy for the South prior to the conflict. At the 1860 Democratic convention, he had even put forward Jefferson Davis as a presidential candidate—albeit as a

ploy to help James Guthrie win the nomination in the hope that
the Kentuckian would be acceptable to both the North and South.
After Lincoln's election, Butler visited the Democratic National
Committee headquarters in Washington and commented that
secession was "now the only thing left for the South to do."[2]

When Fort Sumter was fired upon, Butler became the most
fervent of Union men. He led his Massachusetts soldiers south
to protect Washington. Never shy about self-promotion, he appeared before Lincoln in the "wonderful disguise" of a Bay State
militia general, with "a vast amount of sash, mountainous epau-
lets and a scythe sword with a railway curve in it." An old-style
cocked hat topped off the fanciful get-up which could hardly have
complemented the politician's squat physique.[3]

Acting beyond orders in May 1861, Butler marched his men
into Baltimore and placed artillery on Federal Hill overlooking
the city to quell the activities of secessionist agitators. The action
brought a decidedly mixed response from his Washington superiors. On one hand, as a kind of rebuke, he was transferred out of
Baltimore and sent to command at Fortress Monroe, Virginia. At
the same time, he received a promotion to major general.

At Fortress Monroe, Butler made a lasting contribution to
Civil War nomenclature. Escaped slaves flooded into Union lines
hoping to be rescued from bondage. Under the Fugitive Slave
Law, their masters could demand their return. Butler applied
his legal talents to the problem and came up with a solution.
Slaves were property and, as property, they were being used as
labor to advance the rebellion. Such property could rightfully be
seized as contraband. Butler refused to return the slaves to their
masters and the name of "contraband" stuck to all black refugees
through the remainder of the war.[4]

After the Union navy forced New Orleans to surrender in
April 1862, Butler became its military governor. This was not an
easy post. The largest city in the Confederacy, New Orleans had
sent legendary fighting units like the Louisiana Tigers and Washington Artillery into Southern service. For the city to fall into

Yankee hands barely a year after the war had begun was a rank humiliation.

The residents demonstrated their discontent from the start. Angry mobs roamed the town. Union soldiers and sailors were taunted and threatened. When the "Stars-and-Stripes" was hoisted above the United States Mint, a local man named William Mumford cut down the flag and tossed it to the furious crowd. Accompanied by fife-and-drum music, the Southerners paraded the captured banner through the streets until reaching City Hall where it was torn to pieces. The fragments were tossed at the Yankee occupiers. Told of Mumford's action, Butler declared, "I will make an example of that man by hanging him."[5]

Butler was as good as his word. His soldiers tracked down Mumford and let him swing by the neck in front of the United States Mint where the fatal offense occurred. Butler proceeded with the execution despite a last-minute plea from the condemned's wife. Butler advised her to visit her husband and instruct him to pray for his soul as no last-minute pardon would be granted. After the war, however, when Mumford's widow found herself in dire financial straits, Butler used his influence to get her a government clerkship.

At the beginning of the occupation, New Orleans Mayor Pierre Soule met with Butler at his headquarters in the Customs House. The mayor was there to extract as many guarantees and concessions as possible from the city's conquerors and, as he made his points, the roars of a secessionist mob could be heard outside. Soule tried and failed to quiet them. Then Butler stepped forward and ordered horse-drawn artillery to the front. As the guns were unhitched and turned toward them, the hot-tempered protesters dispersed. Butler recalled that it was the only time he had to move cannon during his tour of duty in the Crescent City.

The petty affronts and insults to the United States troops continued. The locals referred to the commanding general as "Picayune" Butler, after a black New Orleans barber who the wags suggested was Ben's true father. Death threats were common and the general kept a loaded revolver at the ready on his desk.[6]

Hearing that a Catholic priest had refused permission for a U.S. soldier to be buried in his church yard, Butler summoned the holy man to him. The priest confidently informed the general that his information was not at all correct. "I assure you," he said, "that nothing would give me more pleasure than to bury you all."[7]

The secessionist ladies were a particular annoyance. Union navy commander David Farragut reportedly had the contents of a chamber pot dumped on his head as he strolled the picturesque city. Other Federals were spit at and women crossed the street to avoid encountering anyone in blue. Clever cockades containing outlawed Southern symbols were worn as signs of resistance. When some local women turned their backs on Butler, he dryly commented that they knew which side of them looked best.

Eventually, Butler had enough of this foolishness and decided to take action. Arresting every female who gave offense would quickly fill the jails and make martyrs of the ladies. Butler put his lawyer's brain to work and came up with the controversial "General Orders Number 28," which would make him hated throughout the Confederacy.

Head-Quarters, Department of the Gulf

New Orleans, May 15, 1862.

General Orders, No. 28.

As the Officers and Soldiers of the United States have been subject to repeated insults from the women calling themselves ladies of New Orleans, in return for the most scrupulous non-interference and courtesy on our part, it is ordered that hereafter when any Female shall, by word, gesture, or movement, insult or show contempt for any officer or soldier of the United States,

she shall be regarded and held liable to be treated as a
woman of the town plying her avocation.

  By command of Maj. Gen. Butler
  George C. Strong
  A.A.G. Chief of Staff

Despite its lengthy run-on sentence, the order was remarkably effective. The insults and provocations to the Northern soldiers dramatically decreased, for no self-respecting Southern woman would risk the shame of being charged as a prostitute. The illustrated Northern newspaper, *Harper's Weekly*, ran a "before and after" cartoon. It depicted two unattractive New Orleans matrons, one wearing a Rebel flag, scowling while an unfortunate Union officer wipes spittle from his face. The "after" drawing featured pretty ladies smiling courteously to the Union officer who gallantly tips his cap.[8]

The proclamation created an uproar across the Confederacy and even in Europe. Broadsides appeared about the "outrageous insult to the Women of New Orleans" and urging "Southern Men, avenge their wrongs!!!" Chamber pots were sold with engravings of Butler in the bottom of the bowl and he was popularly depicted as having devil's horns. The diarist Mary Chesnut wrote that "Beast" Butler was now "famous or infamous" and that no one "expected from Massachusetts behavior to shame a Comanche." The Charleston, South Carolina, *Courier* offered a $10,000 reward for the general's apprehension.[9]

For all the controversy, Butler's administration of the captured city was not entirely one-sided. He pardoned six Confederate soldiers from the gallows after they were found guilty of violating their paroles as prisoners of war. He executed five Northerners who posed as Yankee soldiers in order to rob houses. To prevent the malaria which plagued the port in the summer, he instituted a comprehensive city sanitation program and banned entry of ships coming from locales where the disease was active.

Butler did not suffer lightly those he deemed to be fools even when they wore Union blue. On September 10, 1862, Union Naval Lieutenant F. A. Roe, on duty near New Orleans, was ordered to take his ship, *Katahdin,* to serve as escort for some infantry on a forging mission. What occurred greatly offended the seaman's sense of propriety and he sent a heated letter of complaint to Commodore Henry Morris.

> *I was overhauled yesterday by Lieutenant Commanding Lowry, of the Sciota, while at Bonnet Carre Point, and directed by him to follow on as convoy of three transports of the United States Army. Upon arriving at Donaldsonville this day the transports landed at the upper part of the town, landed a party of troops, and commenced receiving on board sugar and other merchandise.*
>
> *A few hours after I received positive information that a company of these troops had entered a large mansion, situated near to the landing of the steamer Saint Maurice, had pillaged it in a brutal manner, and carried off wines, liquors, silver plate, and clothing belonging to ladies. I am informed that several of the soldiers were drunk from the use of the liquor and wine thus appropriated. This house was inhabited in the morning.*
>
> *During this time the Katahdin was at anchor, with her guns trained upon shore over the Saint Maurice for her protection. I respectfully request instructions if the guns of the Katahdin are to be used for the protection of soldiers upon a marauding expedition, and if I am to use them in the protection of drunken, undisciplined, and licentious troops in the wanton pillage of a private mansion of wines, plate, silk dresses, and female apparel, to say nothing of the confiscation of sugar, which I believe to be without proper and lawful reasons therefor. I confess, sir, that I blush to report that while the troops of the Saint Maurice were thus engaged in this*

unsoldierly and ungallant, not to say disgraceful, op-
eration I have done today, without an earnest and re-
spectful appeal to your authority. It is disgraceful and
humiliating to me to be ordered on guard duty of sol-
diers employed in pillaging ladies' dresses and petti-
coats, and I respectfully request that I am to be relieved
from such service.

Very respectfully, your obedient servant
F. A. Roe, Lieutenant, Commanding

Commodore Morris forwarded the letter for comment to the
irascible Butler. His sarcastic response was brief and to the point.

The acts of the troops in pillaging (if true) are with-
out palliation or excuse; certainly no more to be justi-
fied than this improper, bombastic, and ridiculous
rhodomontade of a sub-lieutenant of the Navy.

September 13, 1862.
Benj. F. Butler, Major-General, Commanding[10]

Ultimately, Butler became too controversial and lost his
Louisiana post. Ben was never adverse to making money, and
his brother, Andrew, joined him to engage in the lucrative cotton
and sugar cane trade. Stories spread in New Orleans that "no
planter could obtain permission to gather his crop unless he would
agree to share it with Colonel Butler or some of the Yankee officers." There was also an active grey market trade in cotton between the neighboring Confederate countryside and Union-held
territory. Big money could be made and rumor was that the Butler brothers were making it—perhaps as much as $800,000.[11]

Butler denied any wrongdoing when Washington asked him
about the matter. He ordered his brother to leave New Orleans
and requested a full investigation. No inquiry ever took place.

Then there was the matter of the foreign envoys. Cosmopoli-
tan New Orleans had a number of them, claiming to represent the
affairs of various distant capitals in this multi-national city. The

credentials of some of these part-time counsels were suspect and their Confederate affiliations were strong. Butler believed that they were hiding Rebel property and bullion taken from the U.S. Mint. The consuls protested that Butler did not respect diplomatic immunity and eventually their complaints reached Washington. The State Department wrote Butler for an explanation.

He replied, *"A nation may be friendly and its consul quite the reverse, as witness the late Prussian consul, who is now a general in the rebel army, for which he recruited a battalion of his countrymen. When, therefore, I find a consul aiding the rebels I must treat him as a rebel, and the exceptions are very few indeed among the consuls here. Bound up with the rebels by marriage, commercial and social relations, many of the consular offices are only asylums where rebels are harbored and rebellion fostered."*[12]

Butler's words may have been true enough but they were not the language of diplomatic nicety—especially when the United States was working feverishly to keep foreign recognition away from the Confederacy. The last thing Washington wanted was an international incident created by an impetuous politician-cum-general.

And so, in December 1862, Butler was removed from command in New Orleans. Interestingly, no one in official Washington was eager to take responsibility for the removal, despite Butler's best effort to ferret out the offender. He returned home to await reassignment.

That same month, Butler's actions in New Orleans led his former friend, Confederate President Jefferson Davis, to issue a proclamation which read in part:

> *Now therefore I, Jefferson Davis, President of the Confederate States of America, and in their name do pronounce and declare the said Benjamin F. Butler to be a felon deserving of capital punishment. I do order that he be no longer considered or treated simply as a*

public enemy of the Confederate States of America but
as an outlaw and common enemy of mankind, and that
in the event of his capture the officer in command of
the capturing force do cause him to be immediately ex-
ecuted by hanging; and I do further order that no com-
missioned officer of the United States taken captive
shall be released on parole before exchange until the
said Butler shall have met with due punishment for
his crimes.[13]

Though he left New Orleans, Butler took with him ugly rumors and angry allegations that would haunt him for years. This
is where the legend of the stolen spoons originated.

During Butler's administration of the captured city, a Mrs.
S. G. Ferguson was granted permission to pass through the lines
to her family in Baton Rouge. She was, however, to take nothing
with her. Federal soldiers discovered two bundles of New York
and New Orleans newspapers in her carriage along with a pack-
age of silverware. Mrs. Ferguson was charged with smuggling
but released from custody after a few days. The thirty-eight pieces
of cutlery remained in Federal hands.[14]

As Butler was preparing to leave Louisiana, a French citizen, Adolphe Villeneuve, claimed that the silver was his, produc-
ing a bill of sale as proof. He had asked Mrs. Ferguson, as a
favor, to take the flatware through the lines to his brother.
Villeneuve's request for its return was disregarded.

Villeneuve renewed his plea after Butler's departure. He was
told that the silver had been turned over to Butler's financial
agent, who had left with the general.

The Frenchman was not to be denied. Through the French
consul, the claim was appealed to the U.S. State Department. It
floated around in the red tape of official channels for more than a
year until the War Department finally asked Butler about it in
February 1864. Butler sent his brother-in-law to track down the
missing goods. It turned out the silverware had been sold by a

government quartermaster who had been unable to account for it previously due to a mistake in his reports.

For ten months after his return from Louisiana, Butler was a general without a command. His well-publicized activities in New Orleans, however, had made him a popular Northern hero, particularly in his native New England. To capitalize on this, Butler busied himself with a series of tub-thumping political speeches that burnished his image as a "war Democrat"and built up his base for a future run at the White House. In April 1863, he appeared at the New York Academy of Music and was kept bowing for several minutes with a "vast audience rising to their feet and cheering him, while the ladies waved their handkerchiefs" and the band played "Hail to the Chief." The *New York Herald* devoted seventy column inches of coverage to his address.[15]

The man who once had a reputation as a supporter of Southern rights now vilified Southern wrongs. Butler's influential supporters were eager to see him either placed in Lincoln's cabinet or back on the field of battle. Butler himself believed that he could win a military victory that would carry him to the presidency.

The lawyer/general, though a bold and hard-working administrator, rarely distinguished himself during his infrequent experiences as a combat commander. An anti-Lincoln copperhead journal, *The Old Guard*, published an "Epigram on Butler" who, it noted, "during three years of war has never been in but one battle..."

> *How kind has nature unto Butler been*
> *Who gave him dreadful looks and thievish mien;*
> *Gave tongue to swagger—eyes that look which way*
> *And kinder still, gave legs to run away*[16]

On October 28, 1863, Lincoln announced that Butler had been reappointed to his old stand at Fortress Monroe, Virginia. Lincoln recognized the political clout Butler had acquired and he was eager to keep the Democrat under his control. In fact, after Lincoln decided to choose a new running mate for his "National

Union" ticket in 1864, Pennsylvania political boss Simon Cameron was dispatched to determine Butler's interest in the vice presidency. Butler declined. He joked that he would take the second position only if the president would promise to "die or resign" within three months of taking office. As it turned out, Lincoln was assassinated the month following his second inauguration. Unknowingly Butler had passed up the one sure chance to get the job he wanted. Instead, another Democrat, Andrew Johnson, became president.[17]

Ensconced in Fortress Monroe, it was not long before Butler found himself again in controversy. One of Butler's subordinates, Brigadier General Edward Wild, hung a Confederate guerilla during operations in coastal North Carolina. Though a sign around the dead man's neck attributed the action to Wild, the Confederates gave some of the blame to Butler. To retaliate, a Union soldier was executed by the order of Confederate commander George Pickett. In reply, without Butler's permission, Wild burned the homes of two prominent civilians and imprisoned their wives as hostages. This unchivalrous assault on Southern womanhood reminded the Rebels of Butler's infamous "woman order." It was clear that the "Beast" had not changed. Butler diffused the controversy by arranging for the husbands to take the place of their wives, and eventually the menfolk were released. When Wild continued to stir up more unproductive trouble in the field, Butler moved him to an administrative post.[18]

Rumors of profiteering again arose around Butler. As in New Orleans, his command abutted a porous border where the enemy was eager to trade cotton and tobacco for the manufactured goods not readily available in Dixie. Butler prosecuted some of the smugglers but may have turned a blind eye to others. Through his provost office, he sold trade permits to merchants wishing to do business within his jurisdiction. Some of the proceeds were rumored to go to the general and his cronies. Similarly a kickback scheme may have allowed Ben and his boys to cage a share of the profits on any of the goods moving north or south through his domain.

Secretary of War Edwin Stanton tried to get evidence against Butler by planting a spy in his office but Butler was always one step ahead of his pursuers. He had the informant arrested.[19]

The spring campaign of 1864 brought what Ben Butler hoped would be his chance for glory. U. S. Grant was now the overall commander of Union forces and orchestrating a concerted effort to bring the full weight of Northern power against the rebellion. Butler had a prime role, one he had suggested to Grant during meetings at Fortress Monroe. While Grant approached Richmond from the north, Butler would lead his Army of the James up Virginia's peninsula to attack the Confederate capital from the east. In his dreams, the scheming Massachusetts politician saw himself leading the first Federals into the city.

It nearly happened. On May 5, Butler loaded his men onto ships and sailed up the James River to occupy both City Point and the Bermuda Hundred peninsula without the enemy understanding what he had done. His sizeable Yankee army was just fifteen miles south of Richmond, which had but a meager defense force available. By moving quickly, the Rebel capital would fall to the bluecoats and Butler would be the hero of the North.

But then the doubts set in. What would happen after he took the city? Would Bobby Lee send enough soldiers to crush Butler and his command? Would Grant be close enough to support the bold move? After conferring with his quarrelsome subordinates, Butler let the hours slip away, and his opportunity was lost forever.

Instead, Butler contented himself with tearing up the Richmond and Petersburg Railroad, damage which the Southerners soon repaired. By the time Butler did move north against Richmond, precious days had passed and Confederate General Pierre Beauregard had scraped up enough troops to block the way. A subsequent half-hearted attack against strategically important and scantily defended Petersburg was also badly bungled.

Ever since the war, historians have written about Butler being "bottled up" in Bermuda Hundred. Indeed, much of Butler's army was on the inland peninsula facing a strong line of Confederate earthworks to the west and surrounded by the James and Appomattox Rivers in all other directions. But, if Butler was "bottled up," it was a very porous container, for the Union navy allowed Butler's soldiers to come and go at will. More than half of Butler's command floated off to join Grant for the bloodbath at Cold Harbor.

Butler's holding of City Point and Bermuda Hundred also aided Grant's subsequent change of strategy when he moved the Army of the Potomac south of the James River. City Point became Grant's headquarters and a massive supply center that fueled the Northern drive to victory in the war's final months.

Grant's arrival with the Army of the Potomac in Butler's department also created an interesting and potentially dangerous glitch in the chain of command. If Grant left the department, the next general in seniority of rank was not the victor of Gettysburg, George Gordon Meade. Instead it was the rotund politician whose training in the art of war had come from the social events of the Massachusetts militia, Benjamin Franklin Butler!

Being second in seniority of rank offered cold comfort to the ambitious man. Grant would now receive the laurels for any battles won—not that Butler had ever shown much skill in winning battles. Still the wheels of Ben's fertile mind twirled as he searched for ways to wheedle back into the national limelight.

He came up with the idea of digging a canal that would eliminate a horseshoe bend in the James River and allow Union gunships to skirt some of the Confederate defenses. Digging of the 174-yard Dutch Gap passage began in August and continued through December despite heavy shelling from Confederate artillery. On New Year's Day 1865, 12,000 pounds of black gunpowder blew out the bulkhead in an attempt to open the alternate waterway. Nevertheless the canal never served any wartime purpose.[20]

After Lincoln's reelection in November 1864, an army rumor had it that Butler would become secretary of war when and
if Edwin Stanton moved to the Supreme Court as chief justice.
Butler may have been a tolerable choice for that position but
Stanton remained at the War Department when Lincoln appointed his one-time rival and former treasury secretary, Salmon
Chase, to the chief justice slot.[21]

As the war wound down to its final months, Ben Butler made
one last grab for glory. In December 1864, he led an expedition to
capture the Confederate stronghold at Fort Fisher and close the
vital port of Wilmington, North Carolina. Butler's expedition went
badly from the start, suffering from a lack of army and navy
coordination. What's more, Butler's big idea of exploding a gun-
powder-laden ship close to the enemy fort failed totally. The spec-
tacular blast did almost no damage. Butler admitted failure and
sailed his soldiers back to Fortress Monroe. His humiliation was
compounded when another Union expedition captured the fort a
few weeks later.

Butler's army career was over. With his second term secured,
Lincoln no longer had to worry about any political ramifications
and he permitted Grant to remove Butler from command. Butler
returned home to Massachusetts and won election to the U.S.
Congress. The politician who once described himself as "an old
Andrew Jackson Democrat of twenty years standing" was a Re-
publican now. He actively campaigned for the impeachment of
Lincoln's successor, Andrew Johnson, and even implied that
Johnson had a role in Lincoln's assassination.[22]

Though the Confederacy had failed, Butler continued to be
dogged by his wartime actions. He found himself involved in continuing controversy from his days as military commander in New
Orleans.

One of these cases involved the sum of $50,000 in gold which
Butler had confiscated from a Confederate sympathizer, Sam
Smith. Butler began using the gold as stopgap funding whenever
official monies were late in arriving for payment of the troops

and other expenses. After he settled his accounts upon leaving New Orleans, the War Department reimbursed Butler for these advances. The confiscated fifty thousand had fallen into official limbo and, when Butler brought this to the attention of the authorities, he was told to submit a memorandum and, in the meantime, hang on to the money.

Sam Smith, meanwhile, had seen the light, taken the oath of allegiance to the United States and hired two lawyers to get back his gold. The lawyers asked Butler to turn over the funds but Butler said he could only do so if directed by the War Department, and the War Department was preoccupied fighting the war. Butler suggested that Smith should appeal directly to President Lincoln to order the funds released.

As usual, Butler's reputation suffered. His enemies spread stories of the missing fifty thousand, which portrayed Butler in the worst possible light. In October 1864, Smith filed suit against Butler in New York City. The controversy even spilled over into halls of Congress where Representative James Brooks declared the major general was a "gold robber." Butler responded by sending the congressman a note which read very much like a challenge to a duel.

In the end, Butler finally returned the $50,000 in gold to Smith. The general's reputation was again tarred and more was still to come.[23]

While in the Crescent City, Butler had occupied the house of Confederate General David Twiggs. A servant revealed the hiding place of Twiggs' swords and a box of silverware. Butler confiscated the edged weapons and sent them as a trophy to the White House. He put the cutlery to work at his own dining table in Twiggs' dwelling. Leaving New Orleans, he received a government receipt for the house and its contents, but the receipt contained no individual breakdown for the silverware or other personal property.

In 1869, Twiggs' niece sued Butler for the return of the swords and silver. Butler hired a detective to track down the whereabouts of the flatware but the investigation only determined that the silver had probably been sold by the government for its metal value. In any event, Twiggs' niece lost the lawsuit. A decade later, Butler helped arrange for the U.S. Treasury to return the swords to Twiggs' daughter.[24]

In addition to promoting his political career, the general returned to his law office and built a lucrative practice. Thanks to that and other business investments, the poor widow's son became a wealthy man who had a net worth of some $7 million when he died. For relaxation, he enjoyed sailing on his yacht, *America*.

One of Butler's most celebrated postwar cases involved Simon Cameron, the millionaire Pennsylvania political chief who had once offered Butler the vice presidency. Like Butler, the canny Cameron had a tarnished reputation, primarily due to his willingness to make a buck by any means possible. But in 1875, his woes came from a different source: a woman scorned.

Mrs. Mary Oliver, a stylishly eccentric lecturer on phrenology, claimed that Cameron, then in his late seventies, had promised to marry her during a passionate affair in New Orleans. Mrs. Oliver supposedly became pregnant and had an abortion, after which Cameron procured the forty-something female a clerkship in the U.S. Treasury Department. He also gave her $1,000, but no wedding ring. Mrs. Oliver filed suit for breach of promise.

The sensational case made great copy for the newspapers. The aged Cameron did not attend the trial but his attorney did his job well. After two and a-half hours of deliberation, the jury found in favor of the defendant.[25]

Butler ran several times for the Massachusetts governorship and he finally reached the executive's chair in 1882. Once again a Democrat, the general tried for that party's presidential nomination in 1884. When that failed, he ran as the candidate on the Greenback and Anti-Monopoly ticket but only received about 2 percent of the vote.

Butler died in Washington, D.C., on January 11, 1893. On his last evening, dinner conversation turned to Republican politico James Blaine who had been lingering with a mortal illness. Butler declared, "Mark me, Blaine will outlive us all yet." That night Ben Butler passed away into the great unknown.

The irrepressible Dan Sickles and his staff pose for a photo after the general lost a leg at Gettysburg.

CHAPTER TEN
THE HERO OF GETTYSBURG?

Born on October 20, 1819, in New York City, Daniel Edgar Sickles spent the next ninety-four years living a colorful, swashbuckling life in which he generally did just whatever he wished to do. Freewheeling Dan was not the man to let major or minor legalities, social conventions or an empty purse stand in his way.

Following in his father's footsteps, Dan became an attorney in 1843—which was six years after he had been indicted for receiving money under false pretenses. Fortunately for Sickles, the charges were never prosecuted. He would have other scrapes with the law, including the time he was accused of borrowing $800 and then taking back the mortgage which he had given as collateral without repaying the loan. In that case, he won acquittal on a technicality.[1]

None of this held back his political career as a Tammany Hall Democrat. In 1847, Sickles won election to the New York State Assembly, where he created a scandal when he brought his dear friend, an attractive well-known prostitute named Fanny White, to see the legislative process at work. For this he was censured by his fellow solons. Rumor had it that some of the profits from Fanny's horizontal trade had helped finance the new assemblyman's election campaign.[2]

Dan's time in Albany did produce some results. He championed the legislation that created Central Park, in which he remained actively interested throughout his varied career.

On September 27, 1852, the thirty-three-year-old politician married Teresa Bagioli, a teenage beauty whom he had known since she was an infant. This did not mean that Dan would quit seeing other women however. A year later, after wangling appointment as secretary to the American legation in London, he set sail to England in the company of his old friend, Fanny White, and temporarily left behind his pregnant wife. He amused himself further by taking Fanny to the royal court where she was introduced to Queen Victoria as "Miss Bennett of New York"—a private jab at Sickles' enemy, *New York Herald* publisher James Bennett. Later at a July 4th celebration, Sickles set English tongues wagging when he refused to rise and drink a toast to the queen because it came before the toast to George Washington.[3]

Throughout his diplomatic sojourn, Sickles was unable to restrain his natural penchant for intrigue and double-dealing while neglecting the work that he was supposed to do. U.S. Ambassador James Buchanan liked the man personally but recognized that he was a liability as a legation officer. For his part, Sickles was ready to return home and agreed to resign.[4]

When Sickles went back to America, he left behind angry English creditors who had been given drafts for personal expenses which the U.S. Treasury refused to pay. Once stateside, Sickles began working on Buchanan's successful campaign for the White House. In the same 1856 election, Sickles won a seat in Congress representing the Third District of New York.

As a confidant of the new president, Sickles positioned himself to become a man of real influence in national affairs. He installed his pretty young wife in a fashionable mansion on Lafayette Square, just opposite the White House. Teresa became a popular social hostess and was also a favorite of President Buchanan. Sickles plunged into the political wheeling and dealing which he so enjoyed but still found time for the occasional extracurricular dalliance. Life was good.

Enter Phillip Barton Key, a recent widower and son of "Star Spangled Banner" author Francis Scott Key. In her memoirs, society belle Virginia Clay describes him as "the handsomest man in all Washington" and as "a prominent figure at the principal fashionable functions" who became "a favourite with every hostess of the day." Key and Dan Sickles got along well enough that Dan helped secure Key's reappointment as United States Attorney for the District of Columbia. But, as time passed, Key was increasingly absent from his government office, being preoccupied elsewhere in clandestine rendezvous with attractive Teresa Sickles.[5]

The husband is always the last to know. Even when he first heard the rumors of an affair, Dan did not believe them. Then the truth became clear and he confronted his wife on a terrible evening in February 1859. The congressman forced tearful Teresa to write a long and embarrassing confession of her guilt which the servants then signed as witnesses. She told how she had met with Key in a rented house on Fifteenth Street and "did what is usual for a wicked woman to do."

The next day Sickles looked out the window of his cheerless elegant mansion and saw Phillip Barton Key standing in Lafayette Square, trying to get Teresa's attention. This was too much! Seething at the provocation, the wronged husband knew what he had to do to satisfy his honor. Dispatching an ally to waylay the unsuspecting Key, Sickles ran to get his guns.

The congressman stormed from his house and approached the philanderer. He thundered, "Key! You scoundrel! You have dishonored my home! You must die!" Key begged the enraged husband not to shoot, but Sickles fired several times, mortally wounding his wife's lover.[6]

The murder stunned official Washington. A White House page witnessed the shooting and ran to tell Sickles' old friend, James Buchanan. The president gave the boy some money and told him to hightail it home to North Carolina lest he be jailed as a witness. Sickles surrendered himself at the home of Attorney General Jeremiah Black and was locked up in the D.C. jail.

For his defense, the accused assembled a "dream team" of high-priced lawyers, including future Secretary of War Edwin Stanton. They developed what is often called the first use of a "not guilty by reason of temporary insanity" plea. It worked. Sickles walked free.

Nevertheless the episode would follow Dan Sickles for the rest of his life. Returning to Congress, one observer noted that he sat alone, "left to himself as if he had smallpox." Several years later, in 1862, Confederate Lieutenant Charles C. Jones, Jr., wrote to his parents about fighting near Richmond, which included "the brigade of the miserable Dan Sickles of New York notoriety who you will remember shot District Attorney Key in the streets of Washington, D.C."[7]

The controversy was compounded when Sickles forgave Teresa's transgression and they continued on as man and wife. The initial scandal was bad enough but taking back the fallen woman was simply not done in polite Victorian society.

Sickles left Congress when his second term ended in March of 1861. The following month America erupted in civil war with the firing on Fort Sumter, and dashing Dan embarked on a military career by raising his own unit of soldiers, the Excelsior Brigade. In typical Sickles fashion, when the recruits departed New York for Washington one day after the battle of First Bull Run, they left behind an army of creditors who had fed and equipped them but got only Dan's word as collateral.

To continue to command his soldiers, Sickles' nomination as a brigadier general had to be confirmed by the United States Senate. That was a bit of a problem. His murder of Barton Key remained fresh in the minds of many in Congress and there had always been questions about this man's character anyway. Could he truly be trusted with a general's stars? The senators thought not; they rejected the nomination.

Sickles was not about to give up. He began working his political contacts and sweet-talking newspaper editors. His new friend, Abraham Lincoln, resubmitted the nomination and it just barely passed this time on a vote of 19–18.[8]

The resurrected officer rejoined his Excelsior Brigade in Virginia during McClellan's 1862 Peninsula Campaign. Despite being a "political general" with no real military experience, Sickles compiled a record of reasonable competence. Still the past followed like a shadow. When Sickles became a division commander, Colonel Robert McAllister of the 11th New Jersey recalled Key's murder and noted that his new superior had received credit for more fighting than he had ever done thanks to his influential friends at the New York newspapers. Sickles was neither the first nor last man in public life to recognize the power of the press. What's more, he always made for colorful copy.[9]

By the time of the Chancellorsville battle in May 1863, the former congressman had risen to major general in charge of the III Corps, the second largest in the Army of the Potomac. Sickles' 19,000 soldiers sat in the right/center of the Union line, most of them being held in reserve. The army commander, "Fighting Joe" Hooker, had managed to steal a march on Robert E. Lee with 134,000 Yankees moving against 59,000 Rebs. Events boded well for the bluecoat cause.

On the morning of May 2, General David Birney reported to Sickles that a column of Confederate infantry and artillery could be seen moving across his front. Always a man of action, Sickles requested and eventually received permission to "advance cautiously" and "harass the enemy." Sickles attacked, captured some prisoners and came to the conclusion that the Rebels were retreating, an opinion also shared by army commander Hooker.

However, they were wrong. The grey soldiers were not retreating. They were "Stonewall" Jackson's men making a legendary roundabout march which that evening allowed them to launch a devastating surprise assault on the Union right flank. Despite his superior number of soldiers, many of whom had not even been given a chance to engage the enemy, the fight went out of "Fighting Joe" and the Union army retreated.[10]

That memory remained in Dan Sickles' mind two months later at Gettysburg, Pennsylvania. Portions of the Union army had been badly whipped in a terrific fight on July 1; they found refuge in a strong position on high ground south of town. Despite orders to remain in Maryland, Dan Sickles marched most of his troops north when he heard of the battle. They arrived in time to take their place in the center of the Union line for the second day's bloodbath.

But Dan being Dan, he did not like his assigned position. There was higher ground out in front that he wanted to occupy even though that would put his men well forward of the rest of the bluecoats. Dan's pal, Joe Hooker, was no longer in charge; command of the army had been foist upon George Meade only days before. Dan sent word to Meade that he would like permission to move forward.

Sickles did move forward—although without receiving any authorization from his new superior. Colonel Hiram Berdan of the celebrated Berdan's Sharpshooters reported that his men had encountered Rebels toward the front. Shades of Chancellorsville! Might the Confederates be making another flanking movement? Dan decided he wanted that high ground which centered on a peach orchard and sent his corps off to get it.

The move took the rest of the army by surprise. Officers of the adjoining II Corps wondered if they had missed instructions to advance. When General Meade arrived on the scene, he was dumfounded to discover what Sickles had done. The two generals, as Meade later put it, discussed "the propriety of withdrawing" and Dan offered to march his men back to where they had started but time ran out. Confederate artillery was already pounding them. The III Corps would have to stay where it was.[11]

The fierce fighting at Gettysburg on July 2 rivaled Antietam for the dubious honor of "bloodiest single day of the war." Nowhere was the struggle more intense than along Sickles' line. The gallant III Corps took such a pounding that it never fully recovered. When the Army of the Potomac was reorganized before the start of the 1864 campaign, Sickles' old command was absorbed into other units and the III Corps ceased to exist.

Among the casualties that afternoon was the corps commander himself. As his men were being driven back in confusion, a cannonball struck Sickles' right knee. It was a bit of a freak hit; Sickles was mounted at the time but his horse went unhurt by the round shot. Those around the general thought that the wound would prove fatal but, even under these dire circumstances, Dan made a show of puffing on his cigar while being carried from the field. He wanted his men to know that he had not been killed.

At a field hospital, surgeons soon amputated the damaged limb. The next morning, the doctors decided to move the general away from the battlefield. He was too badly injured for the rough ride of a horse-drawn ambulance, so stretcher bearers carefully carried Sickles on a slow, two-day trip to the rail line at Littlestown. It was only eight miles away but the party took back roads to minimize the danger of encountering marauding Rebel cavalry. Once there, Sickles was put on board a waiting train.[12]

As a result, the injured general was one of the first important officers to reach Washington with first-hand knowledge of the crucial battle. When Abraham Lincoln visited his sickroom, Dan wasted no time in spinning his own version of events at Gettysburg—something he would continue to do for the rest of his life. The crafty lawyer recognized that a good offense was the best defense against criticism of his performance.

There are two ways to look at what happened the second day of the Pennsylvania battle. Some feel that Sickles' unauthorized advance blunted the impact of the assault by Longstreet's Confederates and Dan was truly "the hero of Gettysburg." Others contend that Sickles made a major blunder which almost lost the battle and he should have been court-martialed. While the latter is probably the most popular view, the argument has continued on almost since the moment the last gun fired.

When General Meade issued his report on the campaign, he tactfully wrote that Sickles, "not fully apprehending the instructions in regard to the position to be occupied, had advanced, or was in the act of advancing his corps some half a mile or three-quarters of a mile in front of the line of the Second Corps..." Meade's diplomatic wording could have been much worse but it still incensed the ever-sensitive Sickles. The one-legged general was also dismayed that his ongoing requests to be returned to command were shunted aside.[13]

With plenty of time on his hands, Sickles decided to campaign for Meade's removal. In February 1864, he was the first witness to appear before the Joint Congressional Committee on the Conduct of the War. Controlled by radical Republicans, the committee was looking into Meade's handling of the army during the Gettysburg campaign. Dan gave them an earful, defending his own actions, stating he had never received any orders where to place his men and suggesting that Meade had wanted to retreat from Gettysburg. He also praised Joe Hooker, probably in the unlikely long-shot hope that his old friend would be restored to command and bring Dan back too.

Meade was forced to defend himself before the hostile committee. Immediately after Meade's testimony, a rather curious article appeared in the *New York Herald*, which was now part of the Sickles camp.

Written under the pen name Historicus, the author defended Dan's actions at Gettysburg and criticized Meade's handling of the army. To those who had heard Sickles before the Joint Committee, it was all familiar territory. Meade was certain Sickles had written the offending piece and wanted to reply but was dissuaded by the army chief of staff, Henry Halleck. Responses defending Meade appeared from other anonymous officers. Historicus then returned to deliver another blistering broadside.[14]

With a war still to be won, Meade, unlike Sickles, had little time or enthusiasm for the controversy. It would continue on long after Meade's death in 1872, with Meade's son and fellow officers supplying the defense. The debate would rage in the press, in private correspondence between the battle's participants and wherever the old veterans gathered.

Dan Sickles never gave an inch. In 1893, he made one of his many visits back to Gettysburg, on this occasion in the company of former Confederate General James Longstreet and Union General Oliver Howard. All three had been heavily criticized for blundering in the battle. As they toured the first day's field, Howard sought Longstreet's opinion that his actions that day had been correct, and Longstreet, almost deaf, understood enough to assure onlookers that Howard had done just fine. When they reached the second day's field, Sickles asked "Old Pete" his opinion of Sickles' forward movement and the Rebel general assured those present that his former adversary had been entirely correct.[15]

Despite his best efforts, Sickles did not receive another field command for the rest of the war. In January 1865, President Lincoln did send him off on an errand-running tour of the South and then on a mission to Panama and Columbia to explore possible colonization for freed slaves. Sickles was still there when word came of Lincoln's assassination.

During reconstruction, the general served as military governor of the Carolinas. After he defied a federal court, he was removed from office in a tug-of-war between the embattled President Johnson and the radical Republicans of Congress. Sickles sought revenge by joining the radicals to work for Johnson's impeachment.

In 1868, he led the New York delegation at the Republican convention which nominated Ulysses S. Grant for president. When Grant won, Sickles was rewarded with a posting as minister to Spain.

By now, Sickles was a widower, Teresa having suffered an untimely death in 1867. Always a womanizer, the general played the field at his new post in Europe where his conquests included the deposed Queen Isabella II. That liaison won him a nickname as the "Yankee King of Spain." In 1871, Sickles married a young Spanish woman half his age and they had two children together. Dan's infidelities continued, however, and the couple separated in 1879. Sickles returned from Europe to New York City where he continued the practice of law and won another term in the U.S. Congress. There he introduced the legislation which created the national park at Gettysburg in 1895.

On October 30, 1897, the aging general received the Medal of Honor for his actions at Gettysburg. The citation noted that he "displayed most conspicuous gallantry on the field vigorously contesting the advance of the enemy and continuing to encourage his troops after being himself severely wounded." The award could be seen as the ultimate vindication of his actions on July 2, 1863. Yet, like so many things in Dan's career, even this moment caused controversy with charges that undue influence had been used to get the award for Sickles. The Medal of Honor nomination process was subsequently revised.[16]

Throughout his life, Sickles had always shown a reckless disregard for money, living and spending in a grand style whether he had the means to or not. He had gone through millions of dollars and, in his final years, was deep in debt.

In 1908, twenty-nine years after they had separated, Sickles' Spanish wife arrived in America to attempt a belated reconciliation. That effort failed when Sickles refused to fire his female housekeeper with whom he had a close relationship. The long missing Mrs. Sickles set up camp in a suite at the St. Regis Hotel some blocks away from Dan's townhouse. The wife's appearance may have been motivated by hopes of inheritance. Ironically it was she who helped Dan financially—although, ignoring reality, Sickles denied that he had any need of funds.[17]

An ugly episode arose in 1912 when an audit of the New York State Monuments Commission discovered that $28,476 seemed to be missing. The purpose of the commission was to build battlefield memorials at Gettysburg to the Empire State's Civil War veterans. Dan Sickles had served as the chairman for decades and he declared that he was responsible for the shortfall. An embarrassed sheriff came to arrest the ancient warrior but, at the last moment, friends came up with a $30,000 bond to prevent his imprisonment.[18]

In latter years, Sickles spent much time at veterans reunions and reflecting upon his old soldier days. He frequently visited the battlefields and was a regular guest at the Gettysburg Hotel. In 1913, for the battle's fiftieth anniversary, the owner installed an elevator to help his distinguished one-legged guest travel between floors. Sickles refused to use the newfangled lift; instead he insisted on camping in a tent with his fellow veterans. When asked why there was no monument to him at Gettysburg, he unabashedly indicated that the entire battlefield was his monument. In a way, he was right. The man who helped create Central Park had also played a key role in preserving the historic fields of Gettysburg.[19]

He died in 1914 at age 94, having gone through life pretty much on his own terms and having pretty much managed to get away with it.

Mary Lincoln is shown at right during her White House years. The illustration below depicts the attempt to sell her used clothing in New York after her husband's assassination.

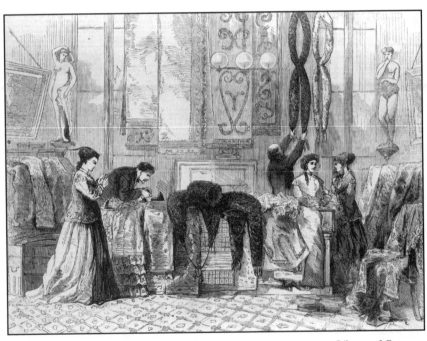

CHAPTER ELEVEN
MARY LINCOLN

Mary was one of the Todds of Kentucky, a slaveholding family from Lexington with social status and political connections. She was intelligent and pretty—though even early photos hint of the plumpness that was to come. Her mother died in 1825 when Mary was just six years old. Her father's subsequent remarriage brought into the household of six children a stepmother who had no experience in parenting. The relationship between the children and their father's second wife was frequently difficult. Life became even more crowded and complex when Robert Todd and his new spouse began production of a large second family.

In 1837, some months after finishing boarding school, Mary Todd started visiting Springfield, Illinois, where two of her older sisters lived. There she met Abraham Lincoln, a gangly attorney and state legislator. It was not love at first sight but eventually blossomed into a true romance. They made an unusual pair, the petite Miss Todd and the long, tall Lincoln; in fact, because of their contrasting shapes, Mary never allowed them to be photographed together. Lincoln made light of their height differences. To Mary's discomfort, he once brought her out before a cheering crowd and announced that they now had "the long and short of it."[1]

Like Mary, Lincoln had lost his mother when he was young. Both suffered bouts of depression. Mary shared Lincoln's keen interest in politics and had actually known the great statesman

Henry Clay when she was a child. The courtship of Abe and Mary was stormy and the pair broke off their engagement for many months before they finally wed on November 4, 1842. Part of the problem was that Mary's sisters felt that she could do better than Mr. Lincoln.

The pair began their married life living in a rented room at Springfield's Globe Tavern. After their first child, Robert, arrived in 1843, they moved to a regular house. Three more boys were born: Edward in 1846, William in 1850 and Thomas in 1853. When Edward died of diphtheria in 1850, both parents were stricken with grief. The loss may have contributed to their lenient parental policy which was summed up as "let the children have a good time." Many observers felt that these very active children had entirely too good a time.[2]

Lincoln continued to work his way up the political ladder. He served one term as a U.S. Congressman and then gave up the seat as custom dictated so that another member of the Whig Party might run. He returned to his law office, spending long hours traveling to the circuit courts and attending political meetings. In 1858, he ran as a Republican against Stephen Douglas for the United States Senate. Lincoln lost but the campaign helped him win national attention and put him on the road to the presidency.

While Lincoln was occupied building his career and reputation, Mary spent many nights alone with their children. She could be a nervous and fearful person, frightened of thunderstorms and strangers. She was ambitious and demanding but sometimes lacked self-confidence. Her demeanor was ever changing, occasionally exploding into unexpected angry tantrums. Because of this, she acquired something of a reputation around Springfield.

Winning the White House in the 1860 elections culminated a life-long dream for both Lincolns. The prairie lawyer of humble origin had always had a burning desire to be somebody; what's more he had the intellectual and emotional make-up to see that it happened. For her part, Mary had long claimed that her husband would someday be president of the United States; she said that if she had not thought so she would not have married him.[3]

Unfortunately, the Lincolns' White House years became something akin to Greek tragedy. For decades, the nation had been sliding toward civil war and the election of a "Black Republican" triggered the crisis in full. South Carolina left the Union shortly after Lincoln's election and was subsequently followed by ten other Southern states.

As the Lincoln family made a triumphant tour of Northern cities en route to Washington, word of death threats arrived from Baltimore. Fearing an assassination plot, Lincoln left his wife and children behind in Pennsylvania while he slipped unannounced into the national capital. Armed troops lined Washington streets on the day of the sixteenth president's inauguration. On April 12, with the firing on Fort Sumter, four years of fratricidal conflict began.

Washington society of that era included strong elements of Eastern snobbery and Southern sympathy. To the former the Lincolns were uncouth Westerners and to the latter they were dangerous abolitionists. Rounding out the picture, many Northerners believed that, as a Kentucky-born Todd, the new first lady was little more than a "spy in the White House." It would have been a difficult situation for anybody but, as one of Mary's allies noted, "a little more diplomacy on her part would have saved her from much adverse criticism." One of the president's aides, John Hay, nicknamed her "Hellcat."[4]

To help adjust to her new social position, Mary made some questionable choices of confidants, including the worldly gadabout Henry Winkoff. Winkoff somehow received advance word on the contents of the chief executive's annual message to the U.S. Congress and the *New York Herald* published his scoop. The leak created an uproar. Winkoff was imprisoned and suspicion fell on Mary as the source of the document. A congressional committee, however, placed the blame on a White House gardener, John Watt, in what was a questionable but nevertheless comfortable resolution of the scandal. Watt was fired and, despite possible Southern sympathies, he found himself shanghaied into the Union army. Watt did deserve some kind of punishment; he had been padding the White House expenses for his own benefit.[5]

The Lincolns arrived in the national capital to find that the executive mansion was in a sad state from years of wear and neglect. For decades, the White House had indeed been the "people's palace" where just about anyone could stop by unannounced with the idea of seeing the president. Public receptions were, in fact, public with muddy shoed, tobacco-spitting citizens welcome to come on in and say howdy. Shortly after the Lincolns took up residence, Union soldiers were being quartered in the hallways and the East Room. The badly abused mansion needed a facelift.

Mary, who had discovered the delights of big city shopping, eagerly undertook the job. She was excited to learn that Congress had routinely provided each recent president with $20,000 for refurbishing and redecorating; however, in recent administrations, the money either was not used to much advantage or had been frittered away on other pursuits.

With this budget, Mary decamped for Philadelphia and New York where she bought beds, chairs, china, wash stands, sofas and books. A beautiful velvet carpet of sea green was found for the East Room. Contractors were hired to apply new paint and wallpaper. Not surprisingly, the $20,000 allowance was soon exhausted but the spending continued nevertheless. Two items alone—a set of china and some French wallpaper—took more than half the appropriation. Even the $6,000 allotted annually for the mansion's internal maintenance was quickly used up.[6]

Exactly how much Mary Lincoln overspent in her redo of the wartime White House is unknown. She struggled to pay the overage through the usual ways of Washington. Money was quietly diverted from other appropriations; a friendly congressman managed to get another $4,500 approved; and there were cutbacks in the executive mansion staff. Mary even sold off some of the house's old secondhand furniture and tried to peddle loads of manure from the presidential stables.[7]

Nevertheless, the extravagant redecoration—no matter how tastefully done—seemed inappropriate at a time when the government was at war. Mary's reputation suffered accordingly in the public's mind.

Her image suffered another blow in February 1862 when the Lincolns hosted a gala ball to which five hundred people were invited. Those who were invited said it was a grand event. Those who were not invited angrily harrumphed about such gaiety during the national crisis.

The elaborate party was a watershed in another way. It embodied everything that a young Mary Lincoln might once have pictured in her White House fantasies. That same evening, however, another drama was taking place in the family quarters. Willie Lincoln was dying.

The worried mother had wanted to cancel the party when Willie became sick but she was assured that her son would be fine. Days later, when he passed away from typhoid fever, both Lincolns were devastated by this loss of a second child. Mary never truly recovered. She never again entered Willie's bedroom or the Green Room where his body had been embalmed. She began patronizing charlatan psychics hoping to contact her lost children in the great beyond. Not until January 1, 1865, did Mary cease to wear black mourning dresses—though even her mourning attire was elegant and expensive.

The war had brought other losses to the Lincolns, too. Early in the conflict's opening days, young Elmer Ellsworth, head of a flashy band of baggy pants Zouave troops, had been gunned down just across the Potomac River in Alexandria. Ellsworth had been such an intimate of the family that he even once caught the measles from the Lincoln children. Colonel Edward Baker, an old friend from long-ago in Illinois, fell during the fighting at Balls Bluff, Virginia. Then, too, there were Mary's brothers.

Kentucky was a border state, split between North and South. Mary's brother, George Todd, served in the Confederate army as a surgeon. Her half brother, Sam, was killed while fighting for the rebellion at Shiloh. Another half brother, David, gained notoriety for his rough treatment of Union prisoners as a jailer in Richmond. A third half brother, Alec, donned grey and died from friendly fire during a Louisiana skirmish in August 1862.

Confederate Brigadier General Ben Helm was married to Mary's half sister, Emily. At the beginning of the war, Lincoln had tried unsuccessfully to stop Helm from going south by offering him a major's commission in the paymaster's department. In September 1863, General Helm received a mortal wound while leading Confederate troops at Chickamauga, Georgia.

Shortly thereafter, the Southern general's widow, affectionately known to the Lincolns as "Little Sis," came to stay at the White House where her presence created an uproar. General Dan Sickles, a presidential family friend, warned Lincoln that he should not have that Rebel in his house. The president replied coolly that he and his wife were in the habit of choosing their own guests and did not need Sickles' assistance in that area. To quiet the criticism, Emily Helm took the oath of allegiance to the United States.[8]

Gossip concerning the first lady's loyalty reached the Committee on the Conduct of the War and some of its members met in a secret session to discuss the matter. Lincoln somehow learned of this and entered the conference unannounced. Looking at the surprised committee members, the president explained that he was appearing before them voluntarily so that they would "know it is untrue that any member of my family holds treasonable communication with the enemy." The president then turned and left as quickly as he had arrived. Abashed, the committee quietly adjourned, ending its investigation.[9]

Throughout the war, Mary's husband was under the continual threat of assassination. Lincoln more or less ignored the danger and tried to keep Mary unaware of the large volume of hate mail that arrived.

On July 2, 1863, the first lady was seriously injured while riding in a carriage going from their summer residence at the Soldiers' Home to the White House. Screws holding the driver's seat had been removed so that the coachman was tossed to the roadway while Mary remained alone in the runaway vehicle. Then she was thrown to the ground and her head struck a rock. It took three weeks of careful nursing before she recovered. Whoever had tampered with the carriage was probably hoping to injure the president.[10]

Mary Lincoln was always jealous of the attention that other women gave to her husband. At White House functions, it was the custom for the president to offer his arm and escort women other than his wife. Mary saw this as an usurpation of her role as first lady and had the practice changed.

On March 23, 1865, President and Mrs. Lincoln sailed on the *River Queen* to visit General Grant's headquarters at City Point, Virginia. Their schedule included a grand review of the Army of the James under the command of Major General Edward Ord. Lincoln rode on horseback with the army officers to the parade ground. Mrs. Lincoln and Mrs. Grant uncomfortably bumped along behind in an army ambulance over a rough log road. At times the mud came up nearly to the vehicle's wheel hubs. As the women traveled, a staff officer mentioned that General Charles Griffin's wife had been granted special permission to stay with the army, and the ever-suspicious Mary jumped to the conclusion that this woman had been alone with the president.

This information—coupled with the difficult journey—put Mary in a foul mood. Her frame of mind did not improve when the ambulance reached the parade ground and the ceremony was already underway. What's more, the first lady learned that her husband had been accompanied on his review of the troops by General Ord's beautiful wife. Her jealously out of control, Mary had to be restrained from jumping out of the ambulance. When the unsuspecting Mrs. Ord came over to present her compliments, Mary delivered a withering rebuke. The first lady remained in an angry and distraught state for the rest of the day, creating an awkward and embarrassing atmosphere for all who were present. Her husband endured repeated verbal attacks delivered right in front of the officers whom he commanded. For the next three days, Mary retreated to her stateroom on the *River Queen* before cutting her trip short and returning alone to Washington.[11]

Through the years, Abraham Lincoln had become accustomed to his wife's sudden and unpredictable mood swings. He had once cautioned her that, if she did not control her emotions, she might someday end up in an asylum. Nevertheless, the tantrums were another burden on an already overburdened president.

Shortly after that incident, Richmond fell to Grant's army and Lee surrendered. Peace was at hand and Lincoln had hope that his second term in office might be less turbulent than the first. On April 14, the last day of their married life, Mary and Abraham went for a carriage ride and talked hopefully of what the future might bring. That evening, the Lincolns visited Ford's Theater for a performance of *Our American Cousin* and Mary saw her husband shot down in cold blood by the pro-Southern actor John Wilkes Booth. Abraham Lincoln died the following morning.

After her husband's assassination, Mary Lincoln remained in the White House for more than a month, trying unsuccessfully to come to terms with her grief. She was too stricken to attend the Washington funeral service or to accompany the coffin back to Illinois. On May 22, heavily swaddled in black, she departed the capital for Chicago with only a few well-wishers to see her off. Mary had turned away many of those who had come to console her during her seclusion. That may be one reason for the lack of a farewell audience. Of the new president, she would later declare that "that miserable inebriate Johnson" had not written her a letter of condolence and had behaved "in the most brutal way"—forgetting that he had generously allowed her to remain undisturbed in the executive mansion for so many weeks. She told friends that she believed Andrew Johnson had knowledge of the plot to kill her husband.[12]

Arriving in Chicago, the former first lady checked into a fashionable hotel but remained there only a week before moving to a less luxurious hotel/boarding house. Money was again a major concern. Lincoln's death had ended his presidential salary and there was no widow's pension. Lincoln's estate was valued at roughly $85,000 in cash, bonds and property but, strangely for a man in his position, he died intestate. The lack of a will meant that everything would be divided equally between Mary and her two surviving children. Each of them would receive between $1,500 and $1,800 a year in interest, with Tad's money going into a trust until he came of age.[13]

Mary was financially strapped. She emotionally could not return to the Springfield house that the family still owned; there were too many memories and, after living in the White House, her former hometown held little appeal. She wanted a grand residence in a major city but that, unfortunately, she could not afford. She envied the mansion in Philadelphia that was given as a gift to General Grant for his role in the war. Didn't she deserve the same for her husband's sacrifice?

Beyond that, Mary still owed large debts to merchants back east—between $10,000 and $20,000 according to the best estimates. While in the White House, she had spent extravagantly on fashionable clothing and other accessories, without her husband's knowledge. After all, she had to maintain her proper appearance as first lady. After the president's reelection, she had felt assured that she could quietly take care of the bills over the course of the next four years. Now Mary was no longer in a position of privilege with shopkeepers eager to extend continual credit; the bills were due with no way to pay.[14]

Mary's best hope for financial security lay with the United States Congress. Her husband's salary through the second term would have been $25,000 a year for a total of $100,000. Unfortunately, when the lawmakers finally acted in December 1865, they allotted only one year's salary to the widow, based upon precedents set when William Henry Harrison and Zachary Taylor had died in office. Of course, neither those men had been assassinated nor even served a full term in the White House.[15]

Using a former family retainer and government employee, Alexander Williamson, as a screen, Mary made overtures to wealthy Northerners to assist her in this time of need. Former

Secretary of War Simon Cameron offered to raise a subscription for the widow but little if any money resulted from it. Mary's plea of poverty had been undercut by both her extravagant public image and published newspaper accounts of the sizeable estate left by the late president.

Through Williamson, she tried negotiating with her merchant creditors to discount the debts. Some, like the famous Washington jewelry concern of Galt & Company, accepted the return of merchandise that she had purchased.

Weary of living in rented rooms, Mary used the congressional windfall to purchase a home in Chicago. This was, however, a home that she could not afford to furnish and maintain. Before long she was forced to sell.

In September 1867, the president's widow went to New York with the idea that she could quietly raise cash by peddling pieces of her wardrobe. She tried to do so using the alias "Mrs. Clarke," but she fell into the hands of some aggressive Broadway commission brokers who convinced her that the clothes' real value lay in the Lincoln name. In what amounted to a quasi-blackmail scheme, these conniving advisers persuaded their famous client to write letters to prominent Republicans explaining that she was selling her clothes to avoid penury. That gambit failed as did a subsequent public sale which brought curiosity seekers but no buyers. Another plan to send an exhibition of her dresses off as a touring road show also collapsed. All Mary received from these efforts was a storm of bad publicity.

Even the site of Lincoln's burial proved troublesome. Immediately after the assassination, an Illinois citizens group called the National Lincoln Monument Association had obtained six acres in downtown Springfield where—without consulting his widow—they planned to bury the town's most famous former resident. Mary insisted that her husband be placed in Springfield's Oak Ridge Cemetery. Otherwise she would haul the body back to Washington and bury Abraham in the unused Capitol crypt that had once been reserved for George Washington. Mary won the battle and Lincoln's remains went to Oak Ridge. In 1876, there was a macabre failed attempt to steal the corpse. A gang of counterfeiters had hoped to hold it for ransom until one of their gang was freed from prison.

There were other troubles, too. Mr. Lincoln's old law partner, Billy Herndon, had decided to make money off his association with the martyred president and had gone on a lecture tour. Needing some sensational insider info to spice up the talks, he told the public of a romance that Lincoln supposedly had with Ann Rutledge, a young woman Lincoln had known in New Salem, Illinois. Ann had died tragically and, according to Herndon, Lincoln lost the love of his life. What's more, Herndon claimed that Lincoln's marriage to Mary Todd was an unhappy one.

Mary never liked Herndon. He had once tried to compliment her by saying that she danced "like a serpent" and Mary took great offense. Never had Herndon been welcome to dine at the Lincoln's Springfield home. Now this evil man was trying to diminish the one true thing that she had left: the memory of life with her husband. She told a friend that she "would not believe an assertion of Herndon's if he would take a thousand oaths, upon the Bible." Herndon would later use Mary's own words to declare that Lincoln was not a "technical Christian" and that the great man may have been born out of wedlock.[16]

Herndon's tale of true love ended by tragedy was well-tailored to Victorian sentiment and was widely taken at face value. Since then, many historians have tended to discount the Rutledge story as legend, the truth of which may never be known.

Seeking a refuge from these storms, Mary took her teenaged son, Tad, and sailed to Germany in October 1868. There she enrolled her boy in boarding school and tried to live economically abroad, often staying at second-rate hotels.

During her absence, the United States Congress again reviewed the financial plight of the "Great Emancipator's" widow. In July 1870, she was granted a lifetime pension of $3,000 annually. Even so, that was not enough for Mary. She felt that the legislators should have made the pension retroactive. Returning to America in May 1871, she bitterly told a friend that, while her husband performed the great work of the war, U. S. Grant—who now occupied the White House—had received all the pecuniary compensation.[17]

Mary Lincoln reached her breaking point in July 1871 when her son, Tad, died from a tubercular-type pleurisy. With his death, she had outlived her husband and all of her children but one—a circumstance that would also be shared by her Confederate counterpart, Varina Davis.

The erratic behavior which Mary had exhibited throughout her life became more pronounced. She had frequent headaches and grew increasingly paranoid. She continued her interest in spiritualism and contacting the dead. She accused her remaining son, Robert, of trying to murder her but, at the same time, feared that he might die and leave her all alone in the world. At one point, she believed that gas lamps came from the devil and would use only candles in her room. Despite her concerns about poverty, she went on grand shopping sprees and repeatedly bought multiples of items for which she had no need. She worried about being poisoned and thought that she was being followed.[18]

On the last count, she was correct. Given his mother's irrational actions, Robert Lincoln hired Pinkerton agents to shadow her. The eldest son was now a successful Chicago attorney and a married family man. His mother, however, would no longer visit his home, due to a quarrel with her daughter-in-law.

Robert became concerned that his mother was truly mentally ill and might spend herself into the poor house. He began proceedings for Cook County Court to find her insane. On May 19, 1875, the unsuspecting woman was taken into custody and hauled before a judge and all-male jury. In what must have seemed to her as the ultimate betrayal, she saw her only living child in the courtroom and learned what he had instigated. The judge ordered the former first lady committed to an asylum and appointed Robert as guardian of her financial affairs.

When Robert approached his mother after the verdict, she said sadly, "Oh Robert, to think that my son would ever have done this." That night, according to one account, Mary tried but failed to commit suicide by poisoning herself.[19]

They sent her to Bellevue Place, a sanitarium thirty-five miles west of Chicago. There she remained for less than four months before her sister, Elizabeth, persuaded the doctors to put Mary into her custody. In June 1876, the court ruled that Mary Lincoln's sanity had been restored. In the public mind, however, this ugly episode confirmed the rumors that Abraham Lincoln's widow was a "crazy lady." Seeking privacy and peace, Mary knew that she could not stay in America and sailed for Europe. She lived there, mainly in the French resort town of Pau, until October 1880.

Not surprisingly, her relationship with her son remained strained. She grew excited when newspapers mentioned him as a possible presidential candidate and was pleased when James Garfield appointed him to be secretary of war. After she returned to America, Robert visited his mother, bringing along her granddaughter. Still the memory of the betrayal remained.

Mary Lincoln would win one last battle in her war for financial security. In January 1882, Congress increased her pension by $2,000 annually and awarded a supplemental sum of $15,000. The impetus had been the assassination of President James Garfield. He left behind a widow and five children to whom the government had given $5,000 a year. The lawmakers agreed that the widow of the great Abraham Lincoln deserved as much as the Garfield family.

Mary spent her final months at her sister's home in Springfield. She was a strange reclusive woman who lived behind drawn shades and feared that others were planning to steal her money. She spent hours going through dozens of storage trunks again and again, examining clothing she had never worn and looking at mementos of her husband and family.

Mary's eyesight began to fail and her health deteriorated. On July 15, 1882, she died, only sixty-four but old beyond her time, worn down by years of emotional trauma. Her funeral was held in the very same room where she had married Abraham Lincoln forty years before.

Robert Lincoln lived until 1926. He served as ambassador to the Court of St. James and president of the Pullman Palace Car Company. In 1901, he oversaw the rebuilding of the family mausoleum at Oak Hill Cemetery and ordered that his father's coffin be opened to ensure that the body had never actually been stolen. The surprisingly lifelike corpse was then reburied under four thousand pounds of burglar-proof cement. In 1922, Robert presided as the honored guest at the dedication of the magnificent Lincoln Memorial in Washington. Four years later, when Abraham and Mary's eldest son passed away, he did not join his parents and brothers in Illinois but instead was buried at Arlington National Cemetery.

No direct descendants of Abraham and Mary Lincoln are alive today. The last of the bloodline, the sixteenth president's great-grandson, Robert Todd Lincoln Beckwith, died on Christmas Eve in 1985.[20]

NOTES

CHAPTER ONE

1. "The (Agri)Cultural Contradictions of Obesity" by Michael Pollan, *New York Times Magazine*, October 12, 2003, p. 41.
2. *The Assassination of Lincoln: History and Myth* by Lloyd Lewis, University of Nebraska Press, Lincoln, 1994, pp. 135–39.
3. *Sword of San Jacinto* by Marshal DeBruhl, Random House, New York, 1993, p. 312.
4. *President James Buchanan* by Philip Shriver Klein, Pennsylvania State University Press, University Park, PA, 1962, pp. 210, 211, 424.
5. *Lincoln* by David Herbert Donald, Simon & Schuster, New York, 1995, p. 171.
6. Ibid., pp. 49, 172.
7. *Abraham Lincoln: The War Years,* Vol. 2, by Carl Sandburg, Harcourt, Brace & Company, New York, 1939, p. 232.
8. *Mary Todd Lincoln: A Biography* by Jean H. Baker, Norton, New York, 1987, p. 114; *Abraham Lincoln: The War Years,* Vol. 2, Sandburg, p. 233.
9. *Lincoln's Virtues* by William Lee Miller, Knopf, New York, 2002, p. 480n147.
10. *Campaigning with Grant* by Horace Porter, Century Company, New York, 1887, p. 217.
11. *Wendell Phillips: Orator & Agitator* by Lorenzo Sears, B. Blom, New York, 1967, p. 184.
12. *Life in the North during the Civil War* by George Winston and Charles Judah, University of New Mexico Press, Albuquerque, 1966, p. 241.
13. *A Battle from the Start: The Life of Nathan Bedford Forrest* by Brian Steel Wills, Harper Perennial, 1993, p. 18.
14. *Stonewall of the West* by Craig L. Symonds, University Press of Kansas, Lawrence, 1997, p. 30.
15. *The Custer Story: The Life and Letters of General George A. Custer and His Wife Elizabeth,* edited by Marguerite Merington, Barnes & Noble, New York, 1994, pp. 48–49; *Custer* by Jeffry D. Wert, Simon & Schuster, New York, 1996, p. 46.
16. *Embattled Confederates* by Bell Wiley, Bonanza Books, New York, 1964, p. 51.
17. *I Rode with Stonewall* by Henry Kyd Douglas, Mockingbird Books, St. Simons Island, GA, 1974, p. 182.
18. *Stonewall Jackson* by James I. Robertson, Jr., Macmillan, New York, 1997, p. 305. Henry Kyd Douglas gives a slightly different version of this story.
19. *A Government of Our Own* by William C. Davis, Free Press, New York, 1994, p. 92; *Robert Toombs of Georgia* by William Thompson, Louisiana State University Press, Baton Rouge, 1966, p. 162.

20. *A Government of Our Own*, Davis, p. 410; *Robert Toombs*, Thompson, p. 257.

21. *Jefferson Davis: The Man and His Hour* by William C. Davis, Harper Perennial, New York, 1992, p. 30.

22. Ibid., p. 34.

23. Ibid., p. 35.

24. Ibid., pp. 87–88.

25. *John Letcher of Virginia* by F. N. Boney, University of Alabama Press, Tuscaloosa, 1966, pp. 108, 148; *Richmond Examiner*, January 2, 1864.

26. *Hood's Texas Brigade: Lee's Grenadier Guards* by Col. Harold B. Simpson, Texian Press, Waco, 1970, p. 78.

27. *Louis T. Wigfall: Southern Fire-eater* by Alvy King, Louisiana State University Press, 1970, pp. 139, 155.

28. *Agriculture and the Civil War* by Paul Gates, Alfred Knopf, New York, 1965, p. 97.

29. *Richmond Examiner*, February 15, 1864.

30. *U. S. Grant Album* by Lawrence A. Frost, Bonanza Books, New York, 1966, pp. 46–47; *Personal Memoirs of U. S. Grant*, Vol. 1, Charles L. Webster & Co., New York, 1885, p. 210.

31. *Ulysses S. Grant* by Brooks D. Simpson, Houghton Mifflin, Boston, 2000, p. 63.

32. *Grant Album*, Frost, pp. 54, 63.

33. *Ulysses S. Grant*, Simpson, pp. 89–90; *Campaigning with Grant*, Porter, Century Company, p. 215.

34. Ibid., Simpson, pp. 206–8.

35. *An Army of Amateurs* by Edward G. Longacre, Stackpole Books, Mechanicsburg, PA, 1997, pp. 177–81.

36. *Abraham Lincoln: The War Years,* Vol. 3, by Carl Sandburg, Harcourt, Brace & Company, New York, 1939, p. 659. Congressman George Julian wrote of this incident.

37. It would be an interesting folklore project to collect all the "Grant drinking" stories that have arisen over the years. The author first heard the Harrisburg tale several decades ago and later saw it in a column written by Harrisburg *Patriot-News* reporter Paul Beers. The Cameron mansion where the episode is said to have occurred is not the one which houses the Dauphin County Historical Society but the stone building at the southern corner of Front Street and State Street. The Lancaster County episode is said to have taken place in Marietta, probably after Grant visited Simon Cameron's nearby estate.

38. *Grant: A Biography* by William S. McFeely, Norton, New York, 1982, pp. 472–73.

39. *Elmira: Death Camp of the North* by Michael Horigan, Stackpole, Mechanicsburg, PA, 2002, p. 14.

40. Ibid., p. 177.

41. *Rebel Private: Front and Rear* by William A. Fletcher, Dutton, New York, 1995, p. 32.

42. *A War of the People*, edited by Jeffrey Marshall, University Press of New England, Hanover, NH, 1999, p. 96, Original letter in the Vermont Historical Society.

43. *Official Records*, Vol. 2, p. 697.

44. *Too Afraid to Cry: Maryland Civilians in the Antietam Campaign* by Kathleen A. Ernst, Stackpole Books, Mechanicsburg, PA, 1999, p. 165.

45. *Fort Lyon to Harpers Ferry: The Civil War Letters and Newspaper Dispatches of Charles H. Moulton*, edited by Lee Drickamer and Karen Drickamer, White Mane Publishing, Shippensburg, PA, 1987, pp. 63–64, 91.

46. "Gettysburg's Preview of War" by Linda G. Black, *Gettysburg Magazine*, July 1990, p. 3; *The Comanches* by Frank M. Myers, Stonewall House reprint, Alexandria, 1985, p. 193.

47. *Hood's Texas Brigade*, Simpson, p. 251; *Rebel Private: Front and Rear*, Fletcher, pp. 71–72.

48. *Diary of Battle*, edited by Allan Nevins, Harcourt, Brace & World, New York, 1962, p. 229.

49. Ibid., p. 271.

50. Ibid., pp. 277–78.

51. Ibid., pp. 489–90.

52. *Army of Amateurs*, Longacre, p. 49.

53. Jacob Claar letter in the possession of the author.

54. *Tarnished Eagles* by Thomas P. Lowry, Stackpole Books, Mechanicsburg, PA, 1997, pp. 116–20.

CHAPTER TWO

1. *Valley of the Shadow* web site at valley.vcdh.virginia.edu; transcription from the original in the Southern Historical Collection, Wilson Library, University of North Carolina, Chapel Hill.

2. Memoir of Captain Albert Hunter. Transcript on the Emmitsburg Maryland Area Historical Society web site at emmitsburg.net/history.

3. *Diary of a Confederate Soldier,* edited by William C. Davis, University of South Carolina Press, Columbia, 1990, p. 104.

4. *History of the Eighth Cavalry Regiment Illinois Volunteers* by Abner Hard, M.D., Morningside Bookshop reprint, Dayton, 1984, p. 68.

5. *Hardtack and Coffee* by John D. Billings, Time-Life reprint, Alexandria, VA, 1982, pp. 139–40; *History of the Forty-Fifth Regiment Pennsylvania Volunteer Infantry 1861–1865*, written by the Comrades, Grit Publishing, Williamsport, PA, 1912, p. 142.

6. *History of the Forty-Fifth Regiment PVI*, p. 142.

7. *Hardtack and Coffee*, Billings, p. 219; *Glory Road* by Bruce Catton, Doubleday, New York, 1952, p. 145.

8. *Hard Marching Every Day: The Civil War Letters of Private Wilbur Frisk, Second Vermont Volunteers,* edited by Emil Rosenblatt and Ruth Rosenblatt, University Press of Kansas, Lawrence, 1992, p. 146.

9. *A War of the People*, Marshall, p. 211. Original letter in the Vermont Historical Society. Tillison drowned a few months later while traveling by boat from City Point to Alexandria, VA.

10. *One of Jackson's Foot Cavalry* by John Worsham, McCowat-Mercer Press, Jackson, TN, 1964, p. 148.

11. *Raiders and Blockaders* by William N. Still, Jr., John M. Taylor and Norman C. Delaney, Brassey's, Dulles, VA, 1998, pp. 72–74, 93.

12. *800 Paces to Hell: Andersonville* by Dr. John W. Lynn, Sgt. Kirkland's Press, Fredericksburg, VA, 1999, p. 21.

13. *Eye of the Storm* by Private Robert Knox Sneden, The Free Press, New York, 2000, pp. 272–73.

14. Ibid., p. 274.

15. *Four Years in the Confederate Artillery: The Diary of Henry Robinson Berkeley*, University of North Carolina, Chapel Hill, 1961, p. 126.

16. "Nurse Pember and the Whiskey War" by Mary C. Meskauskas, *Civil War Times Illustrated*, August 1999. Phoebe Yates Pember recounted these experiences in her memoir, *A Southern Woman's Story*.

17. *Inside the Army of the Potomac: The Civil War Experience of Captain Francis Adam Donaldson*, edited by J. Gregory Acken, Stackpole Books, Mechanicsburg,

PA, 1998, p. 35. This book provides a most interesting and candid account of life in the Army of the Potomac.

18. Ibid., p. 55.

19. Ibid., p. 112.

20. Ibid., pp. 179, 190.

21. Ibid., pp. 207–8.

22. Ibid., pp. 226–27, 246.

23. Ibid., pp. 227, 286, 399.

24. Ibid., pp. 269–70.

25. Ibid., p. 329.

26. Ibid., pp. 337–38.

27. Ibid., p. 439.

28. *Official Records*, Series 1, Vol. 2, Part 1, pp. 438–39; *The Bloodiest Day: The Battle of Antietam* by Ronald H. Bailey and the editors of Time-Life Books, p. 38; *Antietam: Voices of the Civil War* by the editors of Time-Life Books, Alexandria, p. 47.

29. *Diary of Battle*, Nevins, pp. 186 and 189; *Inside the Army of the Potomac*, Acken, pp. 250, 464n27.

30. *The Gettysburg Campaign: A Study in Command* by Edwin B. Coddington, Scribners, New York, 1968, p. 308; *Gettysburg: July 1* by David G. Martin, Combined Publishing, Conshohocken, 1995, pp. 473–74.

31. *To the North Anna* by Gordon C. Rhea, Lousiana State University Press, Baton Rouge, 2000, pp. 338–42.

32. *Official Records*, Vol. 40, pp. 119, 128.

33. *Battle Mountain, Nevada: History and Description* at Nevadaweb.com.

34. *Sherman's Horsemen* by David Evans, Indiana University Press, Bloomington, 1996, p. 472.

35. *Confederate Veteran*, October 1893, pp. 311–12.

36. *Mosby's War Reminiscences* by John S. Mosby, Dodd, Mead & Company, New York, 1898, p. 60.

37. *Memoirs of Colonel John S. Mosby,* edited by Charles Wells Russell, Indiana University Press reprint, Bloomington, 1959, pp. 341–45.

38. *Mosby's Rangers* by James J. Williamson, Kenyon, New York, 1896, pp. 152–53.

39. *Mosby Vignettes*, Vol. 1, privately published by Thomas J. Evans and James M. Moyer, pp. 22–23; *Mosby Vignettes*, Vol. 3, privately published by Thomas J. Evans and James M. Moyer, p. 35. James Williamson in *Mosby's Rangers* writes that this affair took place April 29, but two contemporary accounts place it as April 28.

40. *Bloody Bill Anderson* by Albert Castel and Thomas Goodrich, Stackpole Books, Mechanicsburg, PA, 1998, p. 73; *Quantrill's War* by Duane Schultz, Thomas Dunne, New York, 1997, pp. 284–89; *Gray Ghosts of the Confederacy* by Richard S. Brownlee, Louisiana State University Press, Baton Rouge, 1958, pp. 216–20.

41. *The Confederacy's Last Hurrah* by Wiley Sword, University Press of Kansas, Lawrence, 1992, p. 136.

42. *Shrouds of Glory* by Winston Groom, Pocket Books, New York, 1995, pp. 140–50; *The Gallant Hood* by John P. Dyer, Bobbs-Merrill, New York, 1950, pp. 286–89.

43. *Fightin' Tom Rosser, C.S.A.* by Millard K. Bushong and Dean M. Bushong, Beidel Printing, Shippensburg, PA, 1983, p. 172.

44. *The End of an Era* by John Sergeant Wise, Houghton Mifflin & Company, Boston, 1899, p. 338; *Pickett: Leader of the Charge* by Edward G. Longacre, White Mane, Shippensburg, PA, 1998, p. 11.

45. *Robert E. Lee: A Life Portrait* by David J. Eicher, Taylor Publishing, Dallas, 1997, p. 33.

46. *Pickett's Charge in History and Memory* by Carol Reardon, University of North Carolina Press, Chapel Hill, 1997, p. 156.

47. *Lee and Longstreet at Gettysburg* by Glenn Tucker, Bobbs-Merrill, Indianapolis, 1968, p. 151.

48. *Rosser*, Bushong, p. 195.

49. *Decision in the West: The Atlanta Campaign* by Albert Castel, University Press of Kansas, Lawrence, 1992, pp. 97–98.

50. *Sherman: Fighting Prophet* by Lloyd Lewis, Harcourt, Brace & Company, New York, 1932, p. 368.

51. Ibid., pp. 539–42; *End of an Era*, Wise, pp. 450–53.

52. *End of an Era*, Wise, p. 401.

53. *Recollections of the Civil War* by Charles A. Dana, Collier Books, New York, 1963, p. 108.

54. *Charles Sumner and the Rights of Man* by David Donald, Knopf, New York, 1970, p. 218; *The Day Lincoln Was Shot* by Jim Bishop, Harper & Row, New York, 1955, pp. 33–34.

55. *The Day Lincoln Was Shot*, Bishop, p. 203. Other accounts state that Parker remained in the theater but had left his post to get a better view of the stage. After the shooting, the policeman could not be found for the rest of the evening.

56. *Blood on the Moon* by Edward Streets, Jr., University Press of Kentucky, Lexington, 2001, pp. 192, 199.

CHAPTER THREE

1. The Stratford Hall web site—stratfordhall.org—makes a point of debunking this myth.

2. *Lee* by Douglas Southall Freeman, Collier Books, New York, 1991, pp. 3–8.

3. *The Burning of Washington* by Anthony S. Pitch, Naval Institute Press, Annapolis, 1998, pp. 1–12.

4. Ibid., p. 24; *The Marble Man* by Thomas L. Connelly, Louisiana State University Press, Baton Rouge, 1977, p. 177.

5. Cleydael Virginia landmark web site at cleydael.org.

6. Original document transcribed on line at Stratfordhall.org.

7. *Rebel Raider* by James A. Ramage, University of Kentucky Press, Lexington, 1986, pp. 33–39.

8. Ibid., p. 33; *Black Confederates and Afro-Yankees in Civil War Virginia* by Ervin L. Jordan, Jr., University of Virginia, Charlottesville, 1995, pp. 128–29.

9. *James Buchanan*, Klein, p. 350.

10. *Mary Todd Lincoln*, Baker, p. 88.

11. *General A. P. Hill: The Story of a Confederate Warrior* by James I. Robertson, Jr., Random House, New York, 1987, p. 11.

12. Ibid., p. 28.

13. *Custer*, Wert, p. 34.

14. Ibid., p. 107.

15. Ibid., p. 142; *Kill-Cavalry: The Life and Times of Union General Hugh Judson Kilpatrick* by Samuel J. Martin, Stackpole Books, Mechanicsburg, PA, 2000, p. 128; *The Story the Soldiers Wouldn't Tell: Sex in the Civil War* by Thomas P. Lowry, M.D., pp. 154–55, Stackpole Books, Mechanicsburg, PA, 1994.

16. *Little Big Horn Remembered* by Herman J. Viola, Times Books, New York, 1999, p. 53; *Custer*, Wert, p. 287.

17. *Pickett*, Longacre, p. 40; *The General's Second Family* by Martha M. Boltz, PicketSociety.com web site.

18. *Silk Flags and Cold Steel* by William R. Trotter, John F. Blair, Publisher, Winston-Salem, 1991, pp. 234–40; *Kill-Cavalry*, Martin, pp. 220–23.

19. *Kill-Cavalry*, Martin, p. 230.

20. Ibid., p. 234.

21. Ibid., pp. 238–42.

22. Ibid., p. 248.

23. *Southern Hero: Matthew Calbraith Butler* by Samuel J. Martin, Stackpole Books, Mechanicsburg, PA, 2001, p. 11.

24. Ibid., pp. 66–67.

25. Ibid., pp. 79, 243.

26. Ibid., p. 204.

27. *Memoirs of the Confederate War* by Heros Von Borcke, Vol. 2, Morningside reprint, Dayton, 1985, pp. 15–16.

28. *The Letters of J.E.B. Stuart*, edited by Adele H. Mitchell, Stuart-Mosby Historical Society, Carlisle, PA, 1990, p. 229.

29. *War Years with Jeb Stuart*, by W. W. Blackford, Lousiana State University Press, Baton Rouge, 1993, p. 179.

30. *Letters of J.E.B. Stuart*, Mitchell, p. 270; *Fightin' Tom Rosser, C.S.A.*, Bushong, p. 57.

31. *Lee's Lieutenants* by Douglas Southall Freeman, Scribners, New York, 1944, Vol. 3, p. 52.

32. *Letters of J.E.B. Stuart*, Mitchell, p. 283; *Bold Dragoon* by Emory M. Thomas, Vintage Books, New York, 1988, p. 279.

33. *War Years*, Blackford, p. 155.

34. *War Years*, Blackford, p. 90; "Rebel, Yes But Was She a Useful Spy?" by Peter Cliffe, *Washington Times*, August 16, 2003.

35. *Spies for the Blue and Grey* by Harnett T. Kane, Ace Star, New York, 1954, pp. 109–11.

36. *Siren of the South: Belle Boyd* by Ruth Scarborough, Mercer University Press, Macon, GA, 1997, p. 171.

37. Ibid., pp. 180–81.

38. *Wearing of the Gray* by John Esten Cooke, Old Soldier Books reprint, Gaithersburg, MD, 1988, p. 16; *Spies for the Blue and Grey*, Kane, p. 126.

39. *Spies for the Blue and Grey*, Kane, pp. 188–201.

40. *Stonewall Jackson,* Robertson, Jr., pp. 690–91. Anna Jackson's letter to her sister-in-law can be found in *The Family & Early Life of Stonewall Jackson* by Roy Bird Cook, Old Dominion Press, Richmond, 1924, p. 172.

41. *Jefferson Davis: The Man and His Hour*, Davis, pp. 685–86.

42. *Old Jube* by Millard K. Bushong, Beidel Printing House, Shippensburg, PA, 1985, p. 303.

43. *Richmond during the War*, by Sallie B. Putnam, G. W. Carleton & Co., New York, 1867, p. 234.

44. *Old Jube*, Bushong, pp. 18–19.

45. *Drawn with the Sword: Reflections on the American Civil War* by James McPherson, Oxford University Press, Oxford, 1996, p. 46; *Drawn to the Civil War* by J. Stephen Lang, p. 77, John F. Blair, Publisher, Winston-Salem, 1999; *Damage Them All You Can* by George Walsh, Forge, New York, 2002, p. 189. An interview with one of Early's great-granddaughters, who was then serving in the U.S. armed forces, appeared in the periodical *Civil War News*, in the 1990s.

46. *Citizen Sherman* by Michael Fellman, Random House, New York, 1995, p. 379.

47. Vinnieream.com; *Chicago Republican*, February 19, 1868.
48. *Sickles the Incredible* by W. A. Swanberg, Stan Clark Military Books, Gettysburg, 1991, pp. 298–301.
49. *Citizen Sherman*, Fellman, p. 356.
50. "Vinnie Ream Hoxie at Iowa and Elsewhere" by John J. McDonald, *Books at Iowa 22*, April 1975.
51. *Personal Memoirs of W. T. Sherman*, Charles L. Webster & Company, New York, 1891, Vol. 2, p. 460.
52. *Citizen Sherman*, Fellman, pp. 358–68.
53. *William Tecumseh Sherman* by James M. Merrill, Rand McNally, Chicago, 1971, p. 405.

CHAPTER FOUR

1. *Diary of Gideon Welles*, Vol. 1, Houghton Mifflin, New York, 1911, p. 306.
2. *Kate Chase for the Defense* by Alice Hunt Sokoloff, Dodd, Mead & Company, New York, 1971, pp. 186–91.
3. Ibid., pp. 70–72.
4. *Salmon Chase: A Life in Politics* by Frederick J. Blue, Kent State University Press, Kent, Ohio, 1987, p. 245.
5. *Kate Chase*, Sokoloff, p. 221.
6. *Roscoe Conkling of New York* by David M. Jordan, Cornell University Press, Ithaca, NY, 1971, pp. 309–13.
7. *Kate Chase*, Sokoloff, pp. 232–41.
8. *Reveille in Washington* by Margaret Leech, Harper & Brothers, New York, 1941, pp. 453–54.
9. *Kate Chase*, Sokoloff, pp. 274, 282–85.
10. *Historical Times Illustrated Encyclopedia of the Civil War*, Patricia L. Faust, editor, Harper & Row, New York, 1986, p. 709.
11. Ibid., p. 709.
12. *Charles Sumner and the Rights of Man* by David Donald, Alfred A. Kopf, New York, 1970, pp. 269–77, 289–94, 314.
13. *Mary Todd Lincoln: Her Life and Letters* by Justin G. Turner and Linda Levitt Turner, Knopf, New York, 1972, p. 529.
14. *Harpers Ferry* by Ray Jones, Pelican, Gretna, LA, 1992, p. 129.
15. *Reverend Beecher and Mrs. Tilton* by Altina L. Waller, University of Massachusetts Press, Amherst, 1982, p. 34.
16. Ibid., p. 1.
17. For more on this colorful woman, visit victoria-woodhull.com.
18. "100 Years Later, New View of an Icon" by Linda Wheeler, *Washington Post*, September 6, 1999.
19. *Frederick Douglass* by William S. McFeely, Norton, New York, 1991, p. 322.
20. Ibid., p. 320.
21. *Thaddeus Stevens, Nineteenth-Century Egalitarian* by Hans L. Trefousse, Stackpole Books, Mechanicsburg, PA, 2001, pp. 69, 70, 234, 244.
22. *Abraham Lincoln: The Prairie Years and the War Years* by Carl Sandburg, abridged edition, Harcourt, Brace and Company, New York, 1954, p. 275.
23. *Davis*, Davis, pp. 74–75.
24. *The End of An Era*, Wise, p. 401.

25. *The Long Surrender* by Burke Davis, Random House, New York, 1985, pp. 241–47.

26. Ibid., pp. 249–51; *Davis*, Davis, pp. 669–73.

27. *Davis*, Davis, p. 6; Jefferson Davis Papers on-line at http://jeffersondavis.rice.edu.

28. *The Story the Soldiers Wouldn't Tell*, Lowry, pp. 110–11; *Walt Whitman: A Life* by Juston Kaplan, Simon & Schuster, New York, 1980, p. 281.

29. *The Unrecorded Life of Oscar Wilde* by Rupert Croft-Cooke, McKay, New York, 1972, pp. 75–76.

30. *Oscar Wilde* by Richard Ellman, Knopf, New York, 1988, pp. 167–71.

31. *The Story the Soldiers Wouldn't Tell*, Lowry, pp. 114–17.

32. *Lincoln*, Donald, p. 158.

33. *History of the 150th Regiment Pennsylvania Volunteers* by Lieutenant Colonel Thomas Chamberlin, McManus, Jr., & Co., Philadelphia, 1905, p. 41.

34. Ibid., p. 48.

35. Congressional Biographical Directory online at congress.gov.

36. Ibid.

37. *New York Herald*, April 3, 1863.

38. *Buchanan*, Klein, pp. 408, 414; *New York Daily Tribune*, October 13, 1862.

39. *Buchanan*, Klein, p. 426.

40. *Just South of Gettysburg*, Frederic Shriver Klein, editor, Historical Society of Carroll County, Maryland, 1963, pp. 90–97; "Emmitsburg in the Civil War: General Reynolds and Emmitsburg" by John Allen Miller, Emmitsburg Area Historical Society web site: http://www.emmitsburg.net/archive_list/articles/history_articles/civil_war/general_reynolds.htm.

CHAPTER FIVE

1. "Scientist: Hard heads a key to survival" by Marsha Walton, February 13, 2004. CNN.com. University of Iowa anthropologist Russell Ciochon developed the theory.

2. *Extraordinary Popular Delusions and the Madness of Crowds* by Charles Mackay, Harmony Books, New York, 1980, reprint of 1852 edition, p. 655.

3. Ibid., p. 660.

4. *The Duel: A History of Dueling* by Robert Baldick, Potter, New York; *Noted American Duels and Hostile Encounters* by Hamilton Cochran, Chilton, Philadelphia, 1963, p. 132.

5. *Noted American Duels*, Cochran, p. 146.

6. *Andrew Jackson*, Vol. 2, *The Course of American Freedom* by Robert Remini, History Book Club, 1988, pp. 1–2.

7. *Noted American Duels*, Cochran, p. 250.

8. Preston Brooks detailed his thinking in his July 1856 speech resigning from the House of Representatives. It is available on-line at www.iath.virginia.edu/seminar/unit4/brooks.html.

9. *Charles Sumner and the Coming of the Civil War* by David Donald, pp. 286–308, gives a full account of the Sumner/Butler incident. The complete text of the "Crime Against Kansas" speech can be found on the Internet.

10. *Biographic Directory of the United States Congress*, bio.congress.gov.

11. *Sumner: Coming of Civil War*, Donald, p. 308.

12. *A Belle of the Fifties: Memoirs of Mrs. Clay of Alabama* by Virginia Clay-Clopton, Doubleday, Page & Co., New York, 1905, p. 15.

13. "Jefferson Davis' Speech at Vicksburg," Papers of Jefferson Davis on-line at http://jeffersondavis.rice.edu.

14. *Who Fired the First Shot?* by Ashley Halsey, Jr., Hawthorn Books, New York, 1963, p. 93; *The Duel: A History of Dueling,* Baldick, p. 115; *Jefferson Davis,* William C. Davis, p. 146.

15. *Judah P. Benjamin: The Jewish Confederate* by Eli N. Evans, Free Press, New York, 1988, p. 98; *Jefferson Davis: The Man and His Hour,* Davis, p. 264; *Judah P. Benjamin* by Pierce Butler, Chelsea House reprint, New York, 1980, p. 177.

16. *Mary Todd Lincoln,* Baker, pp. 94–97; *Biographical Directory of the United States Congress,* U.S. Government web site.

17. *Stonewall Jackson,* Robertson, p. 140; *Who Fired the First Shot?* Halsey, Jr., p. 109.

18. *The Letters of John S. Mosby,* edited by Adele S. Mitchell, Stuart-Mosby Historical Society, Carlisle, PA, 1986, p. 173; *Ranger Mosby* by Virgil Carrington Jones, University of North Carolina Press, Chapel Hill, p. 21; *Gray Ghost* by James A. Ramage, University Press of Kentucky, Lexington, 1999, p. 21; *Memoirs of Colonel John S. Mosby,* Russell, pp. 6–10.

19. *Ranger Mosby,* Jones, p. 296; *Gray Ghost,* Ramage, p. 279; *Rebel: The Life and Times of John Singleton Mosby* by Kevin H. Siepel, St. Martin's Press, New York, 1983, p. 187.

20. Ibid.

21. *Noted American Duels,* Cochran, p. 275.

22. Museum of the City of San Francisco web site; *The Duel,* Baldick, p. 115; *Noted American Duels and Hostile Encounters* by Hamilton Cochran, p. 141.

23. *Littleton Washington's Journal: Life in Antebellum Washington, Vigilante San Francisco and Confederate Richmond,* edited by Douglas Lee Gibboney, Xlibris, Philadelphia, 2001, pp. 103–5.

24. *The Duel,* Baldick, p. 115; politicalgraveyard.com.

25. *Reveille in Washington,* Leech, p. 442.

26. *Littleton Washington's Journal,* Gibboney, pp. 148–49.

27. Ibid.

28. *Ashes of Glory,* Furgurson, p. 27.

29. *Littleton Washington's Journal,* Gibboney, pp. 259–63.

30. Ibid., pp. 249–59.

31. *Personal Memoirs of U. S. Grant,* Vol. 1, pp. 59–60.

CHAPTER SIX

1. *The Duel,* Baldick, p. 115; *Noted American Duels,* Cochran, p. 232.

2. *Mary Chesnut's Civil War,* edited by C. Vann Woodward, Yale University Press, New Haven, 1981, pp. 68, 380.

3. *Who Fired the First Shot?* Halsey, p. 100. Also see "Civil War in South Carolina: South Carolina First Artillery Battalion" on-line at www.researchonline.net/sccw/unit1.htm.

4. "The Last Duel in the Confederacy" by Ashley Halsey, Jr., *Civil War Times Illustrated,* November 1962.

5. *Battles and Leaders of the Civil War,* Vol. 3, p. 43; *Historical Times Encyclopedia of the Civil War,* Faust, Editor, p. 523; *Who Fired the First Shot?* Halsey, p. 95.

6. "Betrayal at Ebenezer Creek" by Edward M. Churchill, *Civil War Times Illustrated,* October 1998.

7. *Battle from the Start,* Wills, p. 22.

8. *"First With the Most" Forrest* by Robert Selph Henry, Broadfoot Publishing, Wilmington, p. 143.

9. *Van Dorn* by Robert G. Hartje, Vanderbilt University Press, Nashville, 1967, p. 307.

10. *Battle from the Start,* Wills, p. 122; *Noted American Duels,* Cochran, p. 123; *"First With the Most,"* Henry, pp. 162–63.

11. *Battle from the Start,* Wills, p. 146.

12. *An Unerring Fire: The Massacre at Fort Pillow* by Richards L. Fuchs, Stackpole Books, Mechanicsburg, PA, 2002, p. 28.

13. *Reminiscences of Confederate Service 1861–1865* by Francis W. Dawson, Louisiana State University Press, Baton Rouge, 1980, p. 102.

14. "The Last Duel in the Confederacy" by Ashley Halsey, Jr., *Civil War Times Illustrated,* November 1962.

15. *Reminiscences of Confederate Service,* Dawson, p. 155; *Richmond, the Story of a City* by Virginius Dabney, University Press of Virginia, 1992.

16. *Ashes of Glory,* Furgurson, p. 363.

17. *Reminiscences of Confederate Service,* Dawson, p. xiv; *Noted American Duels,* Cochran, p. 256.

18. *Who Fired the First Shot?* Halsey, p. 110.

19. *A Guide to Civil War Sites in Maryland* by Susan Cooke Soderberg, White Mane, Shippensburg, PA, 1998, p. 213.

CHAPTER SEVEN

1. *Judah P. Benjamin: The Jewish Confederate,* Evans, p. 103.

2. The Benjamin quote is from John Wise's memoir, *The End of an Era,* p. 401.

3. *Richmond during the War,* Putnam, p. 255.

4. *The Confederate State of Richmond* by Emory M. Thomas, University of Texas Press, Austin, 1971, pp. 40, 66; *Mr. Davis's Richmond* by Stanley Kimmel, Bramhall House, 1959, pp. 80, 162.

5. *Richmond During the War,* Putnam, pp. 256–57; *Judah P. Benjamin,* Evans, p. 218.

6. *Confederate State of Richmond,* Thomas, p. 37.

7. *A Diary of Battle,* Nevins, p. 215.

8. *Reminiscences of Confederate Service,* Dawson, p. 87.

9. Ibid., p. 87; *General James Longstreet* by Jeffry D. Wert, Touchstone, New York, 1993, p. 97.

10. *The Gallant Hood* by John Dyer, Konecky & Konecky, New York, pp. 251–52; Sherman, Lewis, p. 383.

11. *Longstreet,* Wert, p. 156.

12. *Official Records,* Vol. 19, p. 722.

13. *Lee and Longstreet at Gettysburg* by Glenn Tucker, Bobbs-Merrill, Indianapolis, 1968, p. 129; *Pickett's Charge! Eyewitness Accounts,* edited by Richard Rollins, Rank and File, Redondo Beach, 1994, p. 65.

14. *Embattled Confederates,* Wiley, p. 51; *The End of An Era,* Wise, p. 338.

15. This document is available on-line through the University of North Carolina "Documenting the American South" project.

16. *The Evils of Gaming: A Letter to a Friend in the Army* by Rev. J. B. Jeter, a wartime pamphlet available on-line through the University of North Carolina "Documenting the American South" project.

17. *Pickett's Charge! Eyewitness Accounts,* Rollins, p. 65.

18. *Official Records,* Vol. 5, pp. 59–69.

19. Transcript of a memoir from Captain Albert S. Hunter, First Maryland Potomac Home Guard, Emmitsburg Maryland Historical Society web site.

20. *Official Records*, Vol. 6, p. 575; *A Sketch of the Battle of Franklin, Tenn.; With Reminiscences of Camp Douglas* by John M. Copley, Euguene Von Boeckmann, Printer, 1893, pp. 164–66. This volume is available on-line through the University of North Carolina "Documenting the American South" project.

21. *History of the 150th Regiment Pennsylvania Volunteers*, Chamberlin, p. 197.

22. *Confederate Veteran*, November 1909.

23. *Company Aytch* by Sam Watkins, Broadfoot reprint, Wilmington, NC, 1994, p. 188.

24. *Life of Billy Yank* by Bell Wiley, Doubleday, New York, 2000, p. 250.

25. *The End of an Era*, Wise, p. 454.

26. *Official Records*, Vol. 46, p. 1289.

27. "The Dreux Battalion" by Col. R. G. Lowe, *Confederate Veteran*, February 1897.

28. *Civil War Letters of General Robert McAllister*, edited by James I. Robertson, Jr., p. 251; findagrave.com.

29. *Glory Road*, Catton, p. 126.

30. Ibid.; *Chancellorsville* by Ernest B. Furgurson, Vintage Books, New York, p. 55; *Historical Times Illustrated Encyclopedia of the Civil War*, Faust, p. 483.

31. "St. Patricks Day in the Union Army's Civil War Irish Regiments" by Kevin O'Beirne, published on Thewildgeese.com web site.

32. *Civil War Firsts*, Gerald Henig and Eric Niderost, Stackpole Books, Mechanicsburg, PA, p. 303.

33. John Minor Botts was a Virginia Unionist who had been imprisoned by Confederate authorities earlier in the war and then exiled to his plantation near Culpeper.

34. *A War of the People*, Marshall, editor, p. 225. Original letter at the University of Vermont.

35. *Abraham Lincoln: The War Years,* Vol. 3, Sandburg, p. 482.

36. *Reveille in Washington*, Leech, p. 261; "Tame by Comparison: Buttoned Down D.C. Has a History of Sexual Excess" by Linda Wheeler, *Washington Post*, May 13, 1999, p. DC 1.

37. *Official Records*, Series 2, Vol. 5, Part 1, p. 628.

38. *Ashes of Glory* by Ernest B. Furgurson, Vintage Books, New York, 1996, p. 100.

39. *Decision in the West: The Atlanta Campaign of 1864* by Albert Castel, University Press of Kansas, Lawrence, 1992; p. 72; *Life of Billy Yank*, Wiley, p. 257.

40. "Abraham Lincoln, John Hay, and the Bixby Letter" by Michael Burlingame, *For the People: A Newsletter of the Abraham Lincoln Association,* Spring 1999.

41. *Lincoln's Scapegoat General* by Richard S. West, Jr., Houghton Mifflin, Boston, 1965, p. 226.

42. *Official Records*, Vol. 42, p. 73.

43. *Civil War Firsts*, Henig and Niderost, pp. 211–12.

44. *Official Records*, Series 1, Vol. 36, Part 1, p. 212; *Tenting Tonight: The Soldier's Life* by James Robertson, Jr., Time-Life Books, Alexandria, VA, 1984, p. 62.

45. *Assassination of Lincoln*, Lewis, p. 248; http://www.worldhistory.com/wiki/B/BostonCorbett.htm.

CHAPTER EIGHT

1. *Profiles from the Susquehanna Valley* by Paul B. Beers, Stackpole Books, Harrisburg, 1973, pp. 154–63.

2. *Official Records*, Series 3, Vol. 2, Part 1, pp. 189–90; *Echoes of Glory: Arms and Equipment of the Union* by the editors of Time-Life Books, Alexandria, 1991, p. 35.

3. *Gould's Millions* by Richard O'Connor, Doubleday, Garden City, NY, 1962, pp. 51–54.

4. *Simon Cameron: Lincoln's Secretary of War* by Erwin Stanley Bradley, University of Pennsylvania Press, Philadelphia, 1966, p. 201.

5. *Don Troiani's Regiments and Uniforms of the Civil War*, Stackpole Books, Mechanicsburg, PA, 2002, pp. 21, 24; *The Civil War Dictionary* by Mark M. Boatner III, Vintage Books, New York, 1991, p. 758; *Recollections of the Civil War*, Dana, p. 151.

6. *Profiles*, Beers, p. 160.

7. *Official Records*, Series 3, Vol. 2, Part 1. The "executive summary" submitted with the committee's final report is on pages 188–95.

8. *Civil War Guns* by William B. Edwards, Thomas Publications, Gettysburg, 1997, pp. 27, 55–57; *United States Senate Election, Expulsion and Censure Cases 1793–1990* by Anne M. Butler and Wendy Wolff, U.S. Senate Historical Office, Washington.

9. Falseclaimsact.com.

10. *Recollections of the Civil War*, Dana, p. 150.

11. *Abraham Lincoln: The Prairie Years and the War Years*, Sandburg, abridged edition, p. 278.

12. *Gould's Millions*, O'Connor, p. 56.

13. *Salmon Chase*, Blue, pp. 168–70.

14. *Kate Chase for the Defense*, Sokoloff, pp. 186–91.

15. *Official Records*, Series 1, Vol. 17, p. 123.

16. *Recollections of the Civil War*, Dana, pp. 39–41.

17. *Official Records*, Series 1, Vol. 34, Part 2, p. 824.

18. *The Blockade Runners* by Dave Horner, Dodd, Mead and Company, New York, 1968, pp. 12, 16, 17.

19. *Britain and the War for the Union*, Vol. 2, by Brian Jenkins, McGill-Queen's University Press, Montreal, 1980, pp. 118–19.

20. *Blockade Runners*, Horner, p. 12; *Richmond during the War*, Putnam, p. 229.

21. *Official Records*, Vol. 29, Part 2, p. 913.

22. *Hardtack and Coffee*, Billings, 130. The commissioner's name was Amos. Billings gives it as Joseph, confusing him, I believe, with another officer who served in the paymaster's department.

23. *Blood on the Moon*, Streets, p. 61.

24. Falseclaimsact.com.

25. *Abraham Lincoln: War Years*, Vol. 3, Sandburg, p. 59.

26. Ibid., p. 123.

27. *A Classification of American Wealth* web site.

28. *Grover Cleveland* by Rexford Tugwell, Macmillan, New York, 1968, p. 34.

29. *Abraham Lincoln: The War Years*, Vol. 3, Sandburg, p. 190.

30. *Harrisburg Patriot and Union*, December 3, 1863.

31. *Official Records*, Series 3, Vol. 3, Part 1, p. 1008.

32. Original document in the possession of the author.

33. Original letter in the possession of the author.

34. *Littleton Washington's Journal*, Gibboney, p. 229.

35. *Statesmen of the Lost Cause* by Burton J. Hendrick, Literary Guild of America, New York, 1939, p. 223.

36. Ibid., p. 227.

37. Ibid., p. 231.

38. *Littleton Washington's Journal*, Gibboney, p. 249.

39. "Last Days of the Confederacy" by Basil W. Duke, *Battles and Leaders*, Castle Books reprint, Edison, NJ, p. 765.

40. Ibid., p. 766.

41. Sources for this section include *The Long Surrender* by Burke Davis, *An Honorable Defeat* by William C. Davis, *Breckinridge* by William C. Davis, Louisiana State University, Baton Rouge, 1974, and *Flight into Oblivion* by A. J. Hanna, Johnson Publishing, Richmond, 1939. The dollar figures associated with the Confederate treasure train are often conflicting and inexact, which is understandable given the circumstances.

42. Sources for this section include: *Historical Times Illustrated Encyclopedia of the Civil War*, Faust, p. 755; *Breckinridge: Statesman, Soldier, Symbol*, Davis, pp. 560–61; *Jefferson Davis*, Davis, p. 651.

43. *William A. Albaugh III: His Life and Writings*, "The Chronology of the Great Seal of the Confederacy," Broadfoot Publishing, Wilmington, NC, 1993, pp. 169–72; *Littleton Washington*, Gibboney, pp. 210, 216.

44. A Houston newspaper published Mrs. Bromwell's claim on May 3, 1912. A transcript of the article can be found on-line at http://pages.prodigy.net/berryman2/_wsn/page3.html.

45. Ibid.

Chapter Nine

1. *Stormy Petrel: General Benjamin F. Butler* by Howard P. Nash, Jr., Fairleigh Dickinson University Press, 1969, p. 29.

2. *Lincoln's Scapegoat General* by Richard S. West, Jr., p. 45; *Littleton Washington's Journal*, Gibboney, p. 178.

3. *Lincoln's Third Secretary: The Memoirs of William O. Stoddard*, Exposition Press, New York, 1955, p. 153.

4. *Lincoln's Scapegoat General*, West, pp. 81–84.

5. *Battles and Leaders of the Civil War*, Vol. 2, "Incidents of the Occupation of New Orleans" by Albert Kautz, Captain, U.S.N., Castle Books reprint, Edison, NJ, pp. 92–93.

6. *Stormy Petrel*, Nash, p. 145.

7. Ibid., p. 14.

8. *Harpers Weekly*, July 15, 1862.

9. A reprint of one of these broadsides can be found on page 131 of *A Pictorial History of the Confederacy* by Lamont Buchanan; One of the Butler chamber pots is shown on p. 76 of *The Coastal War* in Time-Life's multi-volume history of the conflict. *Mary Chesnut's Civil War*, Woodward, p. 378.

10. *Official Records*, Vol. 15, p. 569.

11. *Official Records*, Vol. 5, p. 794, "Statement of Henry Florence" Confederate Secretary of State Judah Benjamin took depositions from Louisiana planters on Andrew Butler's activities. Benjamin's interest may have been personal since he owned a plantation outside New Orleans.

12. *Official Records*, Vol. 2, p. 631.

13. *Officials Records*, Vol. 5, p. 796.

14. A good account of the New Orleans "spoons" incidents can be found in *Stormy Petrel: General Benjamin F. Butler* by Howard Nash, pp. 296–308.

15. *New York Herald*, April 3, 1863.

16. *The Old Guard*, February 1864.

17. *An Army of Amateurs,* Longacre, p. 31.

18. Ibid., pp. 16–18.

19. Ibid., pp. 23–24.

20. *Battles & Leaders of the Civil War*, Vol. 4, p. 575.

21. *Fort Lyon to Harpers Ferry: The Civil War Letters and Newspaper Dispatches of Charles H. Moulton,* p. 217.

22. *New York Herald*, April 3, 1863.

23. *Stormy Petrel*, Nash, pp. 300–305.

24. Ibid., pp. 305–8.

25. *Lincoln's Scapegoat General*, West, p. 316.

CHAPTER TEN

1. *Sickles the Incredible* by W. A. Swanberg, Stan Clark Military Books, Gettysburg, 1991, pp. 81–83.

2. *American Scoundrel* by Thomas Keneally, Talese, New York, 2002, p. 16.

3. *Sickles*, Swanberg, pp. 92, 95, 96.

4. *President James Buchanan*, Klein, pp. 236, 242.

5. *A Belle of the Fifties*, Compton-Clay, p. 97.

6. "Betrayal, Bloodshed in Sight of the White House" by Sarah Mark, *Washington Post*, July 17, 2000.

7. *Mary Chesnut's Civil War*, edited by C. Vann Woodward, p. 379; *The Children of Pride*, edited by Robert Manson Myers, Yale University Press, New Haven, 1984, p. 927.

8. *Sickles*, Swanberg, p. 146.

9. *Civil War Letters of General Robert McAllister*, edited by Robertson, p. 212.

10. *Chancellorsville: Lee's Greatest Battle* by Edward J. Stackpole, Stackpole Company, Harrisburg, 1958, p. 212.

11. *A Caspian Sea of Ink* by Richard A. Sauers, Butternut & Blue, Baltimore, 1996, pp. 35–39; *Official Records*, Vol. 27, p. 116.

12. *Gettysburg: The Second Day* by Harry W. Pfanz, University of North Carolina Press, Chapel Hill, 1987, pp. 333–34, 436.

13. *Official Records*, Vol. 27, p. 116.

14. *Caspian Sea*, Sauers, pp. 41–55.

15. *The Marble Man,* Connelly, pp. 62–63.

16. http://www.army.mil/cmh-pg/mohciv2.htm.

17. *Dan Sickles: Hero of Gettysburg and Yankee King of Spain* by Edgcumb Pinchon, Doubleday, Garden City, NY, 1945, p. 271.

18. *Sickles*, Swanberg, pp. 384–85.

19. *Hero of Gettysburg*, Pinchon, pp. 270–71.

CHAPTER ELEVEN

1. *Mary Lincoln: Biography of a Marriage* by Ruth Painter Randall, Little, Brown and Company, Boston, 1953, p. 202.

2. *Biography of a Marriage*, Randall, p. 273.

3. Ibid., p. 103.

4. *Lincoln's Third Secretary*, Stoddard, pp. 112, 113; *Abraham Lincoln: The Prairie Years and the War Years*, Sandburg, abridged edition, p. 395.
5. *Sickles the Incredible*, Swanberg, pp. 127–28, 136–38.
6. *Mary Todd Lincoln*, Baker, pp. 182, 187.
7. Ibid., p. 190.
8. *Sickles the Incredible*, Swanberg, pp. 240–42.
9. *Abraham Lincoln: The Prairie Years and the War Years*, Sandburg, abridged edition, p. 385.
10. *Biography of a Marriage*, Randall, p. 324.
11. Ibid., pp. 373–74; *Mary Todd Lincoln: Her Life and Letters* by Justin G. Turner and Linda Levitt Turner, Knopf, New York, 1972, pp. 206–8.
12. *Life and Letters*, Turner and Turner, p. 345.
13. Ibid., p. 246. Mary Lincoln biographer Jean Baker gives the lower end estimate of $10,000.
14. Ibid., p. 247.
15. Ibid., p. 307.
16. Ibid., pp. 33, 415, 601.
17. Ibid., p. 589.
18. Ibid., p. 608.
19. *Biography of a Marriage*, Randall, pp. 431–32.
20. Find-a-grave.com.

INDEX

Page numbers in *italics* refer to illustrations.